AF552553

Christ, Rome, 4th century

THE GOLDEN BOOK OF WORLD RELIGIONS

INDIA BOOKVARSITY

LOTUS CHOICES

Editor: Mahendra Kulasrestha

Crown of Humanity

Religion is a great crown made up of numerous jewels of various colours and hues. The skilled jeweller fastens them with the gold of love, in the setting of knowledge, and at the very top he places the Kohinoor of Divine Wisdom, the white diamond which has in it every colour and shows no one hue alone. This crown he will one day place on the brow of humanity which, enthroned on earth, will at last know its unity and that it is one with the divine oneness.

—Annie Besant

Stories and Scriptures of Eight Major Religions

- Hinduism
- Zoroastrianism
- Jainism
- Buddhism
- Judaism
- Christianity
- Islam
- Sikhism

THE GOLDEN BOOK OF WORLD RELIGIONS

Mayan God

Material selected from various sources as well as freshly written, Just enough to understand, compare and derive conclusions

J.N. Farquhar James Dermestter, F. Max Muller, Edwin Arnold, George Sale and Annie Besant

Sources: The Rigveda, Upnishads, Bhagavadgita, Zend-Avesta, Acharanga Sutra, Adi Purana, Dhammapada, Good News Bible, Holy Quran; ***A Primer of Hinduism***, J. N. Farquhar, Oxford University Press, 1904; ***The Song Celestial***, Edwin Arnold, 1885; ***Seven Great Religions***, Annie Besant, Theosophical Publishing House, Adyar, Chennai; Sacred Books of the East, ***Buddhism***, Max Mullar, T. W. Rhys Davids, Samual Beal; Clareudon Press, Oxford U.K.

THE GOLDEN BOOK OF WORLD RELIGIONS

New First Edition: 2016
ISBN: 978-81-8382-325-8 (H/B)

Acknowledgements:

The Material of this volume has been collected from a variety of sources. We greatfully thank them. —*Editor*

Lotus Press : Publishers & Distributors
Unit No. 220, 2nd Floor, 4735/22, Prakash Deep Building,
Ansari Road, Darya Ganj, New Delhi- 110002
Ph.: 23280047, 98118-38000
• E-mail : lotuspress1984@gmail.com
www.lotuspress.co.in

Printed & Published by : **Lotus Press Publishers & Distributors,** New Delhi-02

Editorspeak

The Play of Religion

The story of Religion, or Religions – as there has never been one single religion despite all human beings being the same everywhere – in the world is very interesting. As well as intriguing. Life emerged on the planet–and why did it emerge at all is not clear– and as soon as it had a Mind in the equally mysterious process of Evolution–Thank God (?) that Mind took shape!–life entities acquired a consciousness, taking charge of Existence of their own as well as of others;– moving here and there, organising themselves, building societies and cultures and trying to understand and solve the problems of life–which they had got without their asking, as a kind of compulsion, no less, and which, they found full of various kinds of suffering, chief of which was lack of food to sustain life–dying to exist life being close to impossible–; the bellies were pretty large and needed to be filled at least twice every day. No wonder, they had to kill animals to eat at the beginning of history, after which they developed agri-practices to serve the purpose–though non-vegism is still rampant all over the world–a pity indeed, for the chickens and goats and. . .

There were many more sufferings, some of which provoked the young Gotama to publicly announce that suffering was the central ingredient of life, for which reason it should be totally discontinued; and he provided a complete plan to do it, fixing Nirvana as the final and complete aim.

His was the first religion in history which spread all over the then known world–not by force, which other latter religions did without any sign of remorse–with its message of non-violence and peace. Wow! Religion started opposing life from so long ago.

It is notable that rejection of life has been the central concept of all Indian religions, and salvation its chief aim. And Jainism provides the most dramatic programme to shed it away, being practised till date in right earnest.

• • •

It is clear that Religions emerged to fulfil the basic requirements of life. They depended on the understanding of the human mind, which were different in various settings. To give an extreme and horrible example (of which most of us may not be aware)–the religions of Maya-Aztec-etc. culture **killed their best youth every morning as sacrificial offers, because they believed that otherwise, the sun will not rise**. The sacrificial process was unbelievably gory; on special occasions thouands were killed and offered. Their enormous temples stand within heavily covered forests as witnesses of these remarkable religions. That the Spaniards destroyed these cultures completely was a welcome act in history.

• • •

Religions everywhere acquired an overwhelming importance, totally subduing life and controlling all its actions. Every religion developed its special characteristics—not necessarily good—even fighting among themselves. Karen Armstrong's bulky study of Jerusalem provides a striking example of horrible massacres carried out by all three of its religionists—Juda, Christian and Islam—against each other whenever they had a chance under a ruler of theirs. It did not matter that these three religions belonged to the same group, having similar basic ideas. The Crusades are another strong case to support the point.

But India has been different since its beginnings. Its central religion, named Hinduism, grew as results of thought and enquiry, providing living space to whatever came up and seemed to make a valid point. It had one God, many gods, females as independent goddesses, no god in many major religions—Jainism provides 40+ arguments against the concept of God—the idealised idea of God in the form of Brahman—which was greatly appreciated by Western thinkers when they came to know about it in much later times, and total Atheism. The philosophies of religion were astonishingly various and elaborate, and still are a factor unknown to all other religions, which in most cases depended on one single book. They were also non-violent, especially, after the emergence of Jainism and Buddhism. Even Tantra was accommodated, and modified. They lived as a family, though a pretty large and extended one. In present times, the concept seems to be growing. (Please note the first item appearing with 'Hinduism.')

• • •

From Violence to Tolerance and Acceptance, Religions have played their game on both extremes, and are still doing so. The problem is, that the word 'Religion' has come to be regarded as sacrosanct, and even its patently evil deeds can't be criticised; hurting religious sentiments has come to be the greatest social crime, punishable by immediate imprisonment. It has resulted in Terrorism of the worst kind in modern times, which is taking its toll in a most unprecedented way. The attack on the twin towers at the beginning of the millinnium was an eye-opener—and the eyes did not open as fast as was needed, because of the over-liberalism of the West, and the problem is festering even after the passage of more than a decade.

Christianity has been the most widely accepted religion in history, but with the spread of education, it has almost totally been eliminated in the West—churches in Europe and elsewhere are closed and priests and nuns are not to come by. Vatican is busy diverting its attention to less developed communities in Asia, Africa and S. America. Hindu religions are gaining ground because of their philosophical content, which the educated find more acceptable. Dalai Lama has also made his mark among them, helping Buddhism to an extent. Atheism is strengthening its hold, forming active groups in many places.

There have been six or seven major religions in the world, though many more have been active in various areas and still are, and a few new ones have come up in recent times–from unexpected lands like Japan and Korea, too–but they seem to have faded despite their making great efforts and spending lots of money in a couple of decades. Earlier, a century ago, a major effort to build up a new religion, Theosophy, by Madame Blavatsky, Col. Olcott, Annie Besant, etc., had also failed–whose remnant J. Krishnamurti is now quite respected, because he refused to be anointed as their Messiah and propounded a somewhat new theory. Older religions like Zoroastrianism and Zionism were dessimated by their rival religions long ago–the former had been totally eliminated after the Muslim destruction of the Sassanian dynasty in Persia in 653 A.D., and the latter one is being revived in the land of Israel after the return of the Jews to that land after 1948, wandering to survive all over the world for almost two millennia.

India is credited to have given birth to three major religions–Hinduism, Buddhism and Jainism–and the tradition of Abraham generated the other three–Judaism, Christianity and Islam. The seventh, Zoroastrianism, was a co-product of the early component of Hinduism, the Aryan-Vedic tradition dedicated to Fire (Agni), taken up and developed by the prophet known as Zoroaster–the prophet tradition being indigenous to that country, which did not come to India, but spread in the West, giving birth to Moses, Jesus, Mohammad and many more, described in the Bible and Koran.

Buddhism is very striking in the sense that it spread in a country larger than India, China, and in Korea, Japan, Mongolia, Cential Asia, etc., on its own, influencing many cultures in a very positive way–Kublai Khan deliberately utilised this religion to change the violent attitudes of his own people–and the Chinese seekers walked thousands of miles to India one after the other in search of its basic tenets. It is a most glorious chapter of world history–and perhaps the great religion can play the same role in modern times also in the world–the famous Japanese Monk Fuji Guruji had started to build Peace Pagodas in various countries, several of which have come up in America, Europe, India, etc., but, unfortunately, it has failed in growing into a world movement (the present writer has also been associated with it in the early stages, in Delhi).

Jainism did not make any effort to globalise itself, while Hinduism is not an organised religion and does not believe in making efforts to spread itself.

• • •

The first of the three Abraham-religions, Judaism, has suffered from an evil fate since its beginning, despite its being selected by God (named Yahweh) to specially serve 'the chosen people', to indicate which the rather strange practice of 'circumcision' was started, which meant initiation into the covenant with God. It was preceded by Baptism to wash away one's sins in water, then anointing him with oil blessed by the bishop, and scaling him. The Old Testament of the Bible is full of God's clearcut and fearful instructions to press them to follow these verbatim. Yet these poor people have kept running away from their land, and are now returning to it when things have improved, ever since 72 B.C. when the Assyrians invaded and destroyed Israel; till the mid years of the 19th century–a very very very long period indeed!—when the British almost surreptitiously passed the resolution to let them have some little land in that country to return and settle down, which they are presently in the process of doing.

The second religion in the chain, Christianity, has been totally centred around the person named Jesus, who came to be regarded as Messiah or messenger and son of God, but who was put to cross at the very early age of 33; and whose life-story—as found in the new researches, that he lived in India from age 15 till 30, and then again, from about 45 till his death around 90, in Kashmir; he is believed to have recovered after being hanged, and left Jerusalem with some of his followers—where on the outskirts of Srinagar at Khanyar, his grave still stands.

The German Holger Kersten and a few of his companions have done good work in this area and have published a few well researched books, describing not only the details of his journey to India and stay in Kashmir, but presenting the genuine ideas of Jesus, which do not tally with the ideas associated with official Christianity–which as presented in the New Testament, were promoted by St. Paul, a former adversary of Jesus, who later on came to believe that Jesus was really the son of God. The ideas of Jesus were Buddhist which he had imbibed in India during his first stay in Nepal, Ladakh, etc. The ideas of St. Paul were essentially Jewish, to which community be belonged, and had never even met Jesus while he was around. All these present a rather funny situation, but the religion promoted under his title, Christ, which means Messiah, lived to become the foremost religion of the world, and still remains so, Wow, again, and a longer Wow for that matter!

The third religion, Islam, in my view, was a better one, because it provided a value system aimed at managing society as a whole, which no other religion did. But it, umfortunately, took the wrong road and failed to serve its basic purpose. The recently published autobiography of the Pakistani cricketeer of world fame, Imran Khan—which I had the occasion to translate into Hindi—presents the case most admirably, and leaves the question hanging in air: why did it so happen? I sometimes wish that the truly remarkable prophet Hazrat Mohammad should have lived in India, or in China for that matter, instead of Arabia. The player Imran Khan has formed his own political party and is fighting elections, and says if he wins, he'll also try to put the religion on the right track–Great Good Luck to him!

• • •

The general story of religions in history is very topsy-turvy, and does'nt lead to any positive conclusions, except the hard fact that they are a basic need of human beings, whose existence is neither safe nor sound in their essentials; another fact is that with the emergence of scientific knowledge, religions as they are presently practised, are losing their hold, raisnig the question: What will be the religion of the future? Will there be religion at all? Can there be one single religion for everybody, and can one be developed by joining the best from all? Perhaps this idea has a potential and should be given further thought. There are developing inter-faith groups, which can move in this direction. The Bahai temples offer that men of every religion can hold their prayers etc. in their precincts–a commendable step indeed. They should make further advances and try to develop a worthwhile eclectic religion.

• • •

Finally, does God exist? Or, is there something we call Divine? The idea is totally subjective, a game of human mind, unsupported by hard reality. Kant's 'Pure Reason' rejects it. The basic sufferings and injustices of life do not give hope either. The lack of meaning as well as purpose in life strengthen this negative aspect. Hindu experiments in attaining Brahman are not materialsing–Sri Aurobindo's 40–yrs. practice of Integral Yoga to attain perfection as well as to evolve a new species, failed in late 1950; now another famnus yogi who stayed in Amsterdam, Maharishi Mahesh, and passed away a few years ago, confirms it. There are many more, who prefer to keep quiet. The problem is, that we are not clear about the basic details of the God idea–it is cleverly valued and is supported as such by its progenitors, May it rest there and in peace!

The situation would be good news to us human beings. That the space is vacant for him–he can occupy it–and take charge. Long live human beings!

Fortunately, or unfortunately–depending on one's conditioning–there have been religions of various kinds–god-religions (the most accepted variety because of the easiness of the concept), goddess-religions (not too many), stone religions, animal-and-bird religions, cruel religions, peaceful (rather excessively) religions, funny religions, serious (even overmuch) religions, purely national religions (Juda), universal religions (Christian), idolatory religions, thought-based ones, though very few indeed, etc., etc.;–and in many many names–from Taoism to Tenrikyo, through well known ones like Christianity, Islam, etc., etc.;–though the freedom to select one of personal choice is almost non existent–though it needs to be recognised as everyone's *democratic* right and promoted worldwide–; and, taken together, they perhaps form the most interesting part of real human life. The seven major religions we have undertaken to present in these pages, we hope, will provide a nearly complete picture of the society we live in today.

Everywhere in the world religion started with human beings acquiring the organ of mind in the process of evolution-which helped them to understand what they were seeing with their eyes and feeling with other body-senses. They found nature in its various forms spread and active in their respective ways, friendly as well as enemical, to them. Since then their laws and processes were not known, they decided to make them as friendly as they could and use them for their benefit. Each person and community reacted according to its capabilities and limitations, controlled and guided by a number of factors. There thus arose the concepts of Divinity, powers behind every phenomena, deities, God or gods, providence, predestination, etc. The ideas and practices developing around them were galore, serious, strong, and all consuming; a major part of human life was affected by them. The situation stays till date, though now further movement seems to be emerging. With the nearly unexpected arrival of the Internet and things related to it, the scenario of religion is also likely to change. How, and in what possible ways, is still to express, but the speed is fast, as well as positive. Cheer up all!

❑ ❑ ❑

Contents

1.

Hinduism

Thought-oriented, Many-faceted, Family-natured Religion

THE EVER-FLOWING RIVER

The well known American weekly *Newsweek* in its Aug. 24-31, 2009 issue, published the following note by **Lisa Miller** under the title:

'We Are All Hindus Now'

'America is not a Christian nation. We are, it is true, a nation founded by Christians, and according to a 2008 survey, 76 percent of us continue to identify as Christian (still, that's the lowest percentage in American history). Of course, we are not a Hindu—or Muslim, or Jewish, or Wiccan—nation, either. A million-plus Hindus live in the United States, a fraction of the billions who live on earth. But **recent poll data show that conceptually, at least, we are slowly becoming more like Hindus and less like traditional Christians** in the ways we think about God, ourselves, each other, and eternity.

'The Rig Veda, the most ancient Hindu scripture, says this: "Truth is One, but the sages speak of it by many names." A Hindu believes there are many paths to God. Jesus is one way, the Quran is another, Yoga practice is a third. None is better than any other; all are equal. **The most traditional, conservative Christians have not been taught to think like this. They learn in Sunday schools that their**

religion is true, and others are false. Jesus said, "I am the way, the truth, and the life. No one comes to the Father except through me."

'Americans are no longer buying it. According to a 2008 Pew Forum survey, 65 percent of us believe that "many religions can lead to eternal life"—including 37 percent of white Evangelicals, the group most likely to believe that salvation is theirs alone. Also, the number of people who seek spiritual truth outside church is growing. Thirty percent of Americans call themselves "spiritual, not religious," according to a 2009 *News-week* Poll, up from 24 percent in 2005. **Stephen Prothero, religion professor at Boston University, has long framed the American propensity for "the divine-deli-cafeteria religion" as "very much in the spirit of Hinduism**. You're not picking and choosing from different religions, because they're all the same," he says. "It isn't about orthodoxy. It's about whatever works. If going to Yoga works, great—and if going to Catholic mass works great. And if going to Catholic mass plus the Yoga plus the Buddhist retreat works, that's great, too."

'Then there's the question of what happens when you die. Christians traditionally believe that bodies and souls are sacred, that together they make up the, "self," and that at the end of time they will be reunited in the Resurrection. You need both, in other words, and you need them forever. Hindus believe no such thing. At death, the body burns on a pyre, while the spirit—where identity resides—escapes. In reincarnation, central to Hinduism, selves come back to earth again and again in different bodies. So here is another way in which Americans are becoming more Hindu: **24 percent of Americans say they believe in reincarnation, according to a 2008 Harris poll.** So agnostic are we about the ultimate fates of our bodies that we're burning them—like Hindus—after death. **More than a third of Americans now choose cremation,** according to the Cremation Association of North America, up from 6 percent in 1975. "I do think the more spiritual role religion tends to de-emphasize some of the more starkly literal interpretations of the Resurrection," agrees Diana Eck, professor of comparative religion at Harvard. So let us all say "Om."'

• • •

WHO IS A HINDU?

A MAN is a Hindu because of two things, birth and conformity. In order to be a Hindu, a man must have been born in one of the social groups which historically have become associated together in Hinduism, and which are known as castes. A man born in Hinduism must conform to the usages of the group in which he was born. The customs of the various castes vary to an extraordinary degree. In some castes a great many things are obligatory, in others comparatively few.

The observance of certain domestic ceremonies is binding on every man who wishes to remain a Hindu. They are carried out with the care in every family under the guidance of Brahmin priests. In the code of Manu, as in the older sacred books, twelve domestic rites or sacraments, *samskaras*, are prescribed for the twice-born castes:

(1) *Garbhadhana,* impregnation, following the marriage ceremony.

(2) *Pumsavana,* male-production, about three months after marriage.

(3) *Simantonnayana,* hair-parting, the parting of the woman's hair some time before the birth of her child.

(4) *Jata-karman,* birth-ceremony.

(5) *Nama-karana,* name-giving.

(6) *Nishkramana,* carrying-out. In the fourth month the child was carried out to look on the rising sun.

(7) *Anna-prasana,* food-giving.

(8) *Chauda,* tonsure.

(9) *Kesanta,* hair-cutting.

(10) *Upanayana,* initiation, the ceremony which introduces the boy to his education.

(11) *Samavartana,* home-coming, the return of the student to his home from the house of his teacher.

(12) *Vivaha,* marriage.

Today the twice-born castes usually observe only the following:

(5) *Nama-karana,* name-giving.

(7) *Anna-prasana:,* food-giving.

(10) *Upanayana,* initiation.

(12) *Vivaha,* marriage.

The other castes have corresponding ceremonies.

The Hindu family is patriarchal in form. Modern customs differ a good deal indetail from the customs of the Rigvedic and earlier ages, yet in the main the ideas and the practice are the same.

The Funeral Ceremonies last ten days. The essential element in each day's ceremony is the offering of a *pinda,* i.e., a ball of cooked rice, to the spirit of the deceased. The belief is that the spirit of the deceased through feeding on this food acquires a gross body, *sthula sarira,* and is thereby transformed from a *preta* or wandering ghost into a *pitri,* father.

Sraddha Ceremonies—A man's relatives, male and female, on both his father's and his mother's side, for three generations upward and three generations downward, are called his *sapindas,* i.e., sharers in the *pinda,* because they take part in the *sraddha* ceremonies with him. On the eleventh day, all the *sapindas* gather in the house of the person who is holding the ceremony, and an elaborate ceremony is conducted the central element of which is the offering of a *pinda* to every deceased person within the circle of *sapindas.* A feast follows the ceremony.

The Worship of the Temple. This takes a large place in the lives of all Hindus except modern educated men, who seldom go near a temple at all, at least in the North.

Belief is altogether free. A Hindu is generally understood to believe that the Vedas are inspired, that the Brahmins are divinely appointed priests, and that caste is a divine institution, but a man may declare that he believes none of these things and yet remain a good Hindu, provided he conforms.

Although Hinduism has many gods, many theologies, and many sacred books, **a man remains an orthodox Hindu without believing in any god or any theology, and without knowing or acknowledging a single sacred book**. He must give some sort of practical recognition to some god or gods in the domestic ceremonies and family festivals. but the divinities thus reverenced vary all over India; there is no uniformity. Nor are there any theological conceptions which he need hold: **an orthodox Hindu may be an atheist, or an agnostic**. The sacred books of Hinduism are not read in the services of the temples, nor is the ordinary Hindu expected to study them. The *Ramayana* and the *Mahabharata*, however, are very largely read in the homes of the people.

But although there is no set of beliefs which the Hindu as a Hindu is expected to hold, there are certain ideas or convictions which all or nearly all Hindus will be found to hold. They are, first, the validity of **caste** and the authority of the **Vedas** and the **Brahmins**; second, the doctrine of **transmigration**; and third, the sacredness of the **cow**. Perhaps it may be said that a further general characteristic of Hinduism is to be found in a tendency of thought, feeling, and aspiration of which the logical issue is a **mystic pantheism**.

Most Hindus are also touched at least in some degree with ascetic ideas. The villager, no matter how worldly his own life may be, is ready to affirm that **the things of the world are**

worthless, nothing is of any final value except **God** and the knowledge of God. He therefore holds that the man who does not give up the world in its entirety and become an ascetic does not really love God. He regards the preservation of animal life **(*ahimsa*)** as meritorious.

There are vast multitudes of people both north and south who are regarded as unclean, who in consequence are excluded from all Brahminical temples, and for whom no Brahmin will perform any ceremony. But they have come so largely under Hindu influence that they cannot be excluded. They show this Hindu influence first of all in their caste organization and in their social usages, which are very largely an imitation of high-caste practice; secondly, in their belief in Hindu theology and superstition, and their desire to bring their village divinites into some sort of relation to the gods of the Hindu pantheon.

The Aryan People

In the dim background of history we catch misty glimpses of a great people which had a common culture, a common religion, and a common language, but, which in the following centuries through division and migration split up into many groups and thus **producerl a large number of the leading nations of Europe and of Asia.** In the language, religion, and life of their descendants we can still find traces of the common life lived so long ago by the Aryan race.

Careful comparison of the religions of the various ancient Aryan peoples enables us to realize in some degree what the religion was in the still earlier days of the undivided people. It seems certain, first of all, that **they honoured a vast number of special gods, each of them supposed to oversee some distinct aspect of life.** But in that primitive age these Aryan men had already another group of gods distinguished as the heavenly ones *(deva—deus)* from the vulgar throng. They were all natural phenomena, but they were also all connected one way or another with the sky and with the grandest of nature's operations. It seems clear that the undivided people already worshipped Sky, Sun, Moon, Dawn, Wind, Fire. But though they regarded and worshipped them as gods, they still called them by their significant names; they had not given them proper names or epithets, The usual method of obtaining the help of the gods in those days seems to have been already **prayer and sacrifice of a rudimentary kind**. In both prayer and sacrifice true religious feeling **mingled with belief in the occult power of charmed words and deeds**.

A certain portion of the mighty Aryan family broke away from the main stock—we do not know when or where—and remained a united people for some time, but finally fell in two; **one taking up its abode in Iran, the other moving into the territory on both sides of the upper Indus**. This people, the ancestors of the **Zoroastrians** and of the creators of **Hinduism**, may be designated **Indo-Iranian** during the period while they were still one.

They were a tall, fair people. They were then **soldier-farmers**, constantly at war with the aborigines around them; and they looked eagerly for sunshine and rain to mature their crops and give them fodder for their cattle and herds. **Their women had a great deal of freedom throughout their lives. There was no child-marriage among them and no law against the remarriage of widows.**

They worshipped the heavenly powers, calling them *devas;* and they were very conscious of the great advantage which their knowledge of these gods gave them over the aborigines. They arranged their gods in three groups, according as they belonged to the upper region of light, the atmosphere, or the earth. These three groups were designated Upper, Middle, and Lower. The chief divinities were—Upper: Varuna, Surya, Savitri, Vishnu, Ushas, Aditi, Mitra, Aryaman, the Asvins; Middle: Vata, Indra, Rudra, Parjanya, the Maruts; Lower: Agni, Soma, Yama.

Their worship was largely sacrificial. Animals were often killed in sacrifice; but their most elaborate rites were connected with the offering of the Soma, and of clarified butter, called *ghee.* They were accustomed to have hymns recited at all sacrifices. But, although they laid so much stress on sacrifice, **they had no temples and no images**. Sacrifices were offered in the open air, and the arrangements were very simple.

Already the people seem to have been roughly divided into three groups—warriors, priests, and agriculturists; but they were classes rather than castes. The priest, Brahmin, was already very influential; for he was believed to have great power over the gods.

Austerity, called *tapas* in Sanskrit, was practised in those days. Various forms of self-torture were endured, with a view to securing warlike prowess, invincibility, miraculous powers, or heaven. The *muni,* who practised *tapas,* wore yellow robes.

The worship of ancestors was kept up with great care by the Indo-Aryans. They were called *pitaras,* 'fathers,' were regularly worshipped, and were invited to come to the sacrifice along with the gods. After death it was believed that the souls of the good were conducted by Yama to the place prepared for them, where they enjoyed an immortality of peace and happiness along with the 'fathers' and the gods.

The hymns, which had been composed during the previous centuries, and which were carefully preserved in the great families and believed to be inspired, were now gradually gathered in some priestly school into the great collection which is called the **Rigveda**. Young Brahmins committed these hymns to memory at school, in order to be able to use them at the sacrifices. The collection was universally accepted by the people as their sacred book, every hymn being recognized as a divine utterance revealed to the *rishi,* 'seer,' whose name it bears.

These hymns which form the Rigveda are one of the most interesting groups of literature in all the world. **No other people ever produced a body of religious poetry of such striking originality and beauty at such an early stage of the history.**

A few of the later hymns are philosophical. They ask questions rather than answer them; yet already the conception of the One behind all the gods finds expression, and a number of the ideas which afterwards helped to create the Hindu systems are tentatively put forward.

At a later date a large number of verses were gathered together, and so arranged as to form a special manual for the second order of priests. This collection was called the **Samaveda**. Another manual, consisting partly of verses, partly of sacrificial formulae in prose, was put together for the use of the third order, and was called the **Yajurveda**.

The Aryans continued to advance eastwards during this period, leavening the old population as they went, until by its close nearly the whole of North India had come under their government and civilization. As they went, the **Brahmins brought the aboriginal tribes under their priestly rule, giving each tribe a definite place in their social system**. Large trade sprang up even sea voyages on the Indian Ocean.

During this period the theological ideas of the Brahmins underwent a great change. A deep tendency is manifested towards belief in one God, either the personal Creator, Prajapati, or, more often, a mysterious incomprehensible divine essence diffused through all things. Many of the ancient gods had already fallen into the background, while others had come into great prominence, among whom were Rudra, who now received his more attractive name, Siva, and Vishnu: Siva as the mountain god and Vishnu as the sun-god.

Towards the end of this period **we begin to meet a real order of ascetics. They lived in the forest** and usually built themselves huts of wood or leaves. They were called Vanaprasthas, forest-dwellers, hermits, and a collection of their huts was called an ***asrama,*** hermitage. They wore coats of bark or skin, wound up their hair in matted coils, and lived largely on woodland fare.

The **law of *ahimsa*** (harmlessness), that they **must not kill an animal nor break a living twig from a tree**, gradually arose among them. They continued the worship of the gods and the worship of their ancestors, and they retained their place in the family and in caste, but **did no work of any kind**. They practised various methods of severe austerity, enduring extreme cold and heat, strange food, most painful postures, and such like. The purpose of the endurance of this *tapas* was still in the main the **attainment of miraculous powers**; but moral aims now began to mingle with the older motives.

Atharvaveda

During this period a fourth Veda, the Atharvaveda, was compiled. Although as a collection it is later than the other three, a great deal of the material embodied in it is of early date. It is a more popular work than the other Vedas, reflecting the superstitions of the people, and consists mostly of charms, which are of two classes, those that bring weal and those that bring woe. It was some time hefore the Atharvaveda received equal recognition with the the older collections.

Philosophic Period

Karma and Rebirth

Religion as a whole remained much as it was during the previous period. **But the more intelligent men underwent a revolutionary cbange.**

(a) The old hazy pantheistic faith became clear and was grasped more firmly. The whole world was paltry and unreal in comparison with the One which informed it and was its sole Reality. All the ordinary gods were spoken of as mere temporary manifestations of the unchanging and **actionless Absolute. Yet the worship of the gods went on unchanged**, as the Absolute is unknowable.

(b) The problems raised by the very varying fortunes of men and the extraordinary differences in character met with everywhere were solved for the Indian mind by the doctrine of Transmigration and its pendant, Karma.

The doctrine of Transmigration is that **souls are emanations of the divine spirit**, sparks from the central fire, drops from the ocean of divinity, that **each soul is incarnated in a body times without number**, that the same soul may be in one life a god, in another a man, in a third an animal or even a plant, and that there can be no rest for the soul and no relief from suffering **until it finds release from the necessity of birth and returns to the divine** source whence it came.

The word *karma* means literally action, but the doctrine means the inevitable working out of action in new life. The idea is that a man's body, character, capacities and temperament, his birth, wealth and station, and the whole of his experience in life, whether of happiness or of sorrow, together form the just retribution for his deeds, good and bad, done in earlier existences.

(c) As it is deeds, good or bad, that form *karma,* and thus lead to rebirth, the idea lies ready to hand that, if by any means a man can cease acting, he may thereby get Releaese (liberation or salvation) from the necessity of rebirth. Quite naturally and unreflectingly men took action to mean the business of life; so there arose the universal conviction that, if a man wished to reach Release, he must give up the ordinary life of man with all its gains; pleasures and interests and live an actionless existence, turning away from the unreal world and drawing near the one actionless Reality.

This then is essential Hinduism:

A. The Theory of God and the world, consisting of

1. The one impersonal Reality and the unreal phenomenal world, which undergoes cyclic change. All minor gods are gathered under the pantheistic All.
2. Transmigration and Karma as the explanation of the world.
3. Release from Transmigration and union with the one Reality, the object of all serious men.

The steadily growing culture of the Brahmins and the wider experience of men and things which they were daily acquiring as they went on with the work of reducing the whole population of India under their own religious sway had brought them to this new and far-reaching system of thought. **Under the wide dome of this universal pantheism they were able to gather all the aboriginal worships of the land and by tactful arrangements to give them a certain distinct unity.**

A time came when **there arose a great passion among thinking men in North India to win Release, and the theories as to be true path to Emancipation were proclaimed.**

Many theories of the constitution of the world were formed and taught, but the most important of all is the doctrine of the Upanishads. The ordinary name for the World-soul was **Brahman**, a neuter noun which expresses the common thought of the time, that the World-soul is an impersonal essence present in all things. There were many speculations as to its nature, until some wise thinker called Brahman the *atman,* or Self of the universe. Then, as the soul of the universe was *atman,* and the soul of the individual was *atman,* the conclusion was soon drawn that the two were identical.

The conception of Brahman-Atman in the Upanishads is a great lightning-flash of truth, and it is placed before us in many a noble passage: Brahman is Consciousness: Brahman is the Reality of everything; Brahman is joy; Brahman is incomprehensible; by the command of Brahman all things are done.

Numerous philosophic leaders stand out dimly in the pale historic light, each with his own specialized doctrine and his following of monks. In an old Buddhist book **there is a catalogue of sixty-two different theories of the universe taught at this time in North India.**

Gradually the allegorical teaching given as a preparation for the hermit life, and the philosophic instruction intended for the wandering life, took definite shape and were handed down orally from teacher to pupil in fixed language, each school having its own sacred deposit. The former was called *aranyaka,* or 'forest-teaching', as we have seen; the latter *upanishad,* probably in the sense of 'secret doctrine '. Thus were formed the wonderful treatises which we know as the Aranyakas and the Upanishads.

Towards the end of this period the *Ramayana* in its earliest form, which consisted of only five books (ii-vi), was composed by Valmiki, in the Kingdom of Kosala. In this work Rama is a purely human hero.

This period is scholastic in most of its religious features. Hindu practice became steadily more regular under the unceasing pressure of priestly authority. This is most noteworthy in the realm of social life. At the beginning of the period there was still a considerable amount of caste laxity throughout Norhtern India, but by the close a great advance had taken place. The whole system had hardened and was very much what it has been for centuries. A large number of the secondary castes were already in existence.

Images and temples rose during this period to the place which they have ever since held in Hindu life.

As knowledge grew and the compass and the number of the subjects taught in the Brahminical schools went on increasing, the mass of material to be learned by rote became more and more unmanageable. It became impossible for the student to store in his memory everything which he wanted to know, so long as it was presented to him in the extraordinarily prolific manner of the Brahmins. A new method was therefore invented. AII the knowledge which the student had to acquire was expressed in strings of aphorisms of the briefest and most pregnant description. As time went on and the new method developed, it became a conventional system of technical terms like a modern telegraphic code. These tabloids of condensed knowledge were called *sutras.*

These books, if books they can be called when they were not written down, dealt with all the subjects of a priest's education. They were usually summed up under six heads, called the *vedangas,* or members of the body of the Veda.

Siksha, pronunciation; *kalpa,* ceremonial; *vyakarana,* grammar; *nirukta,* etymology; *chhandas,* metre; *jyotisha,* astronomy.

Of the six, Kalpa, ceremonial, is the most important. Under Kalpa there are three groups of *sutras,* the Srauta Sutras, which deal with the sacrifices, summarising the teaching of the Brahmins; the Grihya Sutras, which deal with domestic ceremonies; and the Dharma Sutras, which provide rules of conduct for the various classes of men and the various stages of life. The Brahminical schools were now more numerous than ever, many of the earlier schools having split into several branches; and each had its own series of *sutras,* dealing in turn with all the subjects comprehended under the six *vedangas.*

In certain of the schools at this time some of the best parts of the old Upanishads were versified and strung together, so as to make new Upanishads. The brief, pointed, aphoristic character of these poems shows plainly that they were put together with a view to their easily committed to memory.

One very noteworthy change occurred in Hinduism at this time. While at the beginning of the fifth century B.C. Rama and Krishna were but human heroes, they were already worshipped in the time of Megasthenes, the Seleucid ambassador at the court of Chandragupta; and by the opening of the second century B.C. they were acknowledged to be incarnations of Vishnu.

During the next three centuries **this rich warm worship of incarnate divinities became entwined with the philosophy of the Atman, and first Krishna and then Rama rose to the lofty position of incarnations of the Supreme.**

Krishna occurs in this guise in the latest parts of the Mahabharata, dating perhaps from the second century A.D., and also in the Bhagavadgita.

Vishnuism

Certain of the old myths of the Vedas and Brahmanas were transformed into incarnations of Vishnu, and others were created. These new forms of faith, so well calculated to stir emotion and to provoke enthusiastic worship, naturally led to a great growth of Vishnuism. The leading school of Vishnuites were called Bhagavatas, i.e., worshippers of the Bhagavan, the Adorable Lord. **Unlike the teachers of the Vedanta, who held that only the three highest castes could reach Release, because they alone were allowed to read the Upamshads, tht Bhagavatas offered salvation to all.**

The Cult of Shiva

But the cult of Siva did not lag behind. The sacred bull became his companion; the trident was connected with him; the phallic symbol, the *linga,* was adopted for his worship; and he was represented as the typical ascetic. Vishnu in his incarnations, and Siva with these fresh attractions, now stand side by side with Brahma.

Six Systems of Philosophy

It was during this period that the six systems of philosophy which are recognized as orthodox by Hindus were worked out in detail. Each took shape in its own school, gradually developed and expounded by a succession of teachers. They expressed the system in sutras in the briefest possible way, and explained the sutras by means of a commentary.

1. The **Karma Mimamsa**, 'work inquiry', the philosophy of sacrifice, founded on the Srauta Sutra. Jaimini wrote the main treatise, the *Karma Mimamsa Sutra.*
2. The **Uttara Mimamsa** 'later inquiry', the philosophy of the Upanishads, the Vedanta, systematised by Badarayana

in his work known as the *Vedanta Sutra,* the *Brahma Sutra,* or the *Sariraka Sutra.*

3. The **Sankhya**, a dualistic atheism, ascribed to the early sage Kapila. No early treatise survives.
4. The **Yoga**. In this system the Sankhya metaphysic is combined with a personal God and with bodily and mental exercises called Yoga. Patanjali, of the second century B.C., is the author of the manual, which is called the *Yoga Sutra.*
5. The **Vaiseshika**. This system classifies all phenomena under logical categories, and attributes the origin of the world to atoms. The author of the manual, which is known as the *Vaiseshika Sutra,* is remembered by the nickname Kanada, 'atom-eater'.
6. The **Nyaya** accepts the metaphysic of the Vaiseshika, and adds a very detailed and acute exposition of formal logic. The manual, which is by Gautama, is called the *Nyaya Sutra.*

Many of these ancient sutra manuals have perished, but several survive, of which the greatest is the manual of the Vedanta school, the **Vedanta-Sutra** of Badarayana.

Ramayana

It seems most likely that the first and the last books of the *Ramayana* were added about the beginning of our period. Here Rama is represented as an incarnation of half the essence of Vishnu and the *Ramayana* thereby becomes a Vishnuite work. About the same time large additions were made to the *Mahabharata,* which made it an epic of 24,000 slokas. In the new text Krishna is a demi-god. The recreation and re-publication of these great works, which glorify Hindu kings and Hindu life and worship, was almost certainly carried out under the patronage of the Sungas.

About four centuries later (A.D. 200) vast quantities of new text were introduced into the *Mahabharata,* transforming the epic into a didactic library. Among the additions was the *Bhagavadgita*. Here and elsewhere in the new matter Krishna is represented as the Atman-incarnate.

The two epics are the earliest popular literature of India. They sprang from the heart of the people; and though the *Ramayana* was edited for a sectarian purpose, and the *Mahabharata* has been changed by the Brahmins into an immeasurable mass of priestly laws and traditions, they are still greatly beloved hy the people; and, unlike the Vedic literature, they may be read by women, and by men of any caste.

Bhagavadgita

The *Bhagavagita* or "Song of the Adorable " which is largely a product of Bhagavata theology, is one of the most noteworthy pieces of literature produced in India. **It is the noblest and purest expressions of modern Hinduism.** The author wished to produce a poem to express his own boundless reverence for Krishna, to gather the best thoughts of the Upanishads and unite them with the most helpful parts of the philosophies, and at the same time to bind people to the ordinary life and worship of Hindu society.

The Puranas

Our period opens with the rise of the great dynasty of the Guptas, who reigned at Patna, but later moved up to Ayodhya. Under their empire North India enjoyed a period *of* really good government, worthy of comparison with the time of Asoka. The two greatest kings of the dynasty were Samudragupta and Chandragupta II Vikramaditya. The latter king conquered Malwa and probably lived from time to time in Ujjain; so that he may be the reality behind all the mythical tales told about the great Vikramaditya of Ujjain.

Hinduism during this period is chiefly marked by a popular sectarianism. The follower of Siva or of Vishnu uses the most extravagant language in praising his own God and curses the devotees of the other heartily. An attempt was made to reconcile all sectaries by the doctrine of the three-fold manifestation of the Supreme in Brahma, Vishnu, and Siva; but the concept never truly laid hold of the Hindu people. The Triad is frequently mentioned, and it is now and then represented in sculpture; but it was Siva and Vishnu that drew the reverence of men. The mythology of the time is extravagant.

In this period the myths about Krishna underwent considerable embellishment. The story of his childhood was told in great detail. His cowherd exploits also took form at this time and captured the masses. All this fresh mythology had its centre in Mathura and Vrindavan. Clearly the cult of Krishna was carried on there with great fervour.

The Guptas were great patrons of literature. The earliest existing Puranas, which embody the sectarian religion of the period, seem to date from their time; and every branch of secular literature rose to splendoui under their fostering care, The word Purana means *archaeo-logica,* and was first used of old-world myths and tales about the origin of things.

The existing Puranas, however, are sectarian in Sanskrit verses, written to catch the popular ear and secure worshippers for Vishnu, Siva, or Brahma. Each begins with an account of the origin of the world, but soon becomes a panegyric of the favourite divinity. Men of any caste, and women too, are allowed to read the Puranas.

The steady rise of Hinduism to supremacy and the corresponding decline of Buddhism are the most prominent features of the religious history of this period.

But when we look more closely, we become aware that a subtle change has passed over Hindu faith and practice. **Modern popular Hinduism has been born. The ancient Vedic sacrifices have fallen almost altogether into disuse. It is the worship of the temples and the annual festivals celebrated at home that hold the affections or the people.**

The Shaktas

During this period a third sect of great importance arose, chiefly in Bengal: the Saktas or worshippers of Kali, the wife of Siva, as his *sakti.* They fall into two groups, the right-hand and the left-hand Saktas. Both groups show many signs of aboriginal influence, notably animal sacrifice and magic rites; and the basis of the whole cult in both is phallic; but, while the right-hand group are respectable in their worship, **the left-hand Saktas are most immoral. Their cult is based on the five M's, or elements of worship the Sanskrit names of which begin with M—flesh, wine, women, fish, and finger-signs.** In other points the Saktas are like Saivaites.

Alvars

The twelve Alvars (often called *Azhvars:* they were wandering teachers and poets of various castes) preached in South India a popular Vishnuism, which drew its inspiration from the Puranic stories of Krishna. They offered salvation through Vishnu to men of any caste. They caught the ear of the people with their beautiful Tamil hymns. These were finally gathered in a collection, the name of which is the *Nalayira Prabandham,* but which is often referred to as the Tamil Veda. These popular lyrics are still used in the daily worship of most of the Vishnuite temples of the south.

Adiyars

Contemporaneously the Adiyars did a similar service for the religion of Siva. The three greatest of them were Appar, Nana Sambandhar, and Sundarar. Their Tamil hymns form the Devaram, or 'Divine Garland', and have exercised a great influence on Saivism. Like the Vishnuites, they offered salvation to all. In the tenth century a still greater man, known as Manikka Vachakar, consecrated his poetic gifts to Siva. He wrote a collection of exquisite Tamil lyrics which form the Tiruvachakam, or Sacred Utterance. Both these collections of hymns are used in the worship of Siva in the temples.

Bhagavatas

In North India the *Bhagavata Purana* or Purana of the Adorable, a rhapsody on Krishna, and by far the most influential of the Puranas, appeared somewhere about the tenth century. Nimbarka, whose followers worship Radha, Krishna's cowherd mistress, as well as Krishna himself, came a little later. Jayadeva, the author of the *Gita Govinda*, or Cowherd Song, which celebrates Krishna in the richest erotic strain, flourished about A.D. 1100.

Vira Shaivas

At Kalyan in the Maratha country in the twelfth century, Basava, the prime minister of the state, founded the Vira Shiva sect. The movement seems to have been essentially a revolt against Brahmin domination. The ancient worship of Siva is retained, but only the *linga* and Siva's bull, Nandi, are very prominent. Members of the sect are distinguished from ordinary Hindus by the wearing of a small *linga* somewhere about the person. Hence they are commonly called Lingayats. Their priests are called Jangamas. At first they renounced caste completely; but the old poison has crept in amongst them again. Caste had been denounced earlier by Kapilar nd Vemana, the first a Tamil, the second a Telugu poet; but **the Vira Shiva sect seems to have been the earliest organized movement that opposed the ancient basis of Hindu society. Similar attempts followed North India.**

Bhakti is one of the most important clements of the teaching of all these sects. Bhakti means 'adoration' directed towards Bhagavan, 'the adorable,' by the Bhakta, 'the adoring devotee.' Bhagavan is used for Vishnu, Krishna, Rama, Siva, or any other god the worshipper adores. All the modern bhakti schools of Vishnuism are called by the common name of Bhagavatas, worshippers of Bhagavan. This was the name of a very early Vishnuite school.

Sankara

A little more than a century later there appeared the great Sankara (A.D. 788 to about 850), the supreme acharya of the Vedanta school. His fame rests on his commentaries on the *Vedanta Sutra,* the *Bhagavadgita,* and the chief Upanishads. He held that the true Vedanta system was *advaita,* i.e., an unqualified monism. **Nothing is real except Brahman. Man's soul is the eternal spirit whole and undivided; and the world is maya, illusion. Hence forward the central school of the Vedanta is advaita,** strictly monistic. His scholarship and immense capacity secured him great influence; and his system of thought was accepted all over India.

From this time onward the central school of the Vedanta accepts the doctrine of incarnations taught in the Gita.

Thus the ancient philosophy attached to itself a theology with the worship of a personal god and the use of idols. Sankara seems also to have accepted and taught the doctrine of the Hindu triad in the philsophic form, viz., that Brahma, Vishnu, and Siva are the triple manifestation of the impersonal One, but that they are not eternal beings.

Ramanuja

It was nearly three centuries later before the worshippers of Vishnu produced a man fit to wrestle with Sankara over this great question. Their protagonist is Ramanuja, whose mean date is A.D. 1100. He carried on the work of the Alvars, and was high-priest of the whole Vaishnava community of the south. His commentary on the *Vedanta Sutra* is known as the *Sribhashya,* and has achieved a popularity almost as great as the work of Sankara. **He calls his system Visishtadvaita, modified monism, and claims that it is the true Vedanta,** the doctrine of the Upanishads. Brahman is Vishnu and is personal. Man's spirit is an *amsa* or portion of God, and even in final union retains its own individuality and consciousness. The doctrine of incarnations is strongly held.

The Muhammadan conquest of India must not be regarded as merely a series of military exploits leading to a vast political change. The conquerors regarded themselves as crusaders, attacking a vast idolatrous paganism in the name of God. Hence, **wherever they went, they destroyed the religious schools, overthrew the temples, smashed the idols, drove away or killed the Buddhist monks and the Hindu priests.** Idolatry was forbidden, and a tax was imposed on non-Muslims.

Buddhism seems to have disappeared almost altogether under the shock.

Yet Hinduism was too deeply rooted in the hearts of the people to be destroyed by adversity. Though changes necessarily arose as a result of the conquest, it is surprising how little alteration was produced in the religion. Indeed it would not be too much to say that the crushing of the Hinduism of the temple and the scholar led to the outbursting of a simpler and more helpful faith from the heart of the people itself.

The religious movements of the north during these centuries fall into three groups, Ramaite, Krishnaite, and deistic; yet all the sects have a great many point in common, inherited from earlier forms of Vaishnavism. They believe in one personal God who is full of love and pity for those who worship him; yet all, except the followers of Kabir, recognize the other gods, and worship idols they all hold that the human soul is a portion of the Divine, and that it will eternally retain its individuality; they offer salvation to men of all castes, demanding faith and *bhakti* toward the Lord.

Ramananda

Of the Ramaite leaders we shall mention the three most notable. Ramananda was a native of South India and was a leader in the Sri Sampradaya, the church of Ramanuja; but in consequence of a quarrel he left the sect and migrated to North India. He gave up all the exclusiveness of Ramanuja, and also his troublesome restrictions ahout food. He preached in Hindi, and admitted all castes, evcn the lowest, to his fold.

Tulsi Das

Tulsi Das belonged to the church of Ramananda. His activity was contemporaneous with the reign of the great Akbar and of his son Jahangir. He alone among the bhakti leaders did not found a sect. He preferred to influence all his fellow-countrymen; and he has won his reward: for the millions of the people of North India today acknowledge Tulsi Das as their guide.

The teaching which he imparted as he wandered over the land he gave permanent form to it in the *Ramacharitmanas,* 'the Lake of the Deeds of Rama'. It is a modern *Ramayana* in the sense that it recounts the old story, but it is shot through and through with bhakti theology and with the healthy moral spirit of the poet. The language is Eastern Hindi. Those who know say that he produced 'some of the most beautiful poetry which has found birth in Asia'; and the common people of the north show by their devotion to his great work that they agree with this high praise.

Krishnaites

The Krishnaite books in Sanskrit were followed up by some very interesting vernacular literature in the latter half of the fifteenth century. Vidyapati wrote many lyrics in the dialect of Bihar; Chandi Das did similar work in Bengali; and in Rajputana, Mira Bai, a princess, wrote beautiful songs, which are extremely popular, in the Braj Bhasha. This is the dialect of the country around Mathura, where Krishna's life among the cowherds is fabled to have been lived. In this very country the first fully systematized form of popular Krishnaism was founded in the early part of the sixteenth century by a Brahmin from the south named Vallabhacharya. In his teaching and among his followers the sensual elements which are present in all the later Krishnaite mythology come to the front and bear their harvest.

Kabir

The deistic movement springs from KabIr, the Muhammadan weaver who was one of the apostles of Ramananda. Here Muhammadan influence makes itself distinctly felt. For, though KabIr was a disciple of Ramananda, though he calls God by the name Rama, and has Vedantic ideas, he will have nothing to do with the doctrine of incarnations, and **he condemns idolatry and caste with unsparing voice.** Yet he is recognized as an incarnation himself by his followers, the Kabirpanthis.

Nanak

No direct influence exerted by Kabir, however, is equal to the indirect influence which has arisen through the founding of the Sikh sect in the Punjab by his disciple, Nanak. From the beginning the chief guru of the church exercised large power; and the tenth guru, named Govind, took such steps as transformed the sect into a military order and finally created a great and warlike nation. But no guru succeeded Govind, and their sacred book, the *Granth,* is now the centre of the faith.

Madhva

In the fourteenth century a new Vishnuite movement appeared at Udipi, in the Kannada country. The founder of the church is known as Madhvacharya, his followers as Srimadhvas. Madhva was a sannyasi, and, like the other acharyas, he made his reputation by a commentary on the Vedanta Sutra. His system is a dualism, and is frankly called dvaita, dualistic.

The Modern Times[1]

When the British conquered India, Hindu society was in a mess owing to historical factors. Long centuries of Muslim oppression had unnerved its constituents, including religion. The period after Aurangzeb was confusion worse confounded, but the Maratha and Sikh efforts were trying to push up resurguence and revival in a most vigorous manner.

1. Added by M.K.

The sudden intervention of the British in the form of traders had injected an unexpected and unusual element in the country's life which was good as well as bad at the same time. It enslaved the country as also freed it and gave it new ideas, including railways, factories, postal system, etc. Christianity came with them, which worked both ways, on the one hand condemning the Hindu religion and practices most severely in order to convert the people as soon as they could, as they and their compatriots had been doing in other parts of the world; and on the other, being themselves influenced by the fineries of Hindu philosophy, which no other country had done to them. This is turn inspired the Hindus themselves to start their own renaissance and revive the country after over a thousand years.

Its first major expression was in Bengal, where the British had concentrated and were active in the academic areas, too. Raja Rammohan Roy started the first movement known as the Brahmo Samaj which promoted a simpler worship influenced by Christianity. Keshav Chandra Sen, Debendranath Tagore and others came up with new ideas and practices, creating a fermentation unknown till date. The Raja also got the practice of Sati outlawed in the country, a ground-breaking contribution in social reform; Rabindranath Tagore, son of Debendranath Tagore, further expanded the awakening through new literature, drama, music and education, by establishing the grand multi-sided experiment, Santiniketan; he won the Nobel Prize in 1913, the first in Asia, which added further laurels to Indian culture and made its high points known to the whole world.

The second great movement was initiated by Swami Dayanand of Gujerat who established the Arya Samaj in 1875, promoting perhaps the most enlightened arm of Hinduism, decrying the rampant idolatry and temple-worship, declaring that the Vedas did not approve of it. He was a great fighter and fought singlehanded the temple-worshipper Sanatanis and those forcibly converting the Hindus, the Muslims and Christians. He provided a near complete agenda of India's change and his movement spread like wild fire in north India, contributing substantially to the slowly emerging freedom movement also. It provided revolutionaries with revolvers as well as non-violent brigades of Gandhiji.

Another movement known as Prarthana Samaj was launched in Bombay and it spread in Maharashtra, with Mahadev Govind Ranade as its leader. Its contribution to women's awakening was remarkable.

Yet another major movement developed in Bengal with the emergence of Ramakrishna Paramahansa, whose simple ways and devotional teaching made him very popular, and whose disciple Vivekananda, won over the American intellectual world by appearing and speaking in the Parliament of Religions in Chicago in 1893. Though quite young at the time, he was an excellent speaker and his scholarship in religious matters was remarkable. He promoted a world religion based on Vedanta which, it is important, attracted attention of many Western intellectuals, many of whom got ready to work for it, and taught Raja Yoga to them, for the first time. But he didn't live long, passing away without reaching 40, and with his demise his great agenda dissolved into thin air.

He was a thinker also, an idea he left in seed form was taken up a decade later by Cambridge-returned revolutionary Aurobindo Ghose, later on famous as Sri Aurobindo–who tried to translate it into reality: a forty years long yogic experiment which he carried out staying in one simple home in Pondicherry. The idea was that with Yoga the next state of human evolution could be acquired. To achieve the objective, he devised a new form of yoga and called it Purna Yoga, or Integral Yoga. A French yoga-practitioner, Mirra Alfassa, joined him in the unusual experiment; she became famous all over the world as the Mother. The news that the new species might take birth at Pondicherry shook the intellectuals in the West and many started flocking to the ashram to participate in it.

The first half of the twentieth century was the period dominated by Tilak, Gokhale and Gandhiji, and also Subhas—of these Gandhi was a giant, a political experimenter in non-violence. He won freedom for India, greatly influenced the whole world, but was killed in 1948. The second half of the century is now past and the twenty-first has started and the country is struggling to stand on her own feet. Hinduism is spreading as a better religious option in the West.

This is the general scenario of modern Hinduism. There has been a successful renaissance, and we are now 'marketing'– is this the correct word?–our achievements. There have been our Yogananda, Osho, Maharishi Mahesh Yogi, Swami Prabhupada, Swami Muktananda, Satya Sai Baba and others, and despite some of their failings, we are making our mark in the market of ideas in the world.

• • •

SELECT SCRIPTURES FROM THE RIGVEDA

KAH : WHO ?
Hiranyagarbha

Kah (qius) meaning Who? that is, the Unknown God, has been applied as a name to Prajapati, and to other gods.

1. In the beginning rose Hiranyagarbha, born Only Lord of all created beings.
   He fixed and holdeth up this earth and heaven. What God shall we adore with our oblation?
2. Giver of vital breath, of power and vigour, he whose commandments all the Gods acknowledge:
   The Lord of death, whose shade is life immortal. What God shall we adore with our oblation?
3. Who by his grandeur hath become Sole Ruler of all the moving world that breathes and slumbers;
   He who is Lord of men and Lord of cattle. What God shall we adore with our oblation?
4. His, through his might, are these snowcovered mountains, and men call sea and Rasa his possession;
   His arms are these, his are these heavenly regions. What God shall we adore with our oblation?

5. By him the heavens are strong and earth is steadfast, by him light's realm and sky-vault are supported;
   By him the regions in mid air were measured. What God shall we adore with our oblation?
6. To him, supported by his help, two armies embattled look while trembling in their spirit;
   When over them the risen Sun is shining. What God shall we adore with our oblation?
7. What time the mighty waters came, containing the universal germ, producing Agni;
   Thence sprang the Gods' one spirit into being. What God shall we adore with our oblation?
8. He in his might surveyed the floods containing productive force and generating Worship.
   He is the God of gods, and none beside him. What God shall we adore with our oblation?
9. Ne'er may he harm us who is earth's Begetter, nor he whose laws are sure, the heavens' Creator,
   He who brought forth the great and lucid waters. What God shall we adore with our oblation?
10. Prajapati! thou only comprehend all these created things, and none beside thee.
    Grant us our hearts' desire when we invoke thee: may we have store of riches in possession.

(X/21)

SRISHTI: CREATION
Prajapati

Whose eye controls this world in highest heaven, heverily knowist, or perhaps he knows not.

1. Then was not non-existent nor existent: there was no realm of air, no sky beyond it.
   What covered in, and where? and what gave shelter? Was water there, unfathomed depth of water?

2. Death was not then, nor was there aught immortal: no sign was there, the day's and night's divider.

   That One Thing breathless, breathed by its own nature: apart from it was nothing whatsoever.

3. Darkness there was : at first concealed in darkness this All was in discriminated chaos.

   All that existed then was void and formless: by the great power of Warmth was born that Unit.

4. Thereafter rose Desire in the beginning, Desire, the primal seed and germ of Spirit.

   Sages who searched with their heart's thought discovered the existent's kinship in the non-existent.

5. Transversely was their severing line extended: what was above it then, and what below it?

   There were begetters, there were nightly forces, free action here and energy up yonder.

6. Who verily knows and who can here declare it, whence it was born and whence comes this creation?

   The Gods are later than this world's Production. Who knows then whence it first came into being?

7. He, the first origin of this creation, whether he formed it all or did not form it.

(X/129)

PURUSA: THE UNIVERSAL SOUL
Narayana

Purusa, embodied spirit, or Man personified and regarded as the soul and original source of the universe, the personal and life-giving principle in all animated beings, is said to have a thousand, that is, innumerable, heads, eyes, and feet, as being one with all created life. A space ten fingers wide: the region of the heart of man, wherein the soul was supposed to reside. Although as the Universal Soul he pervades the universe, as the Individual Soul he is enclosed in a space of narrow dimensions.

1. A thousand heads hath Purusa, a thousand eyes, a thousand feet.
   On every side pervading earth he fills a space ten fingers wide.
2. This Purusa is all that yet hath been and all that is to be;
   The Lord of Immortality which waxes greater still by food.
3. So mighty is his greatness; yea, greater than this is Purusa.
   All creatures are one-fourth of him, three fourths eternal life in heaven.
4. With three-fourths Purusa went up: one-fourth of him again was here.
   Thence he strod out to every side over what eats not and what eats.
5. From him Viraj was born; again Purusa from Viraj was born.
   As soon as he was born he spread eastward and westward o'er the earth.
6. When Gods prepared the sacrifice with Purusa as their offering,
   Its oil was spring, the holy gift was autumn; summer was the wood.
7. They balmed as victim on the grass Purusa born in earliest time.
   With him the Deities and all Sadhyas and Risis sacrificed.
8. From that great general sacrifice the dripping fat was gathered up.
   He formed the creatures of the air, and animals both wild and tame.
9. From that great general sacrifice Richas and Sama-hymns were born:
   Therefrom were spells and charms produced; the Yajus had its birth from it.
10. From it were horses born, from it all cattle with two rows of teeth:

From it were generated kine, from it the goats and sheep were born.

11. When they divided Purusa how many portions did they make?

What do they call his mouth, his arms? What do they call his thighs and feet?

12. The Brahmin was his mouth, of both his arms was the Rajanya made.

His thighs became the Vaishya, from his feet the Shudra was produced.

13. The Moon was gendered from his mind, and from his eye the Sun had birth;

Indra and Agni from his mouth were born, and Vayu from his breath.

14. Forth from his navel came mid-air; the sky was fashioned from his head;

Earth from his feet, and from his ear the regions. Thus they formed the worlds.

15. Seven fencing-sticks had he, thrice seven layers of fuel were prepared,

When the Gods, offering sacrifice, bound, as their victim, Purusa.

16. Gods, sacrificing, sacrificed the victim: these were the earliest holy ordinances.

The Mighty Ones attained the height of heaven, there were the Sadhyas, Gods of old, are dwelling.

(X/90)

MAYABHEDA: ILLUSION

Prajapati

The subject is Mayabheda, the discernment of maya, or illusion, the cause of material creation.

1. The sapient with their spirit and their mind behold the Bird adorned with all an Asura's magic might.

Sages observe him in the ocean's inmost depth: the wise disposers seek the station of his rays.

2. The flying Bird bears Speech within his spirit: erst the Gandharva in the womb pronounced it:
   And at the seat of sacrifice the sages cherish this radiant heavenly-bright invention.
3. I saw the Herdsman, him who never resteth, approaching and departing on his pathways.
   He, clothed in gathered and diffusive splendour, within the worlds continually travels.

(X/177)

DYAVA-PRITHIVI: HEAVEN AND EARTH

Auchathya

1. These, Heaven and Earth, bestow prosperity on all, sustainers of the region, Holy Ones and wise,
   Two Bowls of noble kind: between these Goddesses the God, the fulgent Sun, travels by fIxed decree.
2. Widely-capacious Pair, mighty, that never fail, the Father and the Mother keep all creatures safe:
   The two world-halves, the spirited, the beautiful, because the Father hath clothed them in goodly forms.
3. Son of these Parents, he the Priest with power to cleanse, Sage, sanctifies the worlds with his surpassing power.
   Thereto for his bright milk he milked through all the days the partly-coloured Cow and the prolifIc Bull.
4. Among the skilful Gods most skilled is he, who made the two world-halves which bring prosperity to all;
   Who with great wisdom measured both the regions out, and established them with pillars that shall ne'er decay.
5. Extolled in song, O Heaven and Earth, bestow on us, ye mighty Pair, great glory and high lordly sway,
   Whereby we may extend ourselves ever over the folk; and send us strength that shall deserve the praise of men.

(X/160)

PRITHIVI: EARTH
Atri

1. Thou, of a truth, O' Prithivi, bearest the tool that rends the hills:

   Thou rich in torrents, who with might quickens earth, O Mighty One.

2. To thee, O wanderer at will, ring out the lauds with beams of day,

   Who drivest, like a neighing steed, the swelling cloud, O bright of hue.

3. Who graspest with thy might on earth e'en the strong sovrans of the wood,

   When from the lightning of thy cloud the rainfloods of the heaven descend.

(V/84)

MANAS: SPIRIT
Bandhu

The Hymn is an address to recall the fleeting spirit of a man at the point of death.

1. Thy spirit, that went far away to Yama to Vivasvan's Son,

   We cause to come to thee again that thou mayst live and sojourn here.

2. Thy spirit, that went far away, that passed away to earth and heaven,

   We cause to come to thee again that thou Mayst live and sojourn here.

3. Thy spirit, that went far away, away to the four-cornered earth,

   We cause to come to thee again that thou mayst live and sojourn here.

4. Thy spirit, that went far away to the four quarters of the world,
   We cause to come to thee again that thou mayst live and sojourn here.
5. Thy spirit, that went far away, away unto the billowy sea,
   We cause to come to thee again that thou mayst live and sojourn here.
6. Thy Spirit, that went far away to beams of light that Flash and Flow,
   We cause to come to thee again that thou mayst live and Sojourn here.
7. Thy spirit, that went far away, went to the waters and the plants,
   We cause to come to thee again that thou mayst live and sojourn here.
8. Thy spirit, that went far away, that visited the Sun and Dawn.
   We cause to come to thee again that thou mayst live and sojourn here.
9. Thy spirit, that went far away, away to lofty mountain heights,
   We cause to come to thee again that thou mayst live and sojourn here.
10. Thy spirit, that went far away into this All that lives and moves,
    We cause to come to thee again that thou mayst live and sojourn here.
11. Thy spirit, that went far away to distant realms beyond our ken,
    We cause to come to thee again that thou mayst live and sojourn here.
12. Thy spirit, that went far away to all that is and is to be,
    We cause to come to thee again that thou mayst live and sojourn here.

(X/58)

VAK: SPEECH
Vagambhrani

Vak is Speech personified, the Word, the first creation and representative of Spirit, and the means of communication between men and Gods. The hymn shows that the primary application of the name was to the voice of the hymn, the means of communication between heaven and earth at the sacrifice.

1. I travel with the Rudras and the Vasus, with the Adityas and All-Gods I wander.

   I hold aloft both Varuna and Mitra, Indra and Agni, and the Pair of Asvins.

2. I cherish and sustain high-swelling Soma, and Tvastar I support, Pusan, and Bhaga.

   I load with wealth the zealous sacrificer who pours the juice and offers his oblation.

3. I am the Queen, the gatherer-up of treasures, most thoughtful, first of those who merit worship.

   Thus Gods have established me in many places with many homes to enter and abide in.

4. Through me alone all eat the food that feeds them,—each man who sees, breathes, hears the word outspoken.

   They know it not, but yet they dwell beside me. Hear, one and all, the truth as I declare it.

5. I, verily, myself announce and utter the word that Gods and men alike shall welcome.

   I make the man I love exceeding mighty, make him a sage, a Rishi, and a Brahmin.

6. I bend the bow for Rudra that his arrow may strike and slay the hater of devotion.

   I rouse and order, battle for the people, and I have penetrated Earth and Heaven.

7. On the world's summit I bring forth the Father: my home is in the waters, in the ocean.

   Thence I extend o'er all existing creatures, and touch even yonder heaven with my forehead.

8. I breathe a strong breath like wind and tempest, the while I hold together all existence.

   Beyond this wide earth and beyond the heavens I have become so mighty in my grandeur.

(X/125)

SHRADDHA: FAITH

Kamayani

1. By Faith is Agni kindled, through Faith is oblation offered up.

   We celebrate with praises Faith upon the height of happiness.

2. Bless thou the man who gives, O Faith; Faith, bless the man who fain would give.

   Bless thou the liberal worshippers: bless thou the word that I have said.

3. Even as the Deities maintained Faith in the mighty Asuras,

   So make this uttered wish of mine true for the liberal worshippers.

4. Guarded by Vayu, Gods and men who sacrifice, draw near to Faith.

   Man winneth Faith by yearnings of the heart and opulence by Faith.

5. Faith in the early morning, Faith at noon-day will we invocate,

   Faith at the setting of the Sun. O Faith, endow us with belief.

(X/151)

JNANA: KNOWLEDGE
Brihaspati

Jnana or Knowledge, the subject of this very difficult hymn, is said by Sayana to mean Parama-brahmajnanam, knowledge of the higher truths of Religion, which teaches man his own nature and how he may be reunited to the Supreme Spirit.

1. When men, BrihaspatL giving names to objects, sent out Vak's first and earliest utterances,

   All that was excellent and spotless, treasured within them, was disclosed through their affection.
2. Where, like men cleansing corn flour in a cribble, the wise in spirit have created language,

   Friends see and recognize the marks of friendship: their speech retains the blessed sign imprinted.
3. With sacrifice the trace of Vak they .followed, and found her harbouring within the Rishis.

   They brought her, dealt her forth in many places: seven singers make her tones resound in concert.
4. One man hath ne'er seen Vak, and yet he seeth: One man hath hearing but hath never heard her.

   But to another hath she shown her beauty as a fond well-dressed woman to her husband.
5. One man they call a laggard, dull in friendship: they never urge him on to deeds of valour.

   He wanders on in profitless illusion: the Voice he heard yields neither fruit nor blossom.
6. No part in Vak hath he who hath abandoned his own dear friend who knows the truth of friendship.

   Even if he hears her still in vain he listens; naught knows he of the path of righteous action.
7. Unequal in the quickness of their spirit are friends endowed alike with eyes and hearing.

Some look like tanks that reach the mouth or shoulder, others like pools of water fit to bathe in.

8. When friendly Brahmins sacrifice together with mental impulse which the heart hath fashioned,

They leave one far behind through their attainments, and some who count as Brahmins wander elsewhere.

9. Those men who step not back and move not forward, nor Brahmins nor preparers of libations,

Having attained to Vak in sinful fashion spin out their thread in ignorance like spinsters.

10. All friends are joyful in the friend who cometh in triumph, having conquered in assembly.

He is their blame-averter, food-provider: prepared is he and fit for deed of vigour.

11. One plies his constant task reciting verses: one sings the holy psalm in Shakvari measures.

One more, the Brahmin, tells the lore of being, and one lays down the rules of sacrificing.

(X/71)

AGNI: GOD OF FIRE
Madhucchandas

The first hymn of the Rigveda is ascribed to the Rishi or seer Madhucchandas Vaisvamitra, a son or descendant of the famous Visvamitra. The deity to whom this hymn is addressed is Agni, the God of fire, the most prominent of the deities of the Rigveda. Agni is the messenger and mediator between earth and heaven, announcing to the Gods the hymns, and conveying to them the oblations of their worshippers, inviting them with the sound of his crackling flames and bringing them down to the place of sacrifice.

As concentrating in himself the various sacrificial duties of different classes of human priests, Agni is called the Purohita or chosen priest He is a Ritvij, a priest or minister who sacrifices at the proper seasons, and a Hotar, an invoking priest, a herald who calls the Gods to enjoy the offering. All riches are at his disposal, and he is the most bountiful rewarder, both directly and indirectly, of the pious whose oblations he carries to the Gods.

1. I laud Agni, the chosen Priest, God, minister of sacrifice,
   The hotar, lavishest of wealth.
2. Worthy is Agni to be praised by living as by ancient seers.
   the shall bring hitherward the Gods.
3. Through Agni man obtains wealth, yea, plenty waxing day by day.
   Most rich in heroes, glorious.
4. Agni, the perfect sacrifice which thou encompassest about,
   Verity goeth to the Gods.
5. May Agni, sapient-minded Priest. truthfuL most gloriously great,
   The God, come hither with the Gods.
6. Whatever blessing, Agni, thou wilt grant unto thy worshipper,
   That, Angiras, is indeed thy truth.
7. To thee, dispeller of the night, O Agni, day by day with prayer,
   Bringing thee reverence, we come;
8. Ruler of sacrifices, guard of Law eternal, radiant One,
   Increasing in thine own abode.
9. Be to us easy of approach, even as a father to his son:
   Agni, be with us for our weal.

(I/1)

INDRA: WARRIOR GOD
Madhuchchandas

Indra was the favourite national deity of the Aryan Indians in the Vedic Age, and more hymns are dedicated to his honour than to the praise of any other divinity. He is the God who reigns over the intermediate region or atmosphere; he fights against and conquers with his thunderbolt the demons of draughts and darkness, and is in general the type of noble heroism.

1. As a good cow to him who milks, we call the doer of fair deeds,
   To our assistance day by day.
2. Come thou to our libations, drink of Soma, Soma-drinker thou!
   The rich One's rapture giveth kine.
3. So may we be acquainted with thine innermost benevolence:
   Neglect us not, come hitherward.
4. Go to the wise unconquered One, ask thou of Indra, skilled in song,
   Him who is better than thy friends.
5. Whether the men who mock us say, Depart unto another place,
   Ye who serve Indra and none else;
6. Or whether, God of wondrous deeds, all our true people call us blest
   Still may we dwell in Indra's care.
7. Unto the swift One bring the swift, man-cheering, grace of sacrifice,
   That to the Friend gives wings and joy.
8. Thou, Shatakratu, drankest this and wast the Vritras' slayer; thou
   helpest the warrior in the fray.
9. We strengthen, Shatakratu, thee, yea, thee the powerful in fight,
   That, Indra, we may win us wealth.
10. To him the mighty stream of wealth, prompt friend of him who pours the juice,
    Yea, to this Indra sing your song.

(I/4)

SOMA: ENERGY DRINK
Vishwamitra

Soma is the God who represents and animates the juice of the Soma plant. He was in former times the Indian Dionysus or Bacchus. 'The simple minded Aryan people,' says Professor Whitney, 'whose whole religion was a worship of the wonderful powers and phenomena of nature, had no sooner perceived that Soma juice had power to elevate the spirits, and produce a temporary frenzy, under the influence of which the individual was prompted to and capable of, deeds beyond his natural powers, than they found in it something divine: it was to their apprehension a God, enduring those into whom it entered with godlike powers; the plant which afforded it became to them the king of plants; the process of preparing it became a holy sacrifice.

1. In sweetest and most gladdening stream flow pure, O Soma, on thy way,
   Pressed out for Indra, for his drink.
2. Fiend-queller, Friend of all men, he hath with the wood attained unto
   His place, his iron-fashioned home.
3. Be thou best Vritra-slayer, best granter of bliss, most liberal:
   Promote our wealthy princes' gifts.
4. Flow onward with thy juice unto the banquet of the Mighty Gods:
   Flow hither for our strength and fame.
5. O Indu, we draw nigh to thee, with this one object day by day:
   To thee alone our prayers are said.
6. By means of this eternal fleece may Surya's Daughter purify;
   Thy Soma that is foaming forth.

7. Ten sister maids of slender form seize him within the press and hold
   Him firmly on the final day.
8. The virgins send him forth: they blow the skin musician live and fuse
   The triple foe-repelling meath.
9. Inviolable milch-kine round about him blend for Indra's drink,
   The fresh young Soma with their milk.
10. In the wild raptures of this draught, Indra slays all the Vritras: he,
    The Hero, pours his wealth on us.

(IX/1)

SURYA : THE SUN
Praskanva

1. His bright rays bear him up aloft, the God who knoweth all that lives,
   Surya, that all may look on him.
2. The constellations pass away, like thieves, together with their beams,
   Before the all-beholding Sun.
3. His herald rays are seen afar refulgent o'er the world of men,
   Like flames of fire that burn and blaze.
4. Swift and all beautiful art thou, O Surya, maker of the light,
   Illumine all the radiant realm.
5. Thou goest to the hosts of Gods, thou comest hither to mankind,
   Hither all light to be beheld.
6. With that same eye of thine wherewith thou lookest, brilliant Varuna,
   Upon the busy race of men,

7. Traversing sky and wide mid-air, thou metest with thy beams our days,
   Sun, seeing all things that have birth.
8. Seven Bay Steeds harnessed to thy car bear thee, O thou farseeing One,
   God, Surya, with the radiant hair.
9. Surya hath yoked the pure bright Seven, the daughters of the car; with these,
   His own dear team, he goeth forth.
10. Looking upon the loftier light above the darkness we have come
    To Surya, God among the Gods, the light that is most excellent.
11. Rising this day, O rich in friends, ascending to the loftier heaven,
    Surya, remove my heart's disease, take from me this my yellow hue.
12. To parrots and to starlings let us give away my yellowness,
    Or this my yellowness let us transfer to Haritala trees.
13. With all his conquering vigour this Aditya hath gone up on high,
    Giving my foe into mine hand: let me not be my foeman's prey.

(I/501)

ANNAM: FOOD
Atri

1. Now will I glorify Food that upholds great strength,
   By whose invigorating power Trita rent Vritra limb from limb.
2. O pleasant Food, O Food of meath, thee have we chosen for our own,
   So be our kind protector thou.

3. Come hitherward to us, O Food, auspicious with auspicious help,

   Health-bringing, not unkind, a dear and guileless friend.
4. These juices which, O Food, are thine throughout the regions are diffused.

   Like winds they have their place in heaven.
5. These gifts of thine, O Food, most sweet to taste,

   These savours of thy juices work like creatures that have mighty necks.
6. In thee, O Food, is set the spirit of great Gods.

   Under thy flag brave deeds were done: he slew the Dragon with thy help.
7. If thou be gone unto the splendour of the clouds,

   Even from thence, O Food of meath, prepared for our enjoyment, come.
8. Whatever morsel we consume from waters or from plants of earth,

   O Soma, wax thou fat thereby.
9. What, Soma, we enjoy from thee in milky food or barley-brew,

   Vatapi, grow thou fat thereby.
10. O Vegetable, Cake of meal, be wholesome, firm, and strengthening:

    Vatapi, grow thou fat thereby.
11. O Food, from thee as such have we drawn forth with lauds, like cows, our sacrificial gifts,

    From thee who banquetest with Gods, from thee who banquetest with us.

(I/187)

• • •

ISHA UPANISHAD
God Pervades Everything

This short but valuable Upanishad provides excellent glimpses into the basic ideas of the Vedanta philosophy. It describes the nature and characteristics of Atman, the ethical conduct of one who knows it as well as a view of the beyond. Its unequivocal declaration that the Lord pervades the whole universe and allied beings, one should not covet others' goods and try to live within one's means and help the needy, may be taken as a commandment to human beings.

All this, whatsoever moves on earth, is to be hidden in the Lord. When thou hast surrendered all this, then thou mayest enjoy. Do not covet the wealth of any man!

Though a man may wish to live a hundred years, performing works, it will be thus with him; but not in any other way: work will thus not cling to a man.

There are the worlds of the Asuras covered with blind darkness. Those who have destroyed their self (who perform works, without having arrived at a knowledge of the true Self), go after death to those worlds.

That one, the Self, though never stirring, is swifter than thought. The Devas (senses) never reached it, it walked before them. Though standing still, it overtakes the others who are running. Matarishvan 'the wind, the moving spirit' bestows powers on it.

It strirs and it stirs not; it is far, and likewise near. It is inside of all this, and it is outside of all this.

And he who beholds all beings in the Self, and the Self in all beings, he never turns away from it.

When to a man who understands, the Self has become all things, what sorrow, what trouble can there be to him who once beheld that unity?

He 'the Self' encircled all, bright, incorporeal, scathless, without muscles, pure, untouched by evil; a seer, wise, omnipresent, self-existent, he disposed all things rightly for eternal years.

All who worship what is not real knowledge (good works), enter into blind darkness: those who delight in real knowledge, enter, as it were, into greater darkness.

One thing, they say, is obtained from real knowledge; another, they say, from what is not knowledge. Thus we have heard from the wise who taught us this.

He who knows at the same time both knowledge and not-knowledge, overcomes death through not-knowledge, and obtains immortality through knowledge.

All who worship what is not the true cause, enter into blind darkness: those who delight in the true cause, enter, as it were, into greater darkness.

One thing, they say, is obtained from knowledge of the cause; another, they say, from knowledge of what is not the cause. Thus we have heard from the wise who taught us this.

He who knows at the same time both the cause and the destruction (the perishable body), overcomes death by destruction, and obtains immortality through knowledge of the true cause.

The door of the True is covered with a golden disk. Open that, O Pushan, that we may see the nature of the True.

O Pushan, only seer, Yama (Judge), Surya (sun), son of Prajapati, spread thy rays and gather them! The light which is thy fairest form, I see it. I am what He is, the person in the sun.

Breath to air, and to the immortal! Then this my body ends in ashes. Om! Mind, remember! Remember thy deeds! Mind, remember! Remember thy deeds!

Agni, lead us on to beatitude by a good path, thou, O God, who knowest all things! Keep far from us crooked evil, and we shall offer thee the fullest praise!

• • •

THE ESSENTIAL GITA

Krishna

How hath this weakness taken thee?
Whence springs
The inglorious trouble, shameful to the brave,
Barring the path of virtue? Nay, Arjuna!
Forbid thyself feebleness! it mars
Thy warrior-name! cast off the coward-fit!
Wake! Be thyself! Arise, Scourge of thy Foes!

Arjuna

How can I, in the battle, shoot with shafts
On Bhishma, or on Drona—O thou Chief!—
Better to live on beggar's bread
With those we love alive,
Than taste their blood in rich feasts spread,
And guiltily survive!
Ah! were it worse—who knows?—to be
Victor or vanquished here,
When those confront us angrily

Whose death leaves living drear?
In pity lost, by doubtings tossed,
My thoughts—distracted—turn
To Thee, the Guide I reverence most,
That I may counsel learn:
I know not what would heal the grief
Burned into soul and sense,
If I were earth's unchallenged chief—
A god—and these gone thence!

Sanjaya

So spake Arjuna to the Lord of Hearts,
And sighing, "I will not fight!" held silence then.
To whom, with tender smile, (o Bharata!)
While the prince wept despairing 'twixt those hosts,
Krishna made answer in divinest verse:

Krishna

Thou grievest where no grief should be! thou speak'st
Words lacking wisdom! for the wise in heart
Mourn not for those that live, nor those that die.
Nor I, nor thou, nor anyone of these,
Ever was not, nor ever will not be,
For ever and for ever afterwards.
All, that doth live, lives always! To man's frame
As there come infancy and youth and age,
So come there raisings-up and laying-down
Of other and of other life-abodes,
Which the wise know, and fear not. This that irks—
Thy sense—life, thrilling to the elements—

Bringing thee heat and cold, sorrows and joys,
'Tis brief and mutable! Bear with it, Prince!
As the wise bear.
The soul which is not moved,
The soul that with a strong and constant calm
Takes sorrow and takes joy indifferently,
Lives in the life undying! That which is
Can never cease to be; that which is not
Will not exist.
To see this truth of both
Is theirs who part essence from accident,
Substance from shadow. Indestructible,
Learn thou! the Life is, spreading life through all;
It cannot anywhere, by any means,
Be anywise diminished, stayed, or changed.
But for these fleeing frames which it informs
With spirit deathless, endless, infinite,
They perish.
Let them perish, Prince! and fight!
He who shall say, "Lo! I have slain a man!"
He who shall think, "Lo! I am slain!" those both
Know naught! Life cannot slay. Life is not slain!
Never the spirit was born; the spirit shall cease to be never;
Never was Time it was not; End and Beginning are realms!
Birthless and deathless and changeless remaineth the spirit for ever;
Death hath not touched it at all, dead though the

house of it seems!
Who knoweth it exhaustless, self-sustained,
Immortal, indestructible—shall such
Say, "I have killed a man, or caused to kill?"

Nay, but as when one layeth
His worn-out robes away,
And, taking new ones, sayeth,
"These will I wear to-day!"
So putteth by the spirit
Lightly its garb of flesh,
And passeth to inherit
A residence afresh.

I say to thee weapons reach not the Life;
Flame burns it not, waters cannot O'erwhelm,
Nor dry winds wither it. Impenetrable,
Unentered, unassailed, unharmed, untouched,
immortal, all-arriving, stable, sure,
Invisible, ineffable, by word
And thought uncompassed, ever all itself,
Thus is the Soul declared!
How wilt thou, then,—
Knowing it so,—grieve when thou shouldst not grieve?
How, if thou hearest that the man new-dead
Is, like the man new-born, still living man—
One same, existent Spirit—wilt thou weep?
The end of birth is death; the end of death
Is birth: this is ordained! and mournest thou,

Chief of the stalwart arm! for what befalls
Which could not otherwise befall? The birth
Of living things comes unperceived; the death
Comes unperceived; between them, beings perceive:
What is there sorrowful herein, dear Prince?
Wonderful, wistful, to contemplate!
Difficult, doubtful, to speak upon!
Strange and great for tongue to relate,
Mystical hearing for everyone!

Nor knoweth man this, what a marvel it is,
When seeing, and saying, and hearing are done!
This life within all living things, my Prince!
Hides beyond harm; scorn thou to suffer, then,
For that which cannot suffer. Do thy part! .
Be mindful of thy name, and tremble not!
Nought better can betide a martial soul
Than lawful war;
happy the warrior
To whom comes joy of battle—comes, as now,
Glorious and fair, unsought; opening for him
A gateway unto Heav'n. But, if thou shunn'st
This honourable field—a Kshatriya—
If, knowing thy duty and thy task, thou bidd'st
Duty and task go by—that shall be sin!
And those to come shall speak thee infamy
From age to age; but infamy is worse
For men of noble blood to bear than death!
The chiefs upon their battle-chariots

Will deem't was fear that drove thee from the fray.
Of those who held thee mighty-souled the scorn
Thou must abide, while all thine enemies
Will scatter bitter speech of thee, to mock
The valour which thou hadst; what fate could fall
More grievously than this?
Either—being killed—
Thou wilt win Swarga's safety, or—alive
And victor—thou wilt reign an earthly king.
Therefore, arise, thou Son of Kunti! brace
Thine arm for conflict, nerve thy heart to meet—
As things alike to thee—pleasure or pain,
Profit or ruin, victory or defeat:

So minded, gird thee to the fight, for so
Thou shalt not sin!

❑ ❑ ❑

2.

Zoroastrianism

Parsi Religion of Purity and Goodness

A RELIGION NO MORE

The *Times of India*, 23.9.13, displays the following ad regarding the subject of this religion:

Jiyo Parsi

The scheme for Containing Population Decline of Parsis in India (with active support of Parzor Foundation & Bombay Parsi Panchayet).

Key Features of 'Jiyo Parsi'

- An ambitious 100% Central Sector scheme of Ministry of Minority Affairs to contain population decline of Parsi Community in India.
- A Community-driven programme with participation from Parzor Foundation, Bombay Parsi Panchayat, and local Anjumans.

Target Groups

- Parsi married couples of child-bearing age who seek assistance.
- Adults/Young men/women/Adolescent boys/girls for detection of diseases resulting in infertility with consent of Parents/Legal Guardians.
- Medical interventions under Standard Medical Protocols in empanelled Hospitals/Clinics.

- Advocacy/Outreach programmes with participation of the Parsi Community.
- Confidentiality of the patients to be given ulmost importance by the Ministry of Minority Affairs, Govt. of India.

AN ARYAN RELIGION

Hinduism and Zoroastrianism go back into what history would call 'the night of time,' Hinduism being the more ancient, and Zoroastrianism the second religion in the evolution of the Aryan race.

Some writers place this prophet – called Zoroaster sometimes, and more lately Zarathushtra – as late as 610 BC. That would make him about contemporary with the Buddha and with Plato—a position resting on Muslim authority. Dr L. H. Mills, looked upon as one of the greatest European authorties, made the standard translation of the Gathas and relies on the evidence of language. He says that the Gathas are written in a tongue which is evidently related to the Vedic Sanskrit, the Gathas being 'long after the oldest Riks'.

Then we come to the view taken by the German scholar, Dr. Haug, and he, basing himself on the destruction of the library of Persepolis by Alexander in 329 B.C., argues that, in order that such a vast library be gathered together, we must assume a greater antiquity to give the mere time necessary to write and gather the books. The writing was completed, he thinks, about 400 B.C. It is not posssible, he says, at the very latest, to put the time of Zoroaster after 1000 B.C. and he regards 2800 BC, as a more likely date, while he may be very much older!

Aristote, for instance, places the date of the Prophet at 9600 B.C., putting it 6,000 years before the time of Plato.

The religion which in modern days is called Zoroastrianism, the religion of the Parsis, is the second of the religions of the Aryan stock. The Iranians–coming forth from the same cradle land as the first family, but spreading westwards over that vast extent of territory which includes not only modern Persia but the realm of ancient Persia–were led in their first migration thither by their great prophet Zoroaster, who held to them the same position that Manu held to the original Aryan race.

These ancient Iranians were Aryan and not Semitic. The Iranians came from the Aryan stock and are really a sister race of the Aryans south of the Himalayas. **The ancient Gathas, or hymns, are written in metres that are closely allied to those of the Samaveda**. Their rhythm, their feet, the evident method of their chanting, are closely related to those which still exist among the Hindus. Those wonderful chants of the ancient world, that control the lower intelligences and that rise up to the higher in the language of colour and of music—these Gathas were chanted in that same archaic *svara*.

Turning now from the language of the Avesta to that much contested word **'Zend'**, which some say is a language while others say, it is a commentary. Zend is nothing more than a modern Pahlavi translation and commentary on the ancient writings. The word is certainly constantly applied simply to that translation, made under the Sassanian dynasty in comparatively modem times.

In the time of Alexander it is admitted that there was a vast library at Persepolis, and that, he burned it either in drunkenness or in revenge. Hence he is constantly called 'the accursed Alexander' in all the later writings belonging to the faith of Zoroaster[1]. Now, there is evidence that at that time there were two sets of the complete Zoroastrian literature. One of these was in the library and so was destroyed. The other set was taken possession of by the Greek conquerors and translated into Greek. Little of this survives, but fragments of it remain in the *Nabathaean Agriculture*, in the quotations made from it by Neoplatonic writers, who speak of the Oracles of Zoroaster and of the teachings of that prophet. These traces of the ancient

1. Still he is called "Great" by the West—should History admire destruction? —Ed.

teaching, preserved in the literature of the Greeks, strengthen and corroborate the acknowledged Zoroastrian.

Let us now consider our documents. First comes the **Yasna** of which the most ancient part consists of the Gathas, the hymns and the teachings which came from the mouth of the great prophet himself. They are now only five in number, and, as accepted in the present day, are mere fragments. But they are dignified, sublime and grand, bearing testimony to the nobility of the ancient teaching. These form the first part of the Yasna, the second part consists of prayers and ceremonies—prayers addressed to the supreme Deity, prayers equally addressed to the mighty ones who stand below him, forming the spiritual hierarchy.

After the Yasna, with its two parts, we have the **Visparad**, a collection of preparatory invocations to be used before other prayers and sacrifices. These two, the Yasna and the Visparad, may be regarded as holding the position in Zoroastrianism that is held by the Vedas in Hinduism.

Below these there comes what was once a vast mass of literature of which now only the names for the most part survive. There is one complete book, and same few fragments of the remainder, out of a list of twenty-one treatises, of which the contents, roughly outlined, are also on record—the twenty-one **Nasks**, they are called. These deal with sciences of every kind—with medicine, astronomy, agriculture, botany, philosophy—with the whole range in fact of sciences and laws. They hold the position held by the Vedanga in Hinduism. Of these only one book survives in its entirety, the *Vendidad*, the book of laws affecting the preservation of purity alike in external nature and in man.

Next we have the *Khordah Avesta* or little Avesta consisting of **Yashtas** (invocations) and prayers for the use of the laity rather than of the priests, many of them being the prayers used daily by the modem Parsis. It is a mixed collection—some of the fragments very ancient, some of comparatively recent date.

After the burning of the library of Persepolis came a period of five hundred and fifty years of anarchy and tumult, and it was only at the close of this period that, under the Sassanian monarchs, the surviving fragments of Zoroastrian literature were gathered together. Little marvel that only fragments remained—fragments of a once glorious whole, like pieces of mosaic rent from their bed where they formed part of a great and intelligible picture. Only those who can recover the picture can see where each fragment fitted in, and can thus judge of the original beauty of the whole.

Philosophy and Religion

Let us now turn to the philosophy and the religion.

At the head of the manifested universe stands **Ahura-Mazda**, sometimes translated as the Living Wisdom, sometimes as the Lord of Wisdom, sometimes as the Wise Lord. The cuneiform inscriptions have Auramazda, the Sassanian Auharmazda, and the modem Persian is Hormazd or Ormazd. He is the Supreme, the Universal, the All-pervasive, the Source and the Fountain of Life. In the Zoroastrian religion, he holds the same position as the manifested Brahman of the Upanishads, who came forth at the beginning, the One, the source of life to man. He is described over and over again in the different scriptures, not so fully in the Gathas—though there also in part—as in some of the prayers and invocations. Let us take two specimens that describe this mighty Being, in order that you may realize how sublime is the concept, how lofty this idea of the primeval God.

In the Ormazd Yasht, He proclaims his own qualities something in the same way as Sri Krishna does in the tenth discourse in the *Bhagavadgita*. He proclaims his names which describe his attributes: 'I am the Protector, I am the Creator, I am the Nourisher.'

I am the Knowing, I am the Holiest Heavenly One. My name is the Healing. ...My name is God, My name is Great, Wise One; My name is the Pure. ...I am called the Majestic. ...the Far-seeing. ...I am called the Watcher. ...The Augmenter,' and so on through a list of seventy-two names.

Let us listen to the description of Him in the words of the prophet himself:

He [Ahura-Mazda] first created, through his inborn lustre, the multitude of celestial bodies, and through his intellect the good creatures, governed by the inborn good mind. Thou, Ahura-Mazda, the Spirit who art everlasting, makest them [the good creatures] grow. When my eyes behold Thee, the Essence of Truth, the Creator of life, who manifests his life in his works, then I know Thee to be the primeval Spirit, Thou, Mazda, so high in mind as to create the world, and the father of the good mind.'

Ahura-Mazda is revealed as threefold as we read in the Khordah Avesta: *'Praise to Thee Ahura-Mazda, threefold before other creatures.'* This 'threefold' joins the Zoroastrian concept of the First Being to the threefold or triple Brahman who is so familiar to us in the Upanishads, and it also explains the emanation of two principles which exist in him, and a third completing the Trinity.

Plutarch says: 'Cromasdes [Ahura-Mazda] sprang out of the purest light'; Damasgys writes: 'The Magi and the whole Aryan nation consider, as Eudemos writes, some Space and others Time, as the universal cause out of which the good God as well as the evil spirit were separated, or as others asser' light and darkness before these two spirits arose. Theodors of 'the nefarious doctrine of the Persians, which Zoroastrades introduced, that about Zorouan whom he makes the ruler of the whole universe and calls him Destiny; and who when offering sacrifice in order to generate Hormisdas, produced both Hormisdas and Satan.'

This again comes out in a 'Refutation of Heresies' in the fifth century AD by Ezvik: 'Before anything heaven or earth, or creature of an kind whatever therein, was existing, Zeruan existed....He offered sacrifices for a thousand years in the hope of obtaining a son, Ormiz by name, who was to create heaven, earth, and everything therein.' Dr Haug, who clings to the grammatical blunder theory, acknowledges: 'That Zarvan Akarana was commonly believed in Persia, during the times of the Sassanians.

Let us now return to the threefold Ahura-Mazda, and his unfolding in order that creation might be. We learn that from him duality proceeded, **Spento-Mainyush** and **Angra Mainyush**, two principles that had their root in him, but that were unfolded in order that a manifested universe might be brought into existence. The words 'good' and 'evil' are used to describe these two principles, but they are not the most accurate. The key is given in the Gathas. Good and evil may be said to come into existence only when man during his evolution gains knowledge and the power of choice. The original duality is not of good and evil, but of spirit and matter, of reality and non-reality, of light and darkness, of construction and destruction, the two poles between which the universe is woven, and without which no universe can be.

The second phrase. 'reality and non-reality', is used by Zarathustra himself in the proclamation of this fundamental truth, for we read in the *Gatha Ahunavaiti*, that the prophet standing by the sacred fire, declared: 'In the beginning there was a pair of twins, two spirits, each of a peculiar activity'; He went on to say: 'And these two spirits united and created the first [the material things]; one the reality, the other the non-reality.'

The Prophet goes on to say that one or the other of these must be followed; of these two 'spirits' you must choose one, just as in all ancient teachings it is said that we may choose either spirit or matter. Call them, if you will, good and evil, but good and evil are not the fundamental names; the choice is made between the spiritual and the material.

Various names are given to these two showing how they were understood in the ancient days. In *Gatha Ushatavaiti* (Yasna, xlv) it is said: 'All ye who have come from near and far should now listen and hearken to what I shall proclaim. Now the wise have manifested this universe as a duality....I will proclaim the two primeval spirits of the world, of whom the increaser thus spoke to the destroyer.'

There are two names again that give us the clue to the secret—the 'increaser' and the 'destroyer'. Life is ever pouring forth from the one; the other is the material side which belongs to form and which is ever breaking up in order that life may go on into higher expression. As though to impress this on the people, it is said that the so-called evil spirit is the death by which the body of men is struck away. The destruction of form means the passing on of life into higher condition—not the work of any evil power, but the liberation of the soul, and therefore a part of the divine manifestation of the universe. They are also spoken of as 'the two masters', as 'the two creators', and it is said that the mighty Intelligence Srosh worshipped these 'two creators who create all things'. Surely this great one would not worship evil, though he might reverence the duality in the divine nature.

As though to set the question at rest, they are spoken of as 'my two spirits' by Ahura-Mazda himself. Dr. Haug fully grasps this idea and remarks: 'They are the two moving causes in the universe, united from the beginning, and therefore called "twins" [Yema, *Sans*. Yama]. They are present everywhere: in Ahura-Mazda as well as in man. We never find Angra-Mainyush mentioned as a constant opponent of Ahura-Mazda in the Gathas, as is the case in later writings. Such is the original Zoroastrian notion of the two creative spirits, who form only two parts of the Divine Being.

A little more difficult, perhaps, to trace, more covered over by a change that came in later times, is a third person in this primeval Trinity: Ahura-Mazda, who is the first and from whom all proceeds; the second with the duality which is ever the mark of the second person in the manifested Trinity; the third, the primeval Wisdom or Mind, by which the world was made.

This is **Armaiti**, of whom it is written: 'To succour this life [to increase it] Armaiti came with wealth, the good and true mind; She, the everlasting one, created the material world.' In later days Armaiti became identified with her creation and was worshipped as the goddess of the earth.

Next in order come the hierarchies of the heavenly Intelligences led by the seven presiding gods or Spirits, the **Ameshaspentas**. Sometimes Ahura-Mazda is placed at their head as one of them; sometimes they form the lower septenary above them being the higher Triad.

The seven Ameshaspentas (if Ahura-Mazda be omitted) are: Vohuman, the Good Mind; Asha Vahishta, the Best Holiness; Kshatraver, Power; Spendarmad, Love; Haurvatat, Health; Ameretad, Immortality; and **Fire**, 'the most helpful of the Ameshaspentas'.

To these prayers are continually addressed, hymns are chanted to them, the whole liturgy is permeated by their worship; and yet some oriental scholars—followed in this by only a small minority of modem Parsis—have materialized them into mere attributes of God, instead of the living Intelligences by whom, as it is said in the Gathas, the worlds were made and are sustained.

Dr. Mills degrades them into mere attributes, and in his translation always treats them as such, though occasionally he is forced into very untenable positions by this modern shrinking from the recognition of invisible Intelligences everywhere. Let us see if they can be taken as mere attributes:

Yet the most bounteous Mazda Ahura, and
Piety with Him,
And Asha the settlements furthering, Thou
Good Mind and thou the Dominion,
Hear ye me, all! and have mercy.

The 'qualities', here spelt with capitals, are some of the Aineshaspentas, Spendarmad, Vohuman and Kshatraver, and the plural 'ye', as well as the phrase, 'hear ye me, all!' is a curious way to address a god and his qualities.

Doctrines, Ahura, and actions, tell me which
are the best ones, Mazda,
And the debtor's prayer of the praisers; tell
me this with the Truth and the Good Mind,
And by Sovereign Power and grace bring on
this world's perfection.

The Pahlavi has: 'Do Thou, therefore, O Auharmazd, declare to me that which is the best word and deed, and do ye give that which is Thy debt, O Vohuman, and Thine, O Ashavahisht, for this praise, for through your sovereignty, O Auharmazd, the completion of progress is made manifestly real in the world at will.'

Thus I conceived Thee, bounteous,
Ahura-Mazda;
When with the Good Mind's help, obedience
neared me,
And asked of me: 'Who art thou? Whence thy
coming.
—a curious proceeding for a quality.
These your favours first ask I Thee, Ahura!
Asha! and grant too thine, Aramaiti!

Then take this from the *Yasna Haptanhaiti*, admittedly one of the oldest parts of the Yasna, after the Gathas: 'We worship Ahura-Mazda the righteous, master of righteousness, We worship the Ameshaspentas [the archangels], the possessors of good, the givers of good. We worship the whole creation of the righteous spirit.'

The Visparad begins: 'I invoke and proclaim to 'the Lords of the Heavenly, the Lords of the Earthly' and so on through a long list of gods. Again: 'We make them known: to Ahura-Mazda, to the holy Sraosha, to Rashnu the most righteous, to Mithra with large pastures. To the Ameshaspentas, to the Fravarshis of the pure, to the souls of the pure, to the Fire, the son of Ahura-Mazda, and to the great Lord.'

The Yasna bears its testimony: 'I invoke and proclaim to: the creator Ahura-Mazda, the Brilliant, Majestic, Greatest, Best, most Beautiful, the Strongest, most Intellectual, of the best body, the Highest through holiness; who is very wise, who rejoices afar, who created us, who formed us, who keeps us, the Holiest among the heavenly. I invoke and proclaim to: Vohumano, Ashavahista, Kshathra-Vairya, Spenta-armaiti, Haurvat and Ameritat; the body of the cow, the soul of the cow, the fire the son of Ahura-Mazda, the most helpful of the Ameshaspentas.'

But the Yasnas are full of worship: worship of the highest gods, of Mithra, of the goddess of the waters, of Sraosh—one of the mightiest of the great Intelligences—of the sun, moon, and stars.

Fire as God

We come now to the Fire, the supreme symbol of God, the symbol of divine life, that which is called the Son of Ahura-Mazda, the sacred symbol most reverenced by the Zoroastrians today. As we might expect, we find prayer after prayer addressed to the Fire, worship addressed to it in the plainest, the clearest and the most explicit terms. **The Fire is declared to be the most helpful of all the spiritual Intelligences, the most friendly, coming down from Ahura-Mazda and acquainted with all heavenly secrets**. 'Happy is the man to whom thou comest mightily, Fire, son of Ahura-Mazda. More friendly than the most friendly, more worthy of adoration than the most worthy of honour. 'Mayest thou come helpfully to us at the greatest business. Fire, thou art acquainted with Ahura-Mazda, acquainted with the heavenly. Thou art the holiest of the same [the fire] that bears the name Vazista. O Fire, son of Ahura-Mazda, we draw near to thee.'

In every religion, fire has been the symbol of the supreme God; Brahman is fire; Ahura-Mazda is fire; the Jews saw their god as a pillar of fire, and the Christians proclaim, 'Our God is a consuming fire.'

Everywhere fire has been and is the supreme emblem; for he whose glory is revealed as fire; it blazes out from That which 'is dark by excess of light', and the whole universe is but the outcome of the living flame. Picture Zarathustra, when, standing by the altar, he first spoke to the people, and taught them the truths that the Fire had revealed to him, the Sons of the Fire who sent him to the earth. Remember what is said in one of those 'Oracles' which reproduce the early traditions: 'When thou beholdest a sacred Fire, formless, flashing dazzlingly throughout the world, hear thou the voice of the Fire.'

There was no fire on the altar at his side; there was sandalwood in fragrant heaps, there were perfumes, but no fire. The rod entwined with fire-serpents that the prophet held in his hands is well known to every occultist, for a similar one was used filled with the living fire of the upper spheres, in the Ancient Mysteries.

He raised the rod, pointing it to heaven, and the vault of the blue sky, flames flashed down and fired the altar at his side, and the living fire wreathing round him made him a mass of flame, as he spake 'the Words of the Fire', and proclaimed the everlasting truths.

Zarathustra gave the words of power that could call the fire down from above, and century after century, the fire that blazed on the Zoroastrian altar in the fire-temple was no mere mingling of material flames. The sacred fire was called down from the fiery akasa; at the word of the priest, it fell upon the altar, and blazed there as the living symbol of God. When the lower priesthood had to act (when the higher one was not available), they were given the rod in which the living flame of fire was ever flashing, and when they touched the altar fuel with it, the heavenly fire blazed forth.

Even now, we see how the tradition has come down in the ceremonies by which the fire is lighted on the new altar. There is still a faint echo of the ancient truth, although the power has departed and no Parsi dastur can summon fire from on high. **Fire is gathered from all the different sources in the town** wherein the sacred flame is to be lighted, but the fire is not used as it is gathered from the earthly fuel; for the officiator places above the gathered fire an iron tray heaped with sandalwood, and holding it high so that there shall not be any material contact, the fire below lights the fuel, and a second fire leaps up. **Nine times over that ceremony is repeated**, until the very essence of fire, as it were, is gathered—pure for the pure, and worthy to be the symbol of the divine.

Further, they seek to have the fire of lightning flashing down from heaven, and as they are now unable to call it down for themselves, they have to wait, sometimes for years, before the last fire is gathered, and mingled at last with the others that burn upon the sacred altar. Before that sacred fire every Zoroastrian bows, and in the Zoroastrian home, when sunset falls, a fragment fire is carried through every room in the gathering dusk, emblem of the purifying and protecting power of the Supreme.

Purity a Must

We must now glance at the way in which man is regarded, that we may understand his place in the hierarchy of Intelligences. In him, as in all else, are the two principles—spirit and matter—and he can side with the one or the other. **All the ethic is based on the idea that he shall throw himself on the side of the pure, battle for the pure, maintain the pure.** It may be that the later view of Angra-Mainyush as the enemy was an attempt to stir man into active conflict against evil, to make him feel he was fighting the battle of the 'good spirit' against the 'evil spirit'.

To be in everything actively on the side of purity is a personal duty. The Zoroastrian must keep the earth pure, must till it as a religious duty. He must perform all the functions of agriculture as a service to the gods, for the earth is the pure creature of Ahura-Mazda to be guarded from all pollution. The air must be kept pure; the water must be kept pure; if anything unclean, like a corpse, falls into the water, the good Zoroastrian must remove it so that the pure element may not be fouled. Hence also the objection to burning a dead body, for the touch of the unclean pollutes the fire. Therefore the body is reverently carried to the Tower of Silence, and in that guarded place, open to the heavens, it is laid, that the vultures may swiftly devour it and no pure element may thereby be soiled.

Passing from the purity of external nature, with which a Parsi must not only passively but also actively associate himself, we come to that famous **axiom of their religion: 'Pure thoughts, pure worlds, pure deeds.'** That is the constantly reiterated rule of the Zoroastrian life repeated in his daily prayers, insisted on at every turn.

The first words of the **Khordah Avesta** from the Ashem-Vohu, the most, sacred formula ever repeated: 'Purity is the best good. Happiness is to him—namely, to the best pure in purity.' When Ahura-Mazda is answering Zarathustra as to the recital of the Ashem-Vohu, he declares that the recital of the Ashem-Vohu that is worth all the good things created by himself is 'when one forsakes evil thoughts and evil words and evil deeds.'

Between the ages of seven and fifteen, a child must be initiated, and then is put on him or her for the first time the *kusti*, or sacred thread, and the *sadra*, or white linen shirt, both emblems of purity. The *kusti* is made of seventy-two threads of lamb's wool, and is wound thrice round the waist, signifying the good thoughts, words and deeds incumbent on the wearer; it is knotted twice in front and twice behind.

Truthfulness, chastity, obedience to parents, hospitality, industry, honesty, kindness to domestic animals, are virtues on which special stress is laid, and charity is made an essential part of religion. Charity must be bestowed on the deserving— helping the poor, helping those to marry who cannot afford to do so, helping to educate the children of those unable to perform this duty for themselves are especially recommended.

Ervad Sheriarji Dadabhai Barucha says: 'Just as certain virtues are said to be the peculiar attributes of the four classes of the people, and highly becoming to them, so certain vices are specially to be shunned by them. For the priestly class, hypocrisy, covetousness, negligence, slothfulness, attention to trifles and unbelief in religion are peculiarly unbecoming. The warrior must be above oppression, violence, breach of promise, encouragement of evil, ostentation, arrogance and insolence. The husbandman must fly from ignorance, envy, ill will and malice; and the artisan must avoid incredulity, ingratitude, rudeness and slander.' (Mainyo-i Khart, liX)

It is interesting to notice that when Ahura-Mazda proclaimed 'the righteous [Ahuna-Vairya] both spiritual and earthly', the Ahuna-Vairya had three lines—the four classes, the five chiefs, and a conclusion. The classes were the fourfold order of priests, warriors, agriculturists and artisans, another mark of the close kinship of the Iranians with the first Aryan sub-race.

Other of these marks are interesting: the sacrifice of the home, worshipped as fervently and extolled as highly in the Homa Yash as in the Sama Veda; the names of the priests—the Atharvan, the Zaota (Hota), and the identity by function of the Rathwi with the Adhvaryu; milk, ghee, holy water, sacred twigs, are all used in certain ceremonies. Parsis, like Hindus, have their prayers for the dead at stated intervals. the two faiths are sister faiths, only invasion, oppression and exile have shattered the younger faith to such an extent that much of its ancient birthright has been lost.

The seven principles of the human constitution are clearly mentioned in Yasna, LIV, I: 'Bodies together with bones, vital power and form, strength and consciousness, soul and Fravarshi.' The fIrst three are the dense and etheric bodies with Prana; strength is Kama, consciousness is Manas; Urvan, translated soul, is Buddhi, and Fravarshi is Atma. 'Every being of the good creation, whether living or deceased or still unborn, has its own Fravarshi,' says Dr Haug. But this hardly gives the full idea of the word as it is expounded in the *Fravaridin* Yasht, in which Ahura-Mazda declares that everything good is maintained by their splendour and glory. They are called the 'strong guardian angels of the righteous', and evidently represent the Atma, and in many cases the Atma when Manas and Buddhi have been merged in it.

After death, the soul passes into the intermediate world, 'the time-worn paths which are for the wicked and which are for the righteous', spoken of by Ahura-Mazda as 'the frightful, deadly, destructive path which is the separation of the body and soul,' Kamaloka. The soul of the righteous meets a beautiful maiden, the embodiment of his good thoughts, good words, and good deeds; he crosses the 'bridge of the judge' safely, and reaches heaven. But the soul of the wicked meets a hideous hag, the embodiment of his evil thoughts, evil words and evil deeds, and he fails to cross the bridge and falls into fire.

SELECTIONS FROM THE ZEND-AVESTA

The Creation

Ahura Mazda (wise Lord of Life) spake unto Spitam Zarathustra, saying:

"I have made every land dear to its people, even though it had no charms whatever in it: had I not made every land dear to its people, even though it had no charms whatever in it, then the whole living world would have invaded the Airyana Vaejo.

The first of the good lands and countries which I, Ahura Mazda, created, was the Airyana Vaejo, by the Vanguhi Daitya. Thereupon came Angra Mainyu (spirit of Destruction), who is all death, and he counter-created the serpent in the river, and Winter, a work of the Devas[1]. There are ten winter months there, two summer months; and those are cold for the waters, cold for the earth, cold for the trees. Winters fall there, the worst of all plagues.

The second of the good lands and countries which I, Ahura Mazda, created, was the plain which the Sughdhas

1. The Parsis regarded the Devas as the enemies; they themselves being Asuras (Ahura). Indian mythology describes the Devasura-Sangram in great detail.—Ed.

inhabit. Thereupon came Angra Mainyu, who is all death, and he counter-created the locust, which brings death unto cattle and plants.

The third of the good lands and countries which I, Ahura Mazda, created, was the strong, holy Mouru. Thereupon came Angra Mainyu, who is all death, and he counter-created plunder and sin.

The fourth of the good lands and countries which I, Ahura Mazda, created, was the beautiful Bakhdhi with high-lifted banners. Thereupon came Angra Mainyu, who is all death, and he counter-created the ants and the ant-hills.

The fifth of the good lands and countries which I, Ahura Mazda, created, was Nisaya, that lies between Mouru and Bakhdhi. Thereupon came Angra Mainyu, who is all death, and he counter-created the sin of unbelief.

The sixth of the good lands and countries which I, Ahura Mazda, created, was the house-deserting Haroyu. Thereupon came Angra Mainyu, who is all death, and he counter-created tears and wailing.

The seventh of the good lands and countries which I, Ahura Mazda, created, was Vaekereta, of the evil shadows. Thereupon came Angra Mainyu, who is all death, and he counter-created the Pairika Knathaiti, who crave unto Keresaspa.

The eighth of the good lands and countries which I, Ahura Mazda, created, was Urva of the rich pastures. Thereupon came Angra Mainyu, who is all death, and he counter-created the sin of pride.

The ninth of the good lands and countries which I, Ahura Mazda, created, was Khnenta which the Vehrkanas inhabit. Thereupon came Angra Mainyu, who is all death, and he counter-created a sin for which there is no atonement, the unnatural sin.

The tenth of the good lands and countries which I, Ahura Mazda, created, was the beautiful Harahvaiti. Thereupon came Angra Mainyu, who is all death, and he counter-created a sin for which there is no atonement, the burying of the dead.

The eleventh of the good lands and countries which I, Ahura Mazda, created, was the bright, glorious Haetumant. Thereupon came Angra Mainyu, who is all death, and he counter-created the evil work of witchcraft. And this is the sign by which it is known, this is that by which it is seen at once: wheresoever they may go and raise a cry of sorcery, there the worst works of witchcraft go forth. From there they come to kill and strike at heart, and they bring locusts as many as they want.

The twelfth of the good lands and countries which I, Ahura Mazda, created, was Ragha of the three races. Thereupon came Angra Manyu, who is all death, and he counter-created the sin of utter unbelief.

The thirteenth of the good lands and countries which I, Ahura Mazda, created, was the strong, holy Kakhra. Thereupon came Angra Mainyu, who is all death, and he counter-created a sin for which there is no atonement, the cooking of corpses.

The fourteenth of the good lands and countries which I, Ahura Mazda, created, was the four-cornered Varena, for which was born Thraetaona, who smote Azi Dahaka. Thereupon came Angra Mainyu, who is all death, and he, counter-created abnormal issues in women and barbarian oppression.

The fifteenth of the good lands and countries which I, Ahura Mazda, created, was the Seven Rivers. Thereupon came Angra Mainyu, who is all death, and he counter-created abnormal issues in women and excessive heat.

The sixteenth of the good lands and countries which I, Ahura Mazda, created, was the land by the sources of the Rangha, where people live who have no chiefs. Thereupon came Angra Mainyu, who is all death, and he counter-created Winter, a work of the Devas.

There are still other lands and countries, beautiful and deep, longing and asking for the good, and bright.'

Myth of Yima

Zarathustra asked Ahura Mazda:

'O Ahura Mazda, most beneficent Spirit, Maker of the material world, thou Holy One! Who was the first mortal, before myself, Zarathustra, with whom thou, Ahura Mazda, didst converse, whom thou did teach the Religion of Ahura, the Religion of Zarathustra?'

Ahura Mazda answered:

'The fair Yima, the good shepherd, O holy Zarathustra! he was the first mortal, before thee, Zarathustra, with whom I, Ahura Mazda, did converse, whom I taught the Religion of Ahura, the Religion of Zarathustra.

Unto him, O Zarathustra, I, Ahura Mazda, spake, saying: "Well, fair Yima, son of Vivanghat, be thou the preacher and the bearer of my Religion!"

And the fair Yima, O Zarathustra, replied unto me, saying: "I was not born, I was not taught to be the preacher and the bearer of thy religion."

Then I, Ahura Mazda, said thus unto him, O Zarathustra, "Since thou dost not consent to be the preacher and the bearer of my Religion, then make thou my world increase, make my world grow: consent thou to nourish, to rule, and to watch over my world."

And the fair Yima replied unto me, O Zarathustra, saying: "Yes! I will make thy world increase, I will make thy world grow. Yes! I will nourish, and rule, and watch over thy world. There shall be, while I am king, neither cold wind nor hot wind, neither disease nor death."

Then I, Ahura Mazda, brought two implements unto him: a golden seal and a poniard inlaid with gold. Behold, here Yima bears the royal sway! Thus, under the away of Yima, three hundred winters passed away; and the earth was replenished with flocks and herds, with men and dogs and birds and with red blazing fires, and there was room no more for flocks, herds, and men.

Then I warned the fair Yima, saying: "O fair Yima, son of Vivanghat, the earth has become full of flocks and herds, of men and dogs and birds and of red blazing fire and there is room no more for flocks, herds, and men."

Then Yima stepped forward, in light, southwards, on the way of the sun, and afterwards he pressed the earth with the golden seal, and bored it with the poniard, speaking thus: "O Spenta Armaiti, kindly open asunder and stretch thyself afar, to bear flocks and herds and men."

And Yima made the earth grow larger by one-third than it was before, and there came flocks and herds and men, at their will and wish, as many as he wished. Thus, under the sway of Virna, six hundred winters passed away, and the earth was replenished with flocks and herds, with men and dogs and birds and with red blazing fires, and there was room no more for flocks, herds, and men.

And I warned the fair Yima, saying: "O fair Yima, son of Vivanghat, the earth has become full of flocks and herds, of men and dogs and birds and of red blazing fires, and there is room no more for flocks, herds, and men."

Then Yima stepped forward, in light, southwards, on the way of the sun, and afterwards he pressed the earth with the golden seal, and bored it with the poniard, speaking thus: "O Spenta Armaiti, kindly open asunder and stretch thyself afar, to bear flocks and herds and men."

And Yima made the earth grow larger by two-thirds than it was before, and there came flocks and herds and men, at their will and wish, as many as he wished. Thus, under the sway of Yima, nine hundred winters passed away, and the earth was replenished with flocks and herds, with men and dogs and birds and with red blazing fires, and there was room no more for flocks, herds, and men.

And I warned the fair Yima, saying: "O fair Yima, son of Vivanghat, the earth has become full of flocks and herds, of men and dogs and birds and of red blazing fires, and there is room no more for flocks, herds, and men."

Then Yima stepped forward, in light, southwards, on the way of the sun, and afterwards he pressed the earth with the golden seal, and bored it with the poniard, speaking thus: 'O Spenta Armaiti, kindly open asunder and stretch thyself afar, to beat flocks and herds and men.' And Yima made the earth grow larger by two-thirds than it was before, and there came flocks and herds and men, at their will and wish, as many as he wished.

The Earth

O Maker of the material world, thou Holy One! Which is the first place where the Earth feels most happy?

Ahura Mazda answered: "It is the place whereon one of the faithful steps forward, O Spitama Zarathustra with, the log in his hand, the Baresma in his hand, the milk in his hand, the mortar in his hand, lifting up his voice in good accord with religion, and beseeching Mithra, the lord of the rolling country-side, and Rama Hvastra."

O Maker of the material world, thou Holy One! Which is the second place where the Earth feels most happy?

Ahura Mazda answered: "It is the place whereon one of the faithful erects a house with a priest within, with cattle, with a wife, with children, and good herds within; and wherein afterwards the cattle continue to thrive, virtue to thrive, fodder to thrive, the dog to thrive, the wife to thrive, the child to thrive' the fire to thrive, and every blessing to thrive."

O Maker of the material world thou Holy One! Which is the third place where the Earth feels most happy?

Ahura Mazda answered: "It is the place .where one of the faithful sows most corn, grass, and fruit, O Spitama Zarathustra! where he waters ground that is dry, or drains ground that is too wet."

O Maker of the material world, thou Holy One! Which is the fourth place where the Earth feels most happy?

Ahura Mazda answered: "It is the place where there is most increase of flocks and herds."

O Maker of the material world, thou Holy One! Which is the fifth place where the Earth feels most happy?

Ahura Mazda answered: "It is the place where flocks and herds yield most dung."

O Maker of the material world, thou Holy One! Which is the first place where the Earth feels sorest grief?

Ahura Mazda answered: "It is the neck of Arezura, whereon the hosts of fiends rush forth from the burrow of the Drug."

O Maker of the material world, thou Holy One! which is the second place where the Earth feels sorest grief.

Ahura Mazda answered: "It is the place wherein most corpses of dogs and of men lie buried."

O Maker of the material world, thou Holy One! Which is the third place where the Earth feels sorest grief?

Ahura Mazda answered; "It is the place whereon stand most of those Dakhmas on which the corpses of men are deposited."

O Maker of the material world, thou Holy One! Which is the fourth place where the Earth feels sorest grief.

Ahura Mazda answered: "It is the place wherein are most burrows of the creatures of Angra Mainyu."

O Maker of the material world, thou Holy One! Which is the fifth place where the Earth feels sorest grief?

Ahura Mazda answered: "It is the place whereon the wife and children of one of the faithful, O Spitama Zarathustra! are driven along the way of captivity, the dry, the dusty way, and lift up a voice of wailing."

O Kaker of the material world, thou Holy One What is the food that fills the Religion of Mazda?

Ahura Mazda answered: "It is sowing corn again and again, O Spitama Zarathustra! **He who sows corn, sows righteousness: he makes the Religion of Mazda walk, he suckles the Religion of Mazda** as well as he could do with a hundred man's feet, with a thousand woman's breasts, with ten thousand sacrificial formulas. When barley was created, the Devas started up; when it grew, then fainted the Devas' hearts; when the knots came, the Devas groaned; when the ear came, the Devas flew away. In that house the Devas stay, wherein wheat perishes. It is as though red hot iron were turned about in their throats, when there is plenty of corn. Then let people learn by heart this holy saying: "No one who does not eat, has strength to do heavy works of holiness, strength to do works of husbandry, strength to beget children. By eating every material creature lives, by not eating it dies away."'

Contracts

"He that does not restore a loan to the man who lent it, steals the thing and robs the man. This he doeth every day, every night, as long as he keeps in his house his neighbor's property, as though it were his own."

O Maker of the material world, thou Holy One! How many in number are thy contracts, O Ahura Mazda?

Ahura Mazda answered: "They are six in number, O holy Zarathustra. The first is the word-contract; the second is the hand-contract; the third, is the contract to the amount of a sheep; the fourth is the contract to the amount of an ox; the fifth is the contract to the amount of a man; the sixth is the contract to the amount of a field, a field in good land, a fruitful one, in good bearing. The word-contract is fulfilled by words of mouth. It is cancelled by the hand-contract; he shall give as damages the amount of the hand-contract. The hand-contract is cancelled by the sheep-contract; he shall give as damages the amount of the sheep-contract. The sheep-contract is cancelled by the ox-contract; he shall give as damages the amount of the ox-contract. The ox-contract is cancelled by the man-contract; he shall give as damages the amount of the man-contract. The man-contract is cancelled by the field-contract; he shall give as damages the amount of the field-contract."

O Maker of the material world, thou Holy One! If a man smite another and hurt him sorely, what is the penalty that he shall pay?

Ahura Mazda answered: "Thirty stripes with the Aspahe-astra, thirty stripes with the Sraosho-karana; the second time, fifty stripes with the Aspahe-astra, fifty stripes with the Sraosho-karana; the third time, seventy stripes with the Aspahe-astra, seventy stripes with the Sraosho-karana; the fourth time, ninety stripes with the Aspahe-astra, ninety stripes with the Sraosho-karana."

O Maker of the material world, thou Holy One! Here is a man watering a corn-field. The water streams down the field; it streams again; it streams a third time; and the fourth time, a dog, a fox, or a wolf carries some Nasu into the bed of the stream: what is the penalty that this man shall pay?

Ahura Mazda answered: "There is no sin upon a man for any Nasu that has been brought by dogs, by birds, by wolves, by winds, or by flies. For were there sin upon a man for any Nasu that might have been brought by dogs, by birds, by wolves, by winds, or by flies, how soon all this material world of mine would be one Peshotanu, bent on the destruction of righteousness, whose soul will cry and wail! so numberless are the beings die that upon the face of the earth."

O Maker of the material world, thou Holy One! Does water kill?

Ahura Mazda answered: "Water kills no man: Asto-vidhotu binds him, and, bound, Vayu carries him off; and the flood takes him up, the flood takes him down, the flood throws him ashore; then birds feed upon him. When he goes away, it is by the will of Fate he goes."

O Maker of the material world, thou Holy One! If a worshipper of Mazda, walking, or running, or riding, or driving; come upon a corpse in a stream of running water, what shall he do?

Ahura Mazda answered: "Taking off his shoes, putting off his clothes, while the others wait, O Zarathustra! he shall enter the river, and take the dead out of the water; he shall go down into the water ankle-deep, knee-deep, waist-deep, or a man's full depth, till he can reach the dead body."

O Maker of the material world, thou Holy One! What part of the water in a well does the Drug Nasu defile with corruption, infection, and pollution?

Ahura Mazda answered: "As long as the corpse has not been taken out of the water, so long shall that water be unclean and unfit to drink. They shall, therefore, take the corpse out of the well, and lay it down on the dry ground. And of the water in the well they shall draw off the half, or the third, or the fourth, or the fifth part, according as they are able or not and after the corpse has been taken out and the water has been drawn off, the rest of the water is clean, and both cattle and men may drink of it at their pleasure, as before."

If a dog or a man die under a hut of wood or a hut of felt, what shall the worshippers of Mazda do?

Ahura Mazda answered: "They shall search for a Dakhma, they shall look for a Dakhma all around. If they find it easier to remove the dead, they shall take out the dead, they shall let the house stand, and shall perfume it with Urvasna or Vohu-gaona, or Vohu-kereti, or Hadha-naepata, or any other sweet-smelling plant. If they find it easier to remove the house, they shall take away the house, they shall let the dead lie on the spot, and shall perfume the house with Urvasna, or Voha-gaona, or Vohii-kereti, or Hadha-naepata, or any other sweet-smelling plant."

Zarathustra asked Ahura Mazda: O Maker of the material world, thou Holy One! How shall I fight against that Drug who from the dead rushes upon the living? How shall I fight against that Nasu who from the dead defiles the living?

Ahura Mazda answered: "Say aloud those words in the Gathas that are to be said twice. Say aloud those words in the Gathas that are to be said thrice. Say aloud those words in the Gathas that are to be said four times. And the Drug shall fly away like the well-darted arrow, like the felt of last year, like the annual garment of the earth."

Who is he, O Ahura Mazda! who threatens to take away fulness and increase from the world, and to bring in sickness and death?

Ahura Mazda answered: "It is the ungodly Ashemaogha, O. Spitama Zarathustra, who in this material world cleanses the unclean without knowing the rites of cleansing according to the law of Mazda. For until then, O Spitama Zarathustra! sweetness and fatness would flow out from that land and from those fields, with health and healing, with fulness and increase and growth, and a growing of corn and grass."

O Maker of the material world, thou Holy One! When are sweetness and fatness to come back again to that land and to those fields, with health and healing, with fulness and increase and growth, and a growing of corn and grass?

Ahura Mazda answered: "Sweetness and fatness will never come back again to that land and to those fields, with health and healing, with fulness and increase and growth, and a growing of corn and grass, until that ungodly Ashemaogha has been smitten to death on the spot, and the holy Sraosha of that place has been offered up a sacrifice for three days and three nights, with fire blazing, with Baresma tied up, and with Haoma prepared. Then sweetness and fatness will come back again to that land and to those fields, with health and healing, with fulness and increase and growth, and a growing of corn and grass."

Spells

Zarathustra asked Ahura Mazda: O Ahura Mazda! most beneficent Spirit, maker of the material world, thou Holy One! How shall I fight against that Drug who from the dead rushes upon the living? How shall I fight against that Drug who from the dead defiles the living?

Ahura Mazda answered: "Say aloud those words in the Gathas that are to be said twice: I drive away Angra Mainyu from this house, from this borough, from this town, from this land; from the very body of the man defiled by the dead, from the very body of the woman defiled by the dead; from the master of the house, from the lord of the borough, from the lord of the town, from the lord of the land; from the whole of the world of Righteousness. I drive away the Nasu, I drive away direct defilement, I drive away indirect defilement, from this house, from this borough, from this town, from this land; from the very body of the man defiled by the dead, from the very body of the woman defiled by the dead; from the master of the house, from the lord of the borough, from the lord of the town, from the lord of the land, from the whole of the world of Righteousness.'"

To Fires, Waters, Plants

"We worship thee, the Fire, O Ahura Mazda's son! We worship the fire Berezisavangha (of the lofty use), and the fire Vohu-fryana (the good and friendly), and the fire Urvazista (the most beneficial and most helpful), and the fire Vazista (the most supporting), and the fire Spenista (the most bountiful), and Nairya-sangha the Yazad, of the royal lineage, and the fire which is the house-lord of all houses and Mazda-made, even the son of Ahura Mazda, the holy lord of the ritual order, with all the fires. And we worship the good and best waters Mazda-made, holy, all the waters Mazda-made and holy, and all the plants which Mazda rna4e, and which are holy. And we worship the Mathra-spenta (the bounteous word-of-reason), the Zarathustrian law against the Devas, and its long descent. And we worship Mount Ushi-darena which is Mazda-made and shining with its holiness, and all the mountains shining with holiness, and of abundant glory, and which Mazda-made. And we worship the good and pious prayer for blessings, and these waters and these lands, and all the greatest chieftains, lords of the ritual order; and I praise, invoke, and glorify the good, heroic, bountiful Fravashis of the saints, those of the house, the Vis, the Zantuma, the Dahvyuma, and the Zarathustrotema, and all the holy Yazads!"

To the Fire

"I offer my sacrifice and homage to thee, the Fire, as a good offering, and an offering with our hail of salvation, even as an offering of praise with benedictions, to thee, the Fire, O Ahura-Mazda's son! Meet for sacrifice art thou, and worthy of our homage. And as meet for sacrifice, and thus worthy of our homage, mayest thou be in the houses of men who worship Mazda. Salvation be to this man who worships thee in verity and truth, with wood in hand, and Baresma ready, with flesh in hand, and holding too the mortar. And mayest thou be ever fed with wood as the prescription orders. Yea, mayest thou have thy perfume justly, and thy sacred butter without fail, and thine andirons regularly placed. Be of fullage as to thy nourishment, of the canon's age as to the measure of thy food, O Fire, Ahura Mazda's son! Be now aflame within his house; be ever without fail in flame; be all a-shine within this house; be on thy growth within this house; for long time be thou thus to the furtherance of the heroic renovation, to the completion of all progress, yea, even till the good heroic millennial time when that renovation shall have become complete. Give me, O Fire, Ahura Mazda's son! a speedy glory, speedy nourishment, and speedy booty, and abundant glory, abundant nourishment, abundant booty, an expanded mind, and nimbleness of tongue for soul and understanding, even an understanding continually growing in its largeness, and that never wanders, and long enduring virile power, an offspring sure of foot, that never sleeps on watch, and that rises quick from bed, and likewise a wakeful offspring, helpful to nurture, or reclaim, legitimate, keeping order in men's meetings, yea, drawing men to assemblies through their influence and word, grown to power, skilful, redeeming others from oppression, served by many followers, which may advance my line in prosperity and fame, and my Vis, and my Bantu, and my province, yea, an offering which may deliver orders to the Province as firm and righteous rulers. And mayest thou grant me, O Fire, Ahura Mazda's Son, that whereby instructors may be given me, now and for evermore, giving light to me of

Heaven, the best life of the saints, brilliant, all glorious. And may I have experience of the good reward, and the good renown, and of the long forecasting preparation of the soul.

The Fire of Ahura Mazda addresses this admonition to all for whom he cooks the night and morning meal. From all these, O Spitama! he wishes to secure good care, and healthful care as guarding for salvation, the care of a true praiser. At both the hands of all who come by me, I, the Fire, keenly look: What brings the mate to his mate, the one, who walks at large, to him who sits at home? We worship the bounteous Fire, the swift-driving charioteer. And if this man who passes brings him wood brought with sacred care, or if he brings the Baresma spread with sanctity, or the Hadha-naepata plant, then afterwards Ahura Mazda's Fire will bless him, contented, not offended, and in its satisfaction saying thus: May a herd of kine be with thee, and a multitude of men, may an active mind go with thee, and an active soul as well. As a blest soul mayest thou live through thy life, the nights which thou shall live. This is the blessing of the Fire for him who brings it wood well dried, sought out for flaming, purified with the earnest blessing of the sacred ritual truth. We strive after the flowing on of the good water and their ebb as well, and the sounding of their waves, desiring their propitiation; I desire to appoach them with my praise.

To the Waters and the Sun

"As the sea Vouru-kasha is the gathering place of the waters, rising up and going down, up the aerial way and down the earth, down the earth and up the aerial way: thus rise up and roll along! thou in whose rising and growing Ahura Mazda made the aerial way. Up! rise up and roll along! thou swift-horsed Sun, above Hara Berezaiti, and produce light for the world, and mayest thou, O man! rise up there, if thou art to abide in Garo-nmanem, along the path made by Mazda, along the way made by the gods, the watery way they opened. And the Holy Word shall keep away the evil. Of thee, O child! I will cleanse the birth and growth; of thee, O woman! I will make the body and the strength pure; I make thee rich in children and rich in milk; rich in seed, in milk, in fat, in marrow, and in offspring. I shall bring to thee a thousand pure springs, running towards the pastures that give food to the child."

❑ ❑ ❑

3.

Jainism

Humanity's Oldest Religion of Non-Violence

Note:
Abbe Dubois' article was written over a century ago. It sounds more anthentic and presents an interesting picture of the religion, its practices and social connects with the Hindus. It must be noted that the word 'God' used by him is that context is different—their God is not what is known in modern times; which they totally reject, as is apparent from the last note presented from the Adi Purana—a most unique piece of logic in world religious literature.

—*Editor*

ETERNAL, GODLESS WORLD

The word 'Jain' is a compound word denoting a person who has overcome human infirmities and passions. A true Jain should entirely renounce all thoughts of self. He should rise superior to the scorn or opposition to which he may be subjected on account of his religion, the principles of which he must preserve and guard unaltered even to death, being fully persuaded that it is the one and only true religion on earth, that is, the true primitive religion which was given to all mankind.

Jainism presenls resemblances to both Brahminism and Buddhism, which have been summarized as follows in Elphinstone's *History of India*: 'They agree with the Buddhas in denying the existence, or at least the activity and providence of God; in believing in the eternity of matter; in the worship of deified saints; in their scrupulous care of animal life and all the precautions which it leads to; in disclaiming the divine authority of the Vedas; and in having no sacrifices and no respect for fire. They agree with the Buddhists also in considering a state of impassive abstraction as supreme felicity, and in all the doctrines which they hold in common with the Hindus. They agree with the Hindus in other points, such as division of caste. This exists in full force in the south and west of India, and can only be said to be dormant in the north-east for, though the Jains there do not acknowledge the four classes of the Hindus, yet a Jain converted to the Hindu religion takes his place in one of the castes from which he must all along have retained the proofs of his descent; and the Jains themselves have numerous divisions of their own, the members of which are as strict in avoiding intermarriages and other intercourse as the four classes of the Hindus. Though they reject the scriptural character of the Vedas, they allow them great authority in all matters not at variance with their religion. The principal objections to them are drawn from the bloody sacrifices which they enjoin, and the loss of animal life which burnt-offerings are liable (though undesignedly) to occasion. They admit the whole of the Hindu gods, and worship some of them, though they consider them as entirely subordinate to their own saints, who are, therefore the proper objects of adoration.'

The following is from Mr. J.A. Baines's Census Report for 1891:

'A second offshoot from the earlier Brahminism is found in the Jain, a form of belief that still subsists and flourishes in India to this day. Its origin is veiled from us, but it bears a strong family likeness to the earlier form of Buddhism, and it is a question amongst scholars whether it rose about the same time or a little earlier. At all events it seems to have been unpopular with the Buddhists, and to have diverged less from Brahminic orthodoxy. The monastic system was not countenanced, but ritual was simplified and women were allowed to share in it. As in Buddhism, however, the larger section of the Jains decline to allow that women can attain Nirvana. The latter, however, is with them perpetual bliss, instead of complete annihilation.

'Caste amongst the Jains is maintained, and though they have no special reservation of the priesthood to a class, there is general tendency in that direction, and in some cases Brahmins even are employed in later years. The Jains seem to have competed with the Brahmin in literature and science, so that they fell into disfavour, and would very probably have succumbed but for the advent of the Muslim power. In the north and west of India they are still a cultivated class, most engaged in commerce, whilst in the south where they share with the Buddhists, who preceded them, the credit of forming the Kannada and Tamil literature, they are as a rule agriculturists. Except in a few of the larger cities of the north there seems to be little sectarian hostility between them and the orthodox; and in the west, where they are still closer in customs and observances, the line of division is scarcely traceable. In parts of both tracts, there is, in the present day, a tendency for Jainism to regard itself as a sect of Brahminism, in spite of the non-recognition of the divine authority of the Veda. It is probable that in compliance with this tendency many have referred to their religion as Hindu of the Jain sect, so that where sect is not separately compiled, as in the imperial series of returns, the total of the Jain religion is reduced by that number.'

In the course of time, the primitive religion gradually became considerably corrupted in several essential points, and was superseded by the superstitious and detestable sophistries of Brahminism. The ancient dogmas were forgotten or put aside by the Brahmins, who invented an entirely new system of religion, in which only a shadowy resemblance can be traced to the old Hindu faith.

It is the Brahmins who invented the four Vedas and the eighteen Puranas, the Trimurti, and the fables connected with it, such as the Avatars of Vishnu, the lingam, the worship of the cow and other animals, the sacrifice of the yajna, etc. The Jains not only reject all these spurious additions, but look upon them with absolute horror.

The Brahmins introduced all these innovations very gradually. The Jains were formerly in close communion with the Brahmins both in faith and doctrine, but they opposed these changes from the very first with all their power. Then, seeing that their remonstrances produced no effect and that these religious innovations were daily making progress among the people, they found themselves reduced at last to the sad necessity of an open rupture with the Brahmins. **The immediate cause of this rupture was the introduction of the yajna sacrifice, at which some living creature must be immolated.** This, they contend, is directly opposed to the most sacred and inviolable principles of the Hindu religion; which forbids the destruction of any living thing, for any reason or on any pretext whatever.

From that moment things came rapidly to a climax; and it was then that the defenders of the pure primitive religion took the name of Jain, and formed themselves into a distinct sect, composed of Brahmins, Kshatriyas, Vaisyas, and Sudras. They were the descendants of the Hindus—of all castes who originally banded themselves together to oppose the innovations of the Brahmins, and they alone have preserved the religion of their forefathers intact to the present day.

After the schism the Jains, or true believers, perpetually taunted the Brahmins with their debased religion, and what at first merely furnished subject-matter for scholastic disputes finally became the cause of long and bloody hostilities. For a long time success was on the side of the Jains, but in the end, the majority of the Kshatriyas and other castes having seceded and adopted the innovations of the Brahmins, the latter gained the ascendant and reduced their adversaries to the lowest depths of subjection.

There are very few of the Brahmin caste who hold the opinions of the Jains. There is a village, however, called Maleyur, in South Mysore, which contains between fifty and sixty families of them. They have a famous temple there, of which the guru is a Brahmin Jain. In the other more important temples of the Jains, such as those at Belgola, Madigery, and others, the gurus or priests are recruited from the Vaisyas, or merchants. The Vaisya Jains are regarded by the Brahmins of the same sect as *patitas*, or fallen, because they have thus usurped the priestly office, and also because they have altered the religion of the true Jains by introducing some of the innovations of their

Brahmin adversaries. This divergence of opinion, however, has not led to any serious differences between them.

The Jains are divided into several sects or schools, which differ on the subject of perfect happiness, and on the means of attaining it. One of the sects, known by the name of **Swetambara** (clad in white), teaches that there is no other moksha, that is to say, no other supreme blessedness, than that which is to be obtained from sensual pleasures, particularly that which is derived from sexual intercourse with women. This sect is, it is true, not numerous.

The school of the **Jaina-bassaru** is the most numerous, and it is subdivided into several others. Its tenets differ very little from those of the Vedanta school of Brahminism. It recognizes the different stages of meditation as taught by the latter, and enjoins very much the same means of attaining everlasting felicity, by which they understand reunion with the Godhead.

The Religious System

The Jains acknowledge one **Supreme Being**, to whom they give the names of Jaineswara, Paramatma, Paratparavastu, and several others expressing the infinity of his nature.

It is to this Supreme Being alone that all the prayers, and sacrifices of the true Jains are offered; and it is to him that all the marks of respect which they pay to their holy personages, known as **Saloka-purushas**, and to other sacred objects represented under a human form, are really addressed; for these, on attaining moksha (supreme blessedness) after death, have become united with and incorporated into the Supreme Being.

The Supreme Being is, they say, one and indivisible, a spirit without corporal parts or limitations. His four or principal attributes are:

1. Ananta-jnanam, infinite wisdom.
2. Ananta-darsanam, infinite intuition, omniscience, and ommpresence.

3. Ananta-viryam, omnipotence.
4. Ananta-sukham, infinite blessedness.

This noble being is entirely absorbed in the contemplation of his infinite perfections, and in the uninterrupted enjoyment of the happiness which he finds in his own essence. He has nothing in common with the things of this world, and does not interfere at all in the government of this vast universe. Virtue and vice, good and evil, are indifferent to him.

Virtue being essentially right, those who practise it in this world will find their reward in another life, either by a blessed reincarnation, or by immediate admittance to the delights of Swarga. Vice being essentially bad and wrong, those who give way to it will be punished in another world by an unhappy reincarnation. The worst offenders will go straight to Naraka after death, there to expiate their crimes. But in no case does God intervene in the distribution of punishments or rewards, or pay any attention to the good or evil by men here below.

Matter is eternal and independent of the Godhead. That which exists now has always existed and will always exist. And not only is matter eternal, but also the order and harmony which reign throughout the universe—the fixed and unchanging movements of the stars, the division of light from darkness, the succession and constant renewal of the seasons, the production and reproduction of animal and vegetable life, the nature and properties of the elements; in fact, all things visible are eternal, and will continue to exist just as they have existed from all time.

Metempsychosis

The fundamental doctrine of the Jains is metempsychosis. Their belief in this differs in no way from that of the Brahmins. But they do not agree with the latter with regard to the four lokas or worlds. These they refuse to recognize. They also reject the three principal Abodes of Bliss—Satyaloka, Vaikuntha, and Kailasa, that is to say, the paradises of Brahma, of Vishnu, and of Siva. They recognize three worlds only, which they describe by the generic name of **Jagat-triya**, and which are the Urdhwa-loka or superior world, the Adha-loka or inferior world, which they also call Patala, and the Madhya-loka or middle world, that is to say, the earth where mortals dwell.

Urdhwa-loka

This world, which is also called Swarga, is the first of the Jagat-triya, and **Devendra** is lord of it. There are sixteen distinct abodes in it, in each of which a different degree of happiness is enjoyed in proportion to the merits of the righteous souls who are admitted. The first and highest of these habitations is the Sadhu-dharma. Only the very purest souls have access to this, and they there enjoy unbroken happiness for thirty-three thousand years. The Ashuda-kalpa, which is the last and lowest of the sixteen habitations, is destined for the souls of those who possess exactly the requisite amount of merit, neither more nor less, necessary to procure their admittance into the Urdhwa-loka. They there enjoy for one thousand years the amount of happiness which is their portion. In the other intermediate habitations the degree and duration of happiness are fixed in relative proportion to the merits of those who are admitted.

Women of the rarest beauty adorn these Abodes of Bliss. The blessed, however, have no intercourse with them. The sight alone of these enchanting beauties is sufficient to intoxicate their senses and plunge them into a perpetual ecstasy that is far superior to all mere earthly pleasures. In this respect the Swarga of the Jains differs little from that of the Brahmins.

On leaving the Urddhwa-loka at the expiration of the period assigned to them, the souls of the blessed are born again upon earth and recommence the process of transmigration.

The Adha-loka

The second world of the Jagat-triya is the Adha-loka, also called Naraka, and sometimes Patala. It is the lower or inferior regions, the abode of great sinners; that is, of those whose crimes are so heinous and so manifold that they cannot be expiated by even the lowest forms of reincarnation.

The Adha-loka is divided into seven dwelling-places, in each of which the severity of the punishments is proportionate to the gravity of the offences. The least terrible is the Retna-pravai, where erring souls are tormented for a thousand consecutive years. The torture gradually increases in intensity and duration in the other abodes, until in the Maha-damai-pravai, the seventh, the punishments reach a point of awfulness which is beyond all description. It is there that the most villainous sinners are sent, and their horrible sufferings only terminate at the end of thirty-three thousand years. Women, who from their constitutional weakness are not able to endure such extremes of suffering, are never sent to this awful Maha-damai-pravai, no matter how wicked they may have been.

The Madhya-loka

The middle world, the Madhya-loka, is the third of the Jagat-triya. It is there that mortals live, and that both virtue and vice are to be found.

This world is one reju in extent, a reju being equal to the distance over which the sun travels in six months. **Jambudwipa**, which is the earth on which we live, occupies only a small part of the Madhya-loka. It is surrounded on all sides by a vast ocean, and in the centre of it is an immense lake excluding for a hundred thousand yojanas, or about four hundred thousand eagles. In the middle of this loka rises the famous mountain Mahameru. Jambudwipa is divided into four equal parts, which are placed at the four cardinal points of Mahameru. India is in the part called Bharata-Kshetra.

These four divisions of Jambudwipa are separated from each other by six lofty mountains, which are called Himavata, Maha-Himavata, Nishada, Nila, Arumani, Sikari, all running in the same direction from east to west, stretching across Jambudwipa from one sea to the other.

These mountains are intersected by vast valleys, where the trees, shrubs, and fruits, which all grow wild, are of a beautiful pink colour. These delicious retreats are inhabited by good and virtuous people. Children of either sex living there arrive at maturity forty-eight hours after their birth. The inhabitants are not subject to pain or sickness. Always happy and contented, they live on the succulent vegetables and delicious fruits which nature produces for them without any cultivation. After death they go straight to the delights of Swarga.

A spring lies on the top of Mahameru which feeds fourteen large rivers, of which the principal are the Ganges and the Indus. All these rivers pursue a regular and even course, which never varies. Unlike the false Ganges and the false Indus of the Brahmins, the waters of which rise and fall, the Ganges and Indus of the Jains can never be forced, and their waters always maintain the same level.

The names of the fourteen rivers of the Jains are the Ganges, the Indus, the Rohita, Toya, the Lohita, the Hari-Toya, the Harikanta, the Sitta, the Sitoda, the Nan, the Narikanta, the Swarna-kula, the Rupya-kula, the Rikta, and the Riktoda. The sea which surrounds Jambudwipa is two hundred thousand yojanas, or eight hundred thousand miles long.

Beyond this ocean there are three other continents, separated from each other by an immense sea. They closely resemble Jambu-dwipa, and are also inhabited by human beings.

At the far end of the fourth continent, called Puskaravarta-dwipa, is situated Manushyotraparvata, a very lofty mountain which is the extreme limit of the habitable world. No living being has ever gone beyond this mountain. Its base is washed by an immense ocean, in which are to be found an infinite number of islands which are inaccessible to the human race.

The Succession and Division of Time

Time is divided into six periods, which succeed each other without interruption throughout eternity. At the termination of each period there is an entire revolution in nature, and the world is renewed. The first, called Prathama-kala, lasted for four kotis of kotis, or forty million millions of years; the second Dwitiya-kala, thirty million millions; the third, Tritiya-kala, twenty million millions; the fourth, Chaturtha-kala, ten million millions, minus forty-two thousand years. The fifth period called Panchama-kala, the period of inconstancy and change, is the age in which we are now living. It will last twenty-one thousand years. The present year (1824) of the Christian era is the year 2469 of the Panchama-kala of the Jains.

The comparatively recent date of the commencement of this period seems to me to be worthy of note. I am inclined to think that it is the date of the schism between the Brahmins and the Jains. Such a memorable event may well have been considered as giving birth to a new era. If this conjecture were confirmed it would be easier to fix the time when the principal myths of Hindu theology originated. There is no doubt that the new ideas introduced by the Brahmins into their religion occasioned the schism which exists to this day.

The sixth and last of these periods, the Sashta-kala, will also last twenty-one thousand years. The element of fire will then disappear from the earth, and mankind will subsist entirely on reptiles, roots, and tasteless herbage, which will only grow sparsely here and there. There will then be no caste distinction or subordination, no public or private property, no form of government, no kings, no laws; men will lead the lives of perfect savages.

This period will terminate with a Jala-pralaya, or flood, which will deluge the whole earth, except the mountain of silver, called Vidi-parvata. This flood will be caused by continuous rain for forty-seven days, which will result in a complete upsetting of the elements. A few people living near the silver mountain will take refuge in the caves which are hidden in its sides, and they will be saved amidst the universal destruction. After the catastrophe the elect will come forth from the mountain and will people the earth. Then the six periods will begin over again, and follow each other as they did before.

The Learning of the Jains

The philosophy of the Jains is contained in four Agamas, twenty-four Puranas, and sixty-four Sastras. The Puranas take the names of the twenty-four **Tirthankaras**, or saints. A Purana is assigned to each of them, and contains his history.

The names of the four are Prathamani-yoga, Charanani-yoga, Karanani-yoga, and Dravyani-yoga. These four books were written by Adiswara, the most ancient and most celebrated of all the holy personages recognized by the Jains. He came down from Swarga, took a human form, and lived on earth for a purva-koti, or a hundred million million years. Not only did he compose the Vedas, but it was he who divided men into castes, gave them laws and a form of government, and laid down the lines of social order. In short, Adiswara is to the Jains what Brahma is to the Brahmins, one of them having most probably been modelled from the other.

The Sixty-Three Saloka-Purushas

Besides Adiswara, who is the holiest and most perfect of all beings who have appeared on the earth in human form, the Jains recognize sixty-three others, whom they describe by the generic name of Saloka-purushas, and whom they also worship. Their history is contained in the Prathamani-yoga.

These venerable personages are sub-divided into five classes: twenty-four Tirthankaras, twelve Chakravartis, nine Vasu-devatas, nine Bala-vasu-devatas, and nine Bala-ramas.

The twenty-four Tirthankaras are the holiest, and to them most honour is paid. Their position is the most sublime that a mortal can aspire to. They all lived in the most perfect state of Nirvana. They were subject to no infirmity or sickness; they felt no want, no weakness, and were not even subject to death. After having lived for a long time on earth they voluntarily quitted their bodies and went straight to moksha, where they were united with, and incorporated into, the Godhead.

All the Tirthankaras came down from Swarga and took human forms among the Kshatriya caste; but they were subsequently incorporated into that of the Brahmins by the ceremony of the Diksha (initiation). During their lives they were examples of all the virtues to other men, whom they exhorted by their precepts and their actions to conform strictly to the rules of conduct laid down by Adiswara, and to give themselves up entirely to meditation and penitence.

Some of them lived for millions of years; the last of them, however, only attained the age of eighty-four. They were in existence during the period of Chaturtha-kala. Some were married, but the greater number remained celibate, being professed sannyasis.

The twelve Chakravartis, or emperors, recognized by the Jains were contemporaries of the twenty-four Tirthankaras. They shared amongst them the temporal government of Jambudwipa. They came straight from Swarga, and when on earth, belonged to the noble caste of Kshatriyas. Some were initiated into the Brahmin caste by the ceremony of the diksha, completed their lives as Sannyasi Nirvanis, and after death obtained moksha, or supreme happiness. Others returned to Swarga. But three of them, having lived extremely wicked lives on earth, were condemned to the tortures of Naraka.

The twelve Chakravartis were often at war with one another, but they had more especially to fight against the nine Vasu-devatas, the nine Bala-vasu-devatas and the nine Bala-ramas, who all governed different provinces in India.

The second Agama, or Charanani-yoga, contains the civil laws, also regulations relating to social status, caste, etc.

The third Agama, Karanani-yoga, is a dissertation on the nature, order, and component parts of the Jagat-triya.

The fourth, or Dravyani-yoga, contains the metaphysical theories of the Jains and several controversial subjects.

Sannyasi Nirvani

The most holy and sublime state to which man can possibly attain is that of **Sannyasi Nirvani, which means 'naked**

penitent'. In embracing this state a man ceases to be a man; he begins to be a part of the Godhead. As soon as he has attained the highest degree of perfection in this state, he frees himself voluntarily, without any trouble or pain, from his own self, and obtains moksha, thus becoming incorporated for ever into the Divine Self. There is no real Nirvani existing in this yuga. Those who aspire to this state must pass through twelve successive degrees of meditation and corporal penance, each one more perfect than the last. These degrees are a kind of novitiate, and each of them has a special appellation. Having at last become a Nirvani the penitent no longer belongs to this world. Terrestrial objects make no impression on his senses. He regards the good and evil, virtue and vice, to be found on this earth with equal indifference.

He is freed from all passion. He scarcely feels the wants of nature. He is able to patiently endure hunger, thirst, and privations of all kinds. **He can live without food of any sort for weeks and months together**. When he is obliged to eat he partakes indifferently of the first animal or vegetable substance that comes to hand, however filthy or disgusting it may seem to ordinary people. **He has neither fire nor sleeping place. He always lives in the open on the bare ground**. Though absolutely naked from head to foot, he is insensible to cold and heat, wind and rain. Neither is he subject to sickness or any bodily infirmities. He feels the most profound contempt for all other men, no matter how exalted their rank may be, and he takes no account of their doings, good or bad. He speaks to no one, looks at no one, and is visited by no one. His feelings, his affections, and his thoughts are immutably fixed on the Godhead, of whom he considers himself as already a part. He remains absorbed in the contemplation of God's perfections, all earthly objects being to him as though they did not exist.

By a long course of penance and meditation the material part of the Nirvani gradually dissolves, like camphor when it is put in the fire. At last all that remains of the penitent is the semblance or shadow of a body, an immaterial phantom, so to say. Having arrived at this pitch of perfection, the Nirvani quits this lower world and proceeds to unite himself inseparably with the Godhead where he enjoys eternal and ineffable happiness.

Rules of Conduct

In many respects Jain rules of conduct are similar to those followed by other Hindus, and particularly the Brahmins. The Jains recognize the same observances with regard to defilement and purity. They perform the same ablutions and recite the same prescribed mantras. Most of their ceremonies relating to marriage, funerals, etc., are the same. In fact, all the rules of social etiquette and the general customs in use in ordinary life form part of their education.

The Jains differ from their compatriots in several particulars, of which the following are the most remarkable:

Under no circumstances do they take any solid food between sunset and sunrise. They always take their meals while the sun is above the horizon.

They have no *tithis* or anniversaries in honour of the dead. **As soon as one of them is dead and his funeral is over, they put him out of their memories and speak of him no more**.

They never put ashes on their foreheads, as do most Hindus; they are satisfied with making with sandalwood-paste the little round mark called Bottu, or else a horizontal line. Some devotees put these marks on their forehead, neck, stomach, and both shoulders in the form of a cross, in honour of their five principal Tirthankaras.

The Jains are even stricter than the Brahmins in regard to their food. **Not only do they abstain from all animal food, and from vegetables the stalks or roots of which grow in bulbous shape, such as onions, mushrooms, etc.**, but they also refrain from eating many of the fruits which the Brahmins allow on their tables, such as the *katri-kai,* or brinjal, the *pudalan-kai,* etc. Their motive is the fear of taking the life of some of the insects which are generally to be found in these vegetables and fruits. The principal, and indeed almost the only, articles of food used by the Jains are rice, milk, things made with milk, and peas of various kinds. They particularly dislike asafoetida, to which Brahmins are so partial, and honey is absolutely forbidden.

Whilst they are eating their food some person sits beside them, and, rings a bell, or strikes a gong. The object of this is to prevent the possibility of their hearing the impure conversation of their neighbours, or of the passers-by in the street. Both they and their food would be defiled if any impure words reached their ears while they were eating.

Their fear of destroying life is carried to such a length that the women, before smearing the floor with cow-dung, are in the habit of sweeping it very gently first, so as to remove, without hurting them, any insects that may be there. If they neglected this precaution they would run the risk of crushing one of these little creatures whilst rubbing the floor, which would be the source of the keenest regret to them.

The mouth of the vessel in which water for household purposes is drawn is always covered with a piece of linen, through which the water filters. This prevents the animal, culae, which float or swim on the surface of the well, from getting into the vessel and being afterwards swallowed. **When a Jain traveller wishes to quench his thirst at a tank or stream, he covers his mouth with a cloth, stoops down, and thus drinks by suction**. This cleanly custom is highly to be recommended everywhere, apart from the superstition which prompts the Jains to practise it.

The Jains form a perfectly distinct class. Brahmins never attend any of their religious or civil ceremonies, while they, on their part, never attend those of the Brahmins. They have their own temples, and the priestly office is filled by men professing the same tenets as themselves. Amongst these temples there are some which are richly endowed and very famous. The Jains make pilgrimages to them, sometimes from great distances. There is a very remarkable one in Mysore, at **Sravana Belgola**, a village near Seringapattam. It is between three mountains, on one of which is an enormous statue, about seventy feet high, sculptured out of one solid piece of rock. It must have been a tremendous piece of work; for to execute it, it was necessary to level the ground from the top of the mountain to below the base of the statue, and there form a sort of terrace, leaving in the centre this mass of rock which was to be carved into the shape of the idol. It is a very fine piece of Hindu sculpture.

Many Europeans who have seen it, have greatly admired the correctness of its proportions. It represents a celebrated Nirvani called Gomata, a son of Adiswara. **The figure is absolutely nude, as are most of the idols to which the Jains offer adoration**, and which are always likenesses of ancient penitents belonging to this sect. In those days it would have shocked them to represent these penitents as wearing garments, since they made it a point of duty to go absolutely naked. Childless women may often be seen praying to these idols, in order that they may become mothers.

This temple of Belgola, being only a day's journey from Seringapattam, has been frequently visited by Europeans. It was a great source of grief to the devotees of the sect to see this *punyasthala* (holy place) defiled by a crowd of unbelieving visitors. And what was still worse, these inquisitive foreigners were often accompanied by their dogs and their Pariah servants. In one resting-place they would cook a stew, in another they would roast a piece of beef under the very nose, as it were, of the idol, whose sense of smell, the Jains thought, was infinitely disgusted by the smoke of this abominable style of cooking. At last the guru attached to the temple, shocked at all this desecration, fled from the unhallowed spot, and retired to some solitary place on the Malabar coast. After three years of this voluntary exile, he returned to his former abode on the assurance that Europeans had ceased to visit the place, and that temple had been thoroughly purified.

Now, I ask you whether it is not the duty of any well-conducted man, even if he does not respect them, at least not to openly outrage the prejudices, feelings, and customs of any people amongst whom he may happen to be thrown, no matter how peculiar or ridiculous they may appear to him. What pleasure could be derived, or what good could be gained, by exciting the anger and contempt of those from whom one has nothing to fear, and who cannot retaliate?

An invalid European officer, who was going to the Malabar coast for change of air, on passing near Belgola, was seized with the idea of spending a night in the temple, which he did, in spite of much opposition on the part of the inhabitants. Two days afterwards the officer died on the road, to the great delight of all the natives, who, of course, attributed his death to a miracle, and looked upon it as a direct retribution from their outraged deity. This just and condign punishment, said they would inspire with wholesome fear others who might be tempted to try a similar experiment.

The idols of the Jains differ in many respects from those of the Brahmins. Almost all have curly hair like Negroes. They wear neither ear-rings, necklaces, bracelets, nor bangles on their ankles, whilst the Brahmins, on the other hand, overload the objects of their devotion with such ornaments.

THE BASICS
Acharanga Sutra

O long-lived Jambusvamin! I, Sudharman, have heard the following discourse from the venerable Mahavira:

Here many do not remember whether they have descended in an eastern direction when they were born in this world, or in a southern, or in a western, or in a northern direction, or in the direction from above, or in the direction from below, or in a direction intermediate between the cardinal points, or in a direction intermediate between these and the cardinal points. Similarly, some do not know whether their soul is born again and again or not; nor what they were formerly, nor what they will become after having died and left this world.

Now this is what one should know, either by one's own knowledge or through the instruction of a Tirthankara, or having heard it from others: that he descended in an eastern direction, or in any other direction. Similarly, some know that their soul is born again and again, that it arrives in this or that direction, whatever direction that may be. He believes in soul, believes in the world, believes in reward, believes in action acknowledged to be our own doing in such judgements as these: 'I did it;' 'I shall cause another to do it;' 'I shall allow another to do it.' In the world, these are all the causes of sin, which must be comprehended and renounced.

A man that does not comprehend and renounce the causes of sin, descends in a cardinal or intermediate direction, wanders to all cardinal or intermediate directions, is born again and again in manifold births, experiences all painful feelings. About this the Revered One has taught the truth of comprehension and renunciation. for the sake of the splendour, honour, and glory of this life, for the sake of birth, death, and final liberation, for the removal of pain, all these causes of sin are at work, which are to be comprehended and renounced in this world. He who, in the world, comprehends and renounces these causes of sin, is called a reward-knowing sage. Thus I say.

The Living World is Full of Pain

The living world is afflicted, miserable, difficult to instruct, and without discrimination. In this world full of pain, suffering by their different acts, see the benighted ones cause great pain. See! there are beings individually embodied in earth; not one all-soul. See! there are men who control themselves, whilst others only pretend to be houseless (i.e. monks, such as the Bauddhas, whose conduct differs not from that of householders), because one destroys this earth-body by bad and injurious doings, and many other beings, besides, which he hurts by means of earth, through his doing acts relating to earth.

About this the Revered One has taught the truth: for the sake of the splendour, honour, and glory of this life, for the sake of birth, death, and final liberation, for the removal of pain, man acts sinfully towards earth, or causes others to act so, or allows others to act so. This deprives him of happiness and perfect wisdom.

Injure Not the Water-Bodies

Thus I say: He who acts rightly, who does pious work, who practises no deceit, is called houseless. One should, conquering the world, persevere in that vigour of faith which one had on the entrance in the order; the heroes of faith, humbly bent, should retain their belief in the illustrious road to final liberation and in the world of water-bodies; having rightly comprehended them through the instruction of Mahavira, they should retain that which causes no danger, i.e., self-control. Thus I say. A man should not himself deny the world of water-bodies, nor should he deny the self. He who denies the world of water-bodies, denies the self; and he who denies the self, denies the world of water-bodies.

Injure Not the Fire-Bodies

Thus I say: A man should not of his own accord, deny the world of fire-bodies, nor should he deny the self. He who denies the world of fire-bodies, denies the self; and he who denies the self, denies the world of fire-bodies. He who knows that, viz.,

fire, through which injury is done to the long-living bodies, i.e., plants, knows also that which does no injury, i.e., control; and he who knows that which does no injury, knows also that through which no injury is done to the long-living bodies. This has been seen by the heroes of faith who conquered ignorance; for they control themselves, always exert themselves, always mind their duty.

Injure Not the Plants

'I shall not do acts relating to plants after having entered the order, having recognised the truth about these acts, and having conceived that which is free from danger, i.e., control.'

He who does not acts relating to plants, has ceased from works; he who has ceased from them is called 'houseless.' Quality is the whirlpool and the whirlpool is quality. Looking up, down, aside, eastward, he sees colours, hearing he hears sounds; longing upwards, down, aside, eastward, he becomes attached to colours and sounds. That is called the world; not guarded against it, not obeying the law of the Tirthankaras, relishing the qualities, conducting himself wrongly, he will wantonly live in a hosue, i.e., belong to the world.

Injure Not the Animate Beings

Thus I say: There are beings called the animate, those who are produced from eggs (birds, etc.), from a fetus as elephants, etc., from a fetus with an enveloping membrum as cows, buffaloes, etc., from fluids as worms, etc., from sweat as bugs, lice, etc., by coagulation as locusts, ants, etc., from sprouts as butterflies, wagtails, etc., by regeneration as men gods, hell-beings. This is called the Samsara for the slow, for the ignorant.

Injure Not the Wind-Bodies

He who is averse from all actions relating to wind, knows affliction. Knowing what is bad, he who knows it with regard to himself, knows it with regard to the world outside; and he who knows it with regard to the world outside, knows it with regard to himself: this reciprocity between himself and others one should mind. Those who are appeased, who are free from passion, do not desire to live.

Control Is the Key

A wise man should remove any aversion to control; he will be liberated in proper time. Some, following wrong instructions, turn away from control. They are dull, wrapped in delusion. While they imitate the life of monks, saying, 'We shall be free from attachment,' they enjoy the pleasures that offer themselves. Through wrong instruction the would-be sages trouble themselves for the pleasures; thus they sink deeper and deeper in delusion, and cannot get to this, nor to the opposite shore.

Those who are freed from attachment to the world and its pleasures, reach the opposite shore. Subduing desire by desirelessness, he does not enjoy the pleasures that offer themselves. Desireless, giving up the world, and ceasing to act, he knows, and sees, and has no wishes because of his discernment; he is called houseless.

Neither Glad Nor Angry

'Frequently I have been born in a high family, frequently in a low one; I am not mean, nor noble, nor do I desire social preferment.' Thus reflecting, who would brag about his family or about his glory, or for what should he long?

Therefore, a wise man should neither be glad nor angry about his lot: thou shouldst know and consider the happiness of living creatures. Carefully conducting himself, he should mind this: blindness, deafness, dumbness, one-eyedness, hunchbackedness, blackness, variety of colour he will always experience; because of his carelessness he is born in many births, he experiences various feelings.

A wise man, who knows the world and has cast off the idea of the world, should prudently conquer the obstructions to righteousness. Thus I say.

The hero does not tolerate discontent,
The hero does not tolerate lust.
Because the hero is not careless.

The hero is not attached to the objects of the senses. Being indifferent against sounds and the other perceptions, detest the comfort of this life.

A sage adopting a life of wisdom, should treat his gross body roughly.

The heroes who have right intuition, use mean and rough food.

Such a man is said to have crossed the flood of life, to be a sage, to have passed over the Samsara, to be liberated, to have ceased from all activity. Thus I say.

The Liberated

Some not instructed in the true law make only a show of good conduct; some, though instructed, have no good conduct. Let that not be your case! That is the doctrine of the clever one. Adopting the acharya's views, imitating his indifference for the outer world, making him the guide and adviser in all one's matters, sharing his abode, conquering sinfulness, one sees the truth; unconquered one should be one's own master, having no reliance on anything in the world, who is great and withdraws his mind from the outer world, should learn the teaching of the Tirthankaras through teaching of the acharya; by his own innate knowledge through the instruction of the highest, or having heard it from others.

The current of sin is said to come from above, from below and from the sides; these have been declared to be the current through which, look, there is sinfulness.

'Examining the whirlpool, a man, versed in the sacred lore, should keep off from it.' Leaving the world to avert to current of sin, such a great man, free from acts, knows and sees the truth; examining pleasures he does not desire them. Knowing whence we come and whither we go, he leaves the road to birth and death, rejoicing in the glorious liberation.

Entering Nirvana

Knowing the twofold obstacles, i.e., bodily and mental, the wise ones, having thoroughly learned the law, perceive in due order that the time for their death has come, get rid of Karman.

He should not long for life, nor wish for death; he should yearn after neither, life or death.

He who is indifferent and wishes for the destruction of Karman, should continue his contemplation. Becoming unattached internally and externally, he should strive after absolute purity.

Whatever means one knows for calming one's own life, that a wise man should practise in order to gain time for continuing penance:

In a village or in a forest, examining the ground and recognising it as free from living beings, the sage should spread the straw.

Without food he should lie down and bear the pains which attack him. He should not for too long time give way to worldly feelings which overcome him.

After the Asravas have ceased, he should bear pains as if he rejoiced in them.

When the bonds fall off, then he has accomplished his life.

• • •

This is the highest law, exalted above the preceding method:

Having examined a spot of bare ground he should remain there.

Having attained a place free from living beings, he should there fix himself.

He should thoroughly mortity his flesh, thinking: There are no obstacles in my body.

Knowing as long as he lives the dangers and troubles, the wise and restrained ascetic should bear them as being instrumental to the dissolution of the body.

He should not be attached to the transitory pleasures, nor to the greater ones; he should not nourish desire and greed, looking only for eternal praise.

He should be enlightened with eternal objects, and not trust in the delusive power of the gods; a Brahmin should know of this and cast off all inferiority.

Not devoted to any of the external objects he reaches the end of his life; thinking that patience is the highest good, he should choose one of the described three good methods of entering Nirvana. Thus I say.

THERE IS NO GOD

Based on Adi Purana

The world is eternal. It is also ephemeral. It has its own basic laws which remain unchanged in all situations and circumstances, though its parts keep changing according to needs and requirements. These laws have not been created by any god, and no god either rules these or can destroy them. The concept of a creator or destroyer is unjustified and self-contradictory; it is illogical as also not moral.

The concept that the world must have a creator has its roots in the idea that it is a product. If that were so, then god must also be a product, for the simple reason that his action of creating and destroying must also take place in him. We shall then have to look for the cause of god himself, leading to an endless search backwards in the cause of cause of cause of cause....

Then if it is supposed that the world had a cause, then it would not mean that the cause was a thinking entity. The maker of a product in the world can never be perfect. In that case god should also have a body, because a material object in this world can never be produced without a body having a material base with the activity of thinking, volition and will to produce something.

Everything in this world which is made of matter is changeable and therefore it must suffer. In that case god could neither be unchangeable nor blissful.

If one supposes that god has created the world without a body, by merely his abstract entity, then one cannot depend in any way on the analogies of the world of experience, the practical realities.

If god has produced the world, from what he has done it? Has be produced it from nothing? If he has done so, and if it will also disappear in nothing, then god himself must also arise from nothing and dissolve into nothing. If being (sat) and non being (asat) are absolute opposites, then one cannot arise from the other. If they are not so, then truth and falsehood, virtue and vice, etc., will also be non-existent. Then all philosophy will be meaningless.

If matter and soul are regarded to be eternal which acquire their qualities from their basic nature, and god's action is limited to managing these qualities in the world phenomenon, then one would wonder why the assistance of god was required to do so; why the matter and souls could not do these on their own, with the help of their inherent powers?

If god is the only all-powerful doer in the world, then he will have to be regarded as the cause of all evil that is the essential part of this world. One will then have to conclude that god is not good.

If god is regarded as good who permits evil to operate freely, then we shall have to accept that he is not all powerful.

If god is regarded to have created the souls, then why did he not make them good? Why has he made them evil also? Has he done so to enable him to punish them for the sins they commit in the world?

If god has called the souls to operate in the world and given it to himself to see whether they act correctly or sinfully, then he will have to be regarded as not omniscient, because if he had been omniscient, he should have foreseen it.

All this will have to be regarded as perverse, unworthy of a noble and kind entity—to let persons fall into hell and suffer horrible tortures for actions for which they have not been directly responsible.

If god has created the world, what would have been his motive? If he did it on account of his desire, was he in a state of dissatisfaction before creating the world? If so, he cannot be regarded as eternally blissful and perfect.

If god has created the world on account of his whim, then how can it be regarded as being conducted according to law?

If god has created the world out of love, to lead the unredeemed souls to salvation, then why only a very few souls reach it? Why did he conjure up the torments of the world? He could have acquired his objective in a different, better way, because he is all powerful.

If god created the world to let the souls selected by him enjoy the rewards, and others rejected by him, be condemned to hell, etc., then he will have to be regarded as partial to some and enemical to others. This would question his sense of justice; he will have to be regarded as arbitrary and unjust.

If god created the world for his play, if the world is his *lila,* without a purpose and goal, just for his entertainment, then he must be regarded as a horrible monster who finds pleasure in the sufferings of the innumerable living beings.

If god were omnipresent, he must be present in the hells. If he were omniscient, he would not have created evil beings—and 'people like the Jainas who deny him his existence.'

God's existence cannot be proved by any means of knowledge, perception, inference, revelation, or the absurd theory of Maya.

❑ ❑ ❑

4.

Buddhism

Oldest Religion which Spread All Over the Then Known World

VIVEKANANDA ON BUDDHISM

Buddhism is historically the most important religion because **it was the most tremendous movement that the world ever saw, the most gigantic spiritual wave** ever to burst upon human society. There is no civilization on which its effect has not been felt in some way or other.

The followers of Buddha were most enthusiastic and very missionary in spirit. They were the first among the adherents of various religions not to remain content with the limited sphere of their Mother Church. They spread far and wide. They travelled east and west, north and south. They reached into darkest Tibet; they went into Persia, Asia Minor; they went into Russia, Poland, and many other countries of the Western world. They went into China, Korea, Japan; they went into Burma, Siam, the East Indies, and beyond.

To understand this movement properly one should know what conditions prevailed in India at the time Buddha came, just as to understand Christianity you have to grasp the state of Jewish society at the time of Christ.

When you study the civilization of India, you find that it has died and revived several times; this is its peculiarity. Most races rise once and then decline for ever. **The peaceful nations, India and China, fall down, yet rise**

again; but the others, once they go down, do not come up—they die. Blessed are the peacemakers, for they shall enjoy the earth.

At the time Buddha was born, India was in need of a great spiritual leader, a prophet. There was already a most powerful body of priests. One will understand the situation better if he remembers the history of the Jews—how they had two types of religious leaders, priests and prophets, the priests keeping the people in ignorance and grinding superstition into their minds. All through the Old Testament, you find the prophets challenging the superstitions of the priests.

The priests in India, the Brahmins, possessed great intellectual and psychic powers. It was they who began the spiritual development of India, and they accomplished wonderful things. But the time came when the free spirit of development that had at first actuated the Brahmins disappeared. They began to arrogate powers and privileges to themselves. If a Brahmin killed a man, he would not be punished. Even the most wicked Brahmin must be worshipped!

But while the priests were flourishing, there existed also the poet-prophets called Sannyasins. The Sannyasins have nothing to do with the two thousand ceremonies that the priests have invented. India was full of it in Buddha's day. There were the masses of people, and they were debarred from all knowledge. If just a word of the Vedas entered the ears of a man, terrible punishment was visited upon him. The priests had made a secret of the Vedas.

At last one man could bear it no more. He had the brain, the power, and the heart—a heart as infinite as the broad sky. This man had the brain to discover the means of breaking the bondages of souls. He learnt why men suffer, and he found the way out of suffering. He taught one and all without distinction and made them realize the peace of enlightenment. This was the man Buddha.

Buddha was the triumph in the struggle that had been going on between the priests and the prophets in India. One of his great messages was the equality of man. Buddha was the great preacher of equality. Every man and woman has the same right to attain spirituality. The difference between the priests and the other castes he abolished. Even the lowest were entitled to the highest attainments; he opened the door of Nirvana to one and all. His teaching was bold even for India; it was hard for India to swallow Buddha's doctrine.

The religion of Buddha spread fast. It was because of the marvellous love which, for the first time in the history of humanity, overflowed a large heart and devoted itself to the service not only of all men but of all living things—a love which did not care for anything except to find a way of release from suffering for all beings.

Buddha's idea is that there is no God, only man himself. He repudiated the mentality which underlies the prevalent ideas of God. He found it made men weak and superstitious. Everything independent is happy; everything dependent is miserable.

The life of Buddha has an especial appeal. All my life I have been very fond of Buddha. I have more veneration for that character than for any other—that boldness, that fearlessness, and that tremendous love! He was born for the good of men. Others may seek God, others may seek truth for themselves: he did not even care to know truth for himself. He sought truth because people were in misery. How to help them, that was his only concern.

And consider his marvellous brain! No emotionalism. That giant brain never was superstitious. Believe not because an old manuscript has been produced, because it has been handed down to you from your forefathers, but think for yourself; search truth for yourself; realize it yourself. Then if you find it beneficial to one and many, give it to people.

People were able to appreciate and embrace his teachings, so revolutionary, so different from what they had been taught by the priests through the ages!

And consider his death. If he was great in life, he was also great in death. He ate food offered to him by an outcaste, a *chandal.* Hindus do not touch them, because they eat every-thing indiscriminately. He told his disciples, 'Do not eat this food, but I cannot refuse it. Go to the man and tell him he has done me one of the greatest services of my life—he has released me from the body.'

Buddhistic India

There have been great religions before Buddhism arose, in India and elsewhere, but, more or less, they are confined within their own races. **With Buddhism first begins that peculiar phenomenon of religion boldly starting out to conquer the world.** Within a few centuries of its birth, the barefooted, shaven-headed missionaries of Buddha had spread over all the then known civilized world, and they penetrated even further—from Lapland on the one side to the Philippine Islands on the other. In India itself, the religion of Buddha had at one time nearly swallowed up two-thirds of the population.

Still it has the largest number of followers of any religion, and it has indirectly modified the teachings of all the other religions. A good deal of Buddhism entered into Asia Minor. It was a constant fight at one time whether the Buddhists would prevail or the later sects of Christians.

His method of work and organization was quite striking. **The idea that we have today of Church is his creation**. He organized these monks and made them into a body. Even the voting by ballot is there five hundred and sixty years before Christ. The Church became a tremendous power, and did great missionary work. Then came, three hundred years after, two hundred years before Christ, **the great emperor Asoka,** as he has been called by Western historians, **the divinest of monarchs,** and that man became entirely converted to the idea of Buddha, and he spread the religion worldwide. He sent his own children as well as others to propagate the ideology and set up inscriptions all over.

The first inscription describes the terror and misery of war, and how he became converted to religion. Then said he: "Henceforth let none of my descendants think of acquiring glory by conquering other races. If they want glory, let them help other races; let them send teachers of sciences and teachers of religion." And next you find how he is sending missionaries even to Alexandria. You wonder that you find all over that part of the country sects rising immediately, called Theraputae, Essenes, and all those—extreme vegetarians, and so on. Asoka built hospitals for men and for animals.

Buddhism was the foundation of the Christian religion: the Catholic Church came from Buddhism.

He was the only man who was ever ready to give up his life for animals to stop a sacrifice. He once said to a king, **'If tbe sacrifice of a lamb helps you to go to heaven, sacrificing a man will belp you better: so sacrifice me.** The king was astonished.

To many the path becomes easier if they believe in God. But the life of Buddha shows that even a man who does not believe in God, has no metaphysics, belongs to no sect, and goes not to any church, or temple, and is a confessed materialist, even he can attain to the highest.

It was the great Buddha, who never cared for the dualist gods, and who has been called an atheist and materialist, who yet was ready to give up his body for a poor goat. That Man set in motion the highest moral ideas any nation can have. **Wherever there is a moral code it is a ray of light from that Man.**

DHAMMACHAKKA-PAVATTANA SUTTA

The Wheel of Law

Reverence to the Blessed One, the Holy One, the Fully-Enlightened One.

Thus have I heard. The Blessed One was once staying at Benares, at the hermitage called Migadaya. And there the Blessed One addressed the company of the five Bhikshus, and said:

'There are two extremes, O Bhikkhus, which the man who has given up the world ought not to follow—the habitual practice, on the one hand, of those things whose attraction depends upon the passions, and especially of sensuality—a low and pagan way (of seeking satisfaction) unworthy, unprofitable, and fit only for the worldly-minded—and the habitual practice, on the other hand, of asceticism (or self-mortification), which is painful, unworthy, and unprofitable.

'There is a middle path, O Bhikkhus, avoiding these two extremes, discovered by the Tathagata—a path which opens the eyes, and bestows understanding, which leads to peace of mind, to the higher wisdom, to full enlightenment, to Nirvana!

'What is that middle path, O Bhikkhus, avoiding these two extremes, discovered by the Tathagata—that path which opens the eyes, and bestows understanding, which leads to peace of mind, to the higher wisdom, to full enlightenment, to Nirvana? Verily! it is this noble eightfold path; that is to say:

'Right views;

Right aspirations;

Right speech;

Right conduct;

Right livelihood;

Right effort;

Right mindfulness; and

Right contemplation.

'This, O Bhikkhus, is that middle path, avoiding these two extremes, discovered by the Tathagata—that path which opens the eyes, and bestows understanding, which leads to peace of mind, to the higher wisdom, to full enlightenment, to Nirvana!

Now this, O Bhikkhus, is the noble truth concerning suffering:

'Birth is attended with pain, decay is painful, disease is painful, death is painful. Union with the unpleasant is painful, painful is separation from the pleasant; and any craving that is unsatisfied, that too is painful. In brief, the five aggregates which spring from attachment (the conditions of individuality and their cause) are painful.

'This then, O Bhikkhus, is the noble truth concerning suffering.

'Now this, O Bhikkhus, is the noble truth concerning the origin of suffering:

'Verily, it is that thirst (or craving), causing the renewal of existence, accompanied by sensual delight, seeking satisfaction now here, now there—that is to say, the craving for the gratification of the passions or the craving for a future life, or the craving for success in this present life.

'This then, O Bhikkhus, is the noble truth concerning the origin of suffering.

'Now this, O Bhi'‹khus, is the noble truth concerning the destruction of ›uffering:

'Verily, it is the destruction, in which no passion remains of this very thirst; the laying aside of, the getting rid of the being free from, the harbouring no longer of this thirst.

'This then, O Bhikkhus, is the noble truth concerning the destruction of suffering.

'Now this, O Bhikkhus, O the noble truth concerning the way which leads to the destruction of sorrow. Verily! it is this noble eightfold path; that is to say:

'Right views;

Right aspirations;

Right speech;

Right conduct;

Right livelihood;

Right effort;

Right mindfulness; and

Right contemplation.

'This then, O Bhikkhus, is the noble truth concerning the destruction of sorrow.

'That this was the noble truth concerning sorrow, was not, O Bhikkhus, among the doctrines handed down, but there arose within me the eye to perceive it, there arose the knowledge of its nature, there arose the understanding of its cause, there arose the wisdom to guide in the path of tranquillity, there arose the light to dispel darkness from it.

'And again, O Bhikkhus, that I should comprehend that this was the noble truth concerning sorrow, though it was not amount the doctrines handed down, there arose within me the eye, there arose the knowledge, there arose the understanding, there arose the wisdom, there arose the light.

'And again, O Bhikkhus, that I had comprehended that this was the noble truth concerning sorrow, thought it was not among the doctrines handed down, there arose within me the eye, there arose the knowledge, there arose the understanding, there arose the wisdom, there arose the light.

'That this was the noble truth concerning the origin of sorrow, though it was not among the doctrines handed down, there arose within me the eye, there arose within me the knowledge, there arose the understanding, there arose the wisdom, there arose the light.

'And again, O Bhikkhus that I should put away the origin of sorrow, though the noble truth concerning it was not among the doctrines handed down, there arose within me the eye, there arose the knowledge, there arose the understanding, there arose the wisdom, there arose the light.

And again, O Bhikkhus, that I had fully put away the origin of sorrow, though the noble truth concerning it was not among the doctrines handed down, there arose within me the eye, there arose the knowledge, there arose the understanding, there arose the wisdom, there arose the light.

'That this, O Bhikkhus, was the noble truth concerning the destruction of sorrow, though it was not among the doctrines handed down, there arose within me the eye, there arose the knowledge, there arose the understanding, there arose the wisdom, there arose the light.

'And again, O Bhikkhus, that I should fully realise the destruction of sorrow, though the noble truth concerning it was not among the doctrines handed down, there arose within me the eye, there arose the knowledge, there arose the understanding, there arose the wisdom, there arose the light.

'And again, O Bhikkhus, that I had fully realised the destruction of sorrow, though the noble truth concerning it Was not among the doctrines handed down, there arose within me the eye, there arose the knowledge, there arose the understanding, there arose the wisdom, there arose the light.

'That this was the noble truth concerning the way which leads to the destruction of sorrow, was not, O Bhikkshus, among the doctrines handed down, there arose within me the eye, there arose the knowledge, there arose the under-standing, there arose the wisdom, there arose the light.

'And again, O Bhikkhus, that I should become versed in the way which leads to the destruction of sorrow, though the noble truth concerning it was not among the doctrines handed down, there arose within me the eye, there arose the knowledge, there arose the understanding, there arose the wisdom, there arose the light.

'And again, O Bhikkhus, that I had become versed in the way which leads to the destruction of sorrow, though the noble truth concerning it was not among the doctrines handed down, there arose within me the eye, there arose the knowledge, there arose the understanding, there arose the wisdom, there arose the light.

'So long, O Bhikkhus, as my knowledge and insight were not quite clear, regarding each of these four noble truths in this triple order, in this twelvefold manner—so long was I uncertain whether I had attained to the full insight of that wisdom which is unsurpassed in the heavens or on earth, among the whole race of Samanas and Brahmins, or of gods or men.

'But as soon, O Bhikkhus, as my knowledge and insight were quite clear regarding each of these four noble truths, in this triple order, in this twelvefold manner—then did I become certain that I had attained to the full insight of that wisdom which is unsurpassed in the heavens or on earth, among the whole race of Samanas and Brahmins, or of gods or men.

'And now this knowledge and this insight has arisen within me. Immovable is the emancipation of my heart. This is my last existence. There will now be no rebirth for me!'

• • •

Thus spake the Blessed One. The company of the five Bhikshus, glad at heart, exalted the words of the Blessed One. And when the discourse had been uttered, there arose within the venerable Kondanna the eye of truth, spotless, and without a stain, and he saw that whatsoever has an origin, in that is also inherent the necessity of coming to an end.

And when the royal chariot wheel of the truth had thus been set rolling onwards by the Blessed One, the gods of the earth gave forth a shout, saying:

'In Benares, at the hermitage of the Migadaya, the supreme wheel of the empire of Truth has been set rolling by the Blessed One—that wheel which not by any Samana or Brahmin, not by any god, not by any Brahma or Mara, not by anyone in the universe, can ever be turned back!'

And when they heard the shout of the gods of the earth, the attendant gods of the four great kings, the guardian angels of the four quarters of the globe, gave forth a shout, saying:

'In Benares, at the hermitage of the Migadaya, the supreme wheel of the empire of Truth has been set rolling by the Blessed One—that wheel which not by any Samana or Brahmin, not by any god, not by any Brahma or Mara, not by anyone in the universe, can ever be turned back!'

And thus as the gods in each of the heavens heard the shout of the inhabitants of the heaven beneath, they took up the cry until the gods in the highest heaven of heavens gave forth the shout, saying:

'In Benares, at the hermitage of the Migadaya, the supreme wheel of the empire of Truth has been set rolling by the Blessed One—that wheel which not by any Samana or Brahmin, not by any god, not by any Brahma or Mara, not by anyone in the universe, can ever be turned back!'

And thus, in an instant, a second, a moment, the sound went up even to the world of Brahma: and this great ten-thousand-world-system quaked and trembled and was shaken violently, and an immeasurable bright light appeared in the universe, beyond even the power of the gods!

Then did the Blessed One give utterance to this exclamation of joy: 'Kondanna hath realised it. Kondanna hath realised it!' And so the venerable Kondanna acquired the name of Ajjata-Kondanna ('the Kondanna who realised').

DHAMMAPADA

The Twin Verses

All that we are is the result of what we have thought : it is founded on our thoughts, it is made up of our thoughts. If a man speaks or acts with an evil thought, pain follows him, as the wheel follows the foot of the ox that draws the carriage.

All that we are is the result of what we have thought : it is founded on our thoughts, it is made up of our thoughts. If a man speaks or acts with a pure thought, happiness follows him, like a shadow that never leaves him.

"He abused me, he beat me, he defeated me, he robbed me"—in those who harbour such thoughts hatred will never cease.

"He abused me, he beat me, he defeated me, he robbed me"—in those who do not harbour such thoughts hatred will cease.

For hatred does not cease by hatred at any time: hatred ceases by love—this is an old rule.

The world does not know that we must all come to an end here; but those who know it, their quarrels cease at once.

He who lives looking for pleasures only, his senses uncontrolled, immoderate in his food, idle, and weak, Mara (the temper) will certainly overthrow him, as the wind throws down a weak tree.

He who lives without looking for pleasures, his senses well controlled, moderate in his food, faithful and strong, him Mara will certainly not overthrow, any more than the wind throws down a rocky mountain.

He who wishes to put on the yellow dress without having cleansed himself from sin, who disregards also temperance and truth, is unworthy of the yellow dress.

But he who has cleansed himself from sin, is well grounded in all virtues, and endowed also with temperance and truth, he is indeed worthy of the yellow dress.

They who imagine truth in untruth, and see untruth in truth, never arrive at truth, but follow vain desires.

They who know truth in truth, and untruth in untruth, arrive at truth, and follow true desires.

As rain break through an ill-thatched house, passion will break through an unreflecting mind.

As rain does not break through a well-thatched house, passion will not break through a well-reflecting mind.

The evil-doer mourns in this world, and he mourns in the next; he mourns in both. He mourns and suffers when he sees the evil result of his own work.

The virtuous man delights in this world, and he suffers in the next; he suffers in both. He delights and rejoices, when he sees the purity of his own work.

The evil-doer suffers in this world, and he suffers in the next; he suffers in both. He suffers when he thinks of the evil he has done; he suffers more when going on the evil path.

The virtuous man is happy in this world, and he is happy in the next; he is happy in both. He is happy when he thinks of the good he has done; he is still more happy when going on the good path.

The thoughtless man, even if he can recite a large portion of the law, but is not a doer of it, has no share in the priesthood, but is like a cowherd counting the cows of others.

The followers of the law, even if he can recite only a small portion of the law, but, having forsaken passion and hatred and foolishness, possesses true knowledge and serenity of mind, he, caring for nothing in this world or that to come, has indeed a share in the priesthood.

Earnestness

Earnestness is the path of immortality, Nirvana, thoughtlessness the path of death. Those who are in earnest do not die, those who are thoughtless are as if dead already.

Having understood this clearly, those who are advanced in earnestness delight in earnestness, and rejoice in the knowledge of the elect.

These wise people, meditative, steady, always possessed of strong powers, attain to Nirvana, the highest happiness.

If an earnest person has roused himself, if he is not forgetful, if his deeds are pure, if he acts with consideration, if he restrains himself, and lives according to law—then his glory will increase.

By rousing himself, by earnestness, by restraint and control, the wise man may make for himself an island which no flood can overwhelm.

Fools follow after vanity. The wise man keeps earnestness as his best jewel.

Follow not after vanity, nor after the enjoyment of love and lust! He who is earnest and meditative, obtains ample joy

When the learned man drives away vanity by earnestness, he, the wise, climbing the terraced heights of wisdom, looks down upon the fools: free from sorrow he looks upon the sorrowing crowd, as one that stands on a mountain looks down upon them that stand upon the plain.

Earnest among the thoughtless, awake among the sleepers, the wise man advances like a racer, leaving behind the hack.

By earnestness did Maghavan (Indra) rise to the lordship of the gods. People praise earnestness; thoughtlessness is always blamed.

A Bhikshu who delights in earnestness, who looks with fear on thoughtlessness, moves about like fire, burning all his fetters, small or large.

A Bhikshu who delights in reflection, who looks with fear on thoughtlessness, cannot fall away from his perfect, state—he is close upon Nirvana.

Thought

As a fletcher makes straight his arrow, a wise man makes straight his trembling and unsteady thought, which is difficult to guard, difficult to hold back.

As a fish taken from his watery home and thrown on the dry ground, our thought trembles all over in order to escape the dominion of Mara, the tempter.

It is good to tame the mind, which is difficult to hold in and flighty; rushing wherever it listeth; a tamed mind brings happiness.

Let the wise man guard his thoughts, for they are difficult to perceive, very artful, and they rush wherever they list; thoughts well guarded bring happiness.

Those who bridle their mind which travels far, moves about alone, is without a body, and hides m the chamber of the heart, will be free from the bonds of Mara, the tempter.

If a man's faith is unsteady, if he does not know the true law, if his peace of mind is troubled, his knowledge will never be perfect.

If a man's thoughs are not dissipated, if his mind is not perplexed, if he has ceased to think of good or evil, then there is no fear for him while he is watchful.

Knowing that this body is fragile like a jar, and making his thought firm like a fortress, one should attack Mara, the tempter, with the weapon of knowledge, one should watch him when conquered, and should never rest.

Before long, alas! this body will lie on the earth, despised, without understanding, like a useless log.

Whatever a hater may do to a hater, or an enemy to an enemy, a wrongly-directed mind will do him greater mischief.

Not a mother, not a father, will do so much, nor any other relatives; a well-directed mind will do us greater service.

Flowers

Who shall overcome this earth, and the world of Yama, the lord of the departed, and the world of the gods? Who shall find out the plainly shown path of virtue, as a clever man finds the right flower?

The disciple will overcome the earth, and the world of Yama, and the world of the gods. The disciple will find the plainly shown path of virtue, as a clever man finds the right flower.

He who knows that this body is like froth, and has learnt that it is as unsubstantial as a mirage, will break the flower-pointed arrow of Mara, and never see the king of death.

Death carries off a man who is gathering flowers, and whose mind is distracted, as a flood carries off a sleeping village.

Death subdues a man who is gathering flowers, and whose mind is distracted, before he is satiated in his pleasures.

As the bee collects nectar and departs without injuring the flower, or its colour or scent, so let a sage dwell in his village.

Not the perversities of others, not their sins of commission or omission, but his own misdeeds and negligences should a sage take notice of.

Like a beautiful flower, full of colour, but without scent, are the fine but fruitless words of him who does not act accordingly.

But, like a beautiful flower, full of colour and full of scent, are the fine and fruitful words of him who acts accordingly.

As many kinds of wreaths can be made from a heap of flowers, so many good things may be achieved by a mortal when once he is born.

The scent of flowers does not travel against the wind, nor that of sandalwood, or the Tagara and Mallika flowers; but the odour of good people travels even against the wind: a good man pervades every place.

Sandalwood or Tagara, a lotus-flower, or a Vassiki, among these sorts of perfumes, the perfume of virute is unsurpassed.

Mean is the scent that comes from Tagara and sandalwood; the perfume of those who possess virtue rises up to the gods as the highest.

Of the people who possess these virtues, who live without thoughtlessness, and who are emancipated through true knowledge, Mara, the tempter, never finds the way.

As on a heap of rubbish cast upon the highway the lily will grow full of sweet perfume and delight, thus among those who are mere rubbish, the disciple of the truly enlightened Buddha shines forth by his knowledge above the blinded worldling.

The Fool

Long is the night to him who is awake; long is a mile to him who is tired; long is life to the foolish who do not know the true law.

If a traveller does not meet with one who is his better, or his equal, let him firmly keep to his solitary journey; there is no companionship with a fool.

"These sons belong to me, and this wealth belongs to me," with such thoughts a fool is tormented. He himself does not belong to himself; how much less sons and wealth?

The fool who knows his foolishness, is wise at least so far. But a fool who thinks himself wise, he is called a fool indeed.

If a fool be associated with a wise man even all his life, he will perceive the truth as little as a spoon perceives the taste of soup.

If an intelligent man be associated for one minute only with a wise man, he will soon perceive the truth, as the tongue perceives the taste of soup.

Fools of poor understanding have themselves for their greatest enemies, for they do evil deeds which bear bitter fruits.

That deed is not well done of which a man must repent, and the reward of which he receives crying and with a tearful face.

No, that deed is well done of which a man does not repent, and the reward of which he receives gladly and cheerfully.

As long as the evil deed does not bear fruit the fool thinks, it is like honey; but when it ripens, then the fool suffers grief.

Let a fool month after month eat his food like an ascetic with the tip of a blade of Kusa-grass, yet is he not worth the sixteenth particle of those who have well weighed the law.

An evil deed, like newly-drawn milk, does not turn suddenly; smouldering, like fire covered by ashes, it follows the fool.

And when the evil deed, after it has become known, turns to sorrow for the fool, then it destroys his bright lot, nay, it cleaves his head.

Let the fool wish for a false reputation, for precedence among the Bhikshus, for lordship in the convents, for worship among other people!

"May both the layman and he who has left the world think that this is done by me; may they be subject to me in everything which is to be done or is not to be done, thus is the mind of the fool, and his desire and pride increase.

"One is the road that leads to wealth, another the road that leads to Nirvana"—if the Bhikshu, the disciple of Buddha, has learnt this, he will not yearn for honour, he will strive after separation from the world.

The Wise Man

If you see a man who shows you what is to be avoided who administers reproofs, and is intelligent, follow that wise man as you would one who tells of hidden treasures; it will be better, not worse, for him who follows him.

Let him admonish, let him teach, let him forbid what is improper!—he will be beloved of the good, by the had he will be hated.

Do not have evil-doers for friends, do not have low people for friends: have virtuous people for friends, have for friends the best of men.

He who drinks in the law lives happily with a serene mind: the sage rejoices always in the law, as preached by the elect.

Well-makers lead the water wherever they like; fletchers bend the arrow; carpenters bend a log of wood; wise people fashion themselves.

As a solid rock is not shaken by the wind, wise people falter not amidst blame and praise.

Wise people, after they have listened to the laws, become serene, like a deep, smooth, and still lake.

Good men indeed walk warily under all circumstances; good men speak not out of a desire for sensual gratification; whether touched by happiness or sorrow wise people never appear elated or depressed.

If, whether for his own sake, or for the sake of others, a man wishes neither for a son, nor for wealth, nor for lordship, and if he does not wish for his own success by unfair means, then he is good, wise, and virtuous.

Few are there among men who arrive at the other shore, become Arhats; the other people here run up and down the shore.

But those who, when the law has been well preached to them, follow the law, will pass over the dominion of death, however difficult to cross.

A wise man should leave the dark state of ordinary life, and follow the bright state of the Bhikshu. After going from his home to a homeless state, he should in his retirement look for enjoyment where enjoyment seemed difficult. Leaving all pleasures behind, and calling nothing his own, the wise man should purge himself from all the troubles of the mind.

Those whose mind is well grounded in the seven elements of knowledge, who without clinging to anything, rejoice in freedom from attachment, whose appetites have been conquered, and who are full of light, they are free even in this world.

The Venerable

There is no suffering for him who has finished his journey and abandoned grief, who has freed himself of all sides, and thrown off all fetters.

They exert themselves with their thoughts well-collected, they do not tarry in their abode; like swans who have left their lake, they leave their house and home.

Men who have no riches, who live on recognized food who have perceived void and unconditioned freedom, Nirvana, their path is difficult to understand, like that of birds in the air. He whose appetites are stilled, who is not absorbed in enjoyment, who has perceived void and unconditioned freedom, Nirvana, his path is difficult to understand, like that of birds in the air.

The gods even envy him whose senses, like horses well broken in by the driver, have been subdued, who is free from pride, and free from appetites; such a one who does his duty is tolerant like the earth, or like a threshold; he is like a lake without mud; no new births are in store for him.

His thought is quiet, quiet are his word and deed, when he has obtained freedom by true knowledge, when he has thus become a quiet man.

The man who is free from credulity, but knows the uncreated, who has cut all ties, removed all temptations, renounced all desires, he is the greatest of men.

In a hamlet or in a forest, on sea or on dry land, wherever venerable persons (Arhant) dwell, that place is delightful.

Forests are delightful; where the world finds no delight, there the passionless will find delight, for they look not for pleasures.

The Thousands

Even though a speech be of a thousand words, but made up of senseless words, one word of sense is better, which if a man hears, he becomes quiet.

Even though a Gatha (poem) be of a thousand words, but made up of senseless words, one word of a Gatha is better, which if a man hears, be becomes quiet,

Though a man recite a hundred Gathas made up of senseless words, one word of the law is better, which if a man hears, he becomes quiet.

If one man conquer in battle a thousand times a thousand men and if another conquer himself, he is the greatest of conquerors.

One's own self conquered is better than all other people; not even a god, a Gandharva, not Mara could change into defeat the victory of a man who has vanquished himself, and always lives under restraint.

If a man for a hundred years sacrifice month by month with a thousand, and if he but for one moment pay homage to a man whose soul is grounded in true knowledge, better is that homage than a sacrifice for a hundred years.

If a man for a hundred years worship Agni in the forest, and if he but for one moment pay homage to a man whose soul is grounded in true knowledge, better is that homage than sacrifice for a hundred years.

Whatever a man sacrifice in this world as an offering or as an oblation for a whole year in order to gain merit, the whole of it is not worth a quarter of a pence; reverence shown to the righteous is better.

He who always greets and constantly reveres the aged, four things will increase to him: life, beauty, happiness, power.

But he who lives a hundred years, vicious and unrestrained, a life of one day is better if a man is virtuous and reflecting.

And he who lives a hundred years, ignorant and unrestrained, a life of one day is better if a man is wise and reflecting.

And he who lives a hundred years, idle and weak, a life of one day is better if a man has attained firm strength.

And he who lives a hundred years, not seeing beginning and end, a life of one day is better if a man sees beginning and end.

And he who lives a hundred years, not seeing the immortal place, a life of one day is better if a man sees the immortal place.

And he who lives a hundred years, not seeing the highest law, a life of one day is better if a man sees the highest law.

Evil

A man should hasten towards the good, and should keep his thought away from evil; if a man does what is good slothfully, his mind delights in evil.

If a man commits a sin, let him not do it again; let him not delight in sin: the accumulation of evil is painful.

If a man does what is good, let him do it again; let him delight in it: the accumulation of good is delightful.

Even an evil-doer sees happiness so long as his evil deed does not ripen; but when his evil deed ripens, then does the evil-doer see evil.

Even a good man sees evil days so long as his good deed does not ripen; but when his good deed ripens, then does the good man see good things.

Let not man think lightly of evil, saying in his heart, it will not come nigh unto me, Even by the falling of water-drops a water-pot is filled; the fool becomes full of evil, even if he gather it little by little.

Let no man think lightly of good, saying in his heart, it will not come nigh unto me. Even by the falling of water-drops a water-pot is filled; the wise man becomes full of good, even if he gather it little by little.

Let a man avoid evil deeds, as a merchant, if he has few companions and carries much wealth, avoids a dangerous road; a man who loves life avoids poison.

He who has no wound on his hand, may touch poison with his hand; poison does not affect one who has no wound; nor is there evil for one who does not commit evil.

If a man offend a harmless, pure, and innocent person, the evil falls back upon that fool, like light dust thrown up against the wind.

Some people are born again; evil-doers go to hell; righteous people go to heaven; those who are free from all worldly desires attain Nirvana.

Not in the sky, not in the midst of the sea, not if we enter into the clefts of the mountains, is there known a spot in the whole world where a man might by freed from an evil deed.

Not in the sky, not in the midst of the sea, not if we enter into the clefts of the mountains, is there known a spot in the whole world where death could not overcome the mortal.

Punishment

All men tremble at punishment, all men fear death; remember that you are like unto them, and do not kill, nor cause slaughter.

All men tremble at punishment, all men love life; remember that thou art like unto them, and do not kill, nor cause slaughter.

He who, seeking his own happiness, punishes or kills beings who also long for happiness, will not find happiness after death.

He who, seeking his own happiness, does not punish or kill beings who also long for happiness, will find happiness after death.

Do not speak harshly to anyone; those who are spoken to will answer thee in the same way. Angry speech is painful: blows for blows will touch thee.

If, like a shattered gong, thou utter nothing, then thou hast reached Nirvana; anger is not known to thee.

As a cowherd with his staff drives his cows into the stable, so do Age and Death drive the life of men.

A fool does not know when he commits his evil deeds: but the wicked man burns by his own deeds, as if burnt by fire.

He who inflicts pain on innocent and harmless will soon come to one of these ten states:

He will have cruel suffering, loss, injury of the body, heavy affliction, or loss of mind.

A misfortune coming from the king, or a fearful accusation, or loss of relations, or destruction of treasures.

Lightning-fire will burn his houses; and when his body is destroyed, the fool will go to hell.

Not nakedness, not platted hair, not dirt, not fasting, or lying on the earth, not rubbing with dust, not sitting motionless, can purify a mortal who has not overcome desires.

He who, though dressed in fine apparel, exercises tranquillity, is quiet, subdued, restrained, chaste, and has ceased to find fault with all other beings, he indeed is a Brahmin, a Sramana, a Bhikshu.

Is there in this world any man so restrained by shame that he does not provoke reproof, as a noble horse the whip?

Like a noble horse when touched by the whip, be ye strenuous and eager, and by faith, by virtue, by energy, by meditation, by discernment of the law, you will overcome this great pain, perfect in knowledge and in behaviour, and never forgetful.

Well-makers lead the water wherever they like; fletchers bend the arrow; carpenters bend a log of wood; good people fashion themselves.

Old Age

How is there laughter, how is there joy, as this world is always burning? Do you not seek a light, ye who are surrounded by darkness?

Look at this dressed-up lump, covered with wounds, joined together, sickly, full of many schemes, but which has not strength, no hold!

This body is wasted, tull of sickness, and frail; this heap of corruption breaks to pieces, life indeed ends in death.

After one has looked at those gray bones, thrown away like gourds in the autumn, what pleasure is there left in life!

After a stronghold has been made of the bones, it is covered with flesh and blood, and there dwell in it old age and death, pride and deceit.

The brilliant chariots of kings are destroyed, the body also approaches destruction, but the virute of good people never approaches destruction—thus do the good say to the good.

A man who has learnt little, grows old like an ox; his flesh grows, but his knowledge does not grow.

Looking for the maker of this tabernacle, I have run through a course of many births, not finding him; and painful is birth again and again. But now, maker of the tabernacle, thou hast been seen; thou shalt not make up this tabernacle again. All thy rafters are broken, thy ridge-pole is sundered; the mind, approaching the Eternal, Nirvana, has attained to the extinction of all desires.

Men who have not observed proper discipline, and have not gained wealth in their youth, perish like old herons in a lake without fish.

Men who have not observed proper discipline, and have not gained wealth in their youth, lie, like broken bows, sighing after the past.

Self

If a man hold himself dear let him watch himself carefully; during one at least out of the three watches a wise man should be watchful.

Let each man direct himself first to what is proper, then let him teach others; thus a wise man will not suffer.

If a man make himself as he teaches others to be, then, being himself well subdued he may subdue others; for one's own self is difficult to subdue.

Self is the lord of self, who else could be the lord? With self well subdued, a man finds a lord such as few can find.

The evil done by one's self, self-forgotten, self-bred, crushes the foolish, as a diamond breaks even a precious stone.

He whose wickedness is very great brings himself down to that state where his enemy wishes him to be, as a creeper does with the tree which it surrounds.

Bad deeds, and deeds hurtful to ourselves, are easy to do; what is beneficial and good, that is very difficult to do.

The foolish man who scorns the rule of the Arhat, of the Arya, of the virtuous, and follows a false doctrine, he bears fruit to his own destruction, like the fruits of the Katthaka reed.

By one's self the evil is done, by one's self one suffers; by one's self evil is left undone, by one's self one is purified. The pure and the impure stand and fall by themselves, no one can purify another.

Let no one forget his own duty for the sake of another's however great; let a man, after he has discerned his own duty, be always attentive to his duty.

The World

Do not follow the evil law! Do not live on in thoughtlessness! Do not follow false doctrine! Be not a friend of the world.

Rouse thyself! do not be idle! Follow the law of virtue! The virtuous rest in bliss in this world and in the next.

Follow the law of virtue; do not follow that of sin. The virtuous rest in bliss in this world and in the next.

Look upon the world as you would on a bubble, look upon it as you would on a mirage: the king of death does not see him who thus looks down upon the world.

Come, look at this world, glittering like a royal chariot; the foolish are immersed in it, but the wise do not touch it.

He who formerly was reckless and afterwards became sober, brightens up this world, like the moon when freed from clouds.

He whose evil deeds are covered by good deeds, brightens up this world, like the moon when freed from clouds.

This world is dark, few only can see here; a few only go to heaven, like birds escaped from the net.

The swans go on the path of the sun, they go miraculously through the ether; the wise are led out of this world, when they have conquered Mara and his train.

If a man has transgressed the one law, and speaks lies, and scoffs at another world, there is no evil he will not do.

The uncharitable do not go to the world of the gods; foolls only do not praise liberality; a wise man rejoices in liberality, and through it becomes blessed in the other world.

Better than sovereignty over the earth, better than going to heaven, better than lordship over all the worlds, is the reward of Sotapatti, the first step in holiness.

Buddha—The Awakened

He whose conquest cannot be conquered again, into whose conquest no one in this world enters, by what track can you lead him, the Awakened, the Omniscient, the trackless?

He whom no desire with its snares and poisons can lead astray, by what track can you lead him, the Awakened, the Omniscient, the trackless?

Even the gods envy those who are awakened and not forgetful, who are given to meditation, who are wise, and who delight in the repose of retirement from the world.

Difficult to obtain is the conception of men, difficult is the life of mortals, difficult is the hearing of the True Law, difficult is the birth of the Awakened, the attainment of Buddhahood.

Not to commit any sin, to do good, and to purify one's mind, that is the teaching of all the awakened.

The Awakened call patience the highest penance, long-suffering the highest Nirvana; for he is not an anchorite who strikes others, he is not an ascetic who insults others.

Not to blame, not to strike, to live restrained under the law, to be moderate in eating, to sleep and sit alone, and to dwell on the highest thoughts—this is the teaching of the Awakened.

There is no satisfying lusts, even by a shower of gold pieces; he who knows that lusts have a short taste and cause pain, he is wise; even in heavenly pleasures he finds no satisfaction, the disciple who is fully awakened delights only in the destruction of all desires.

Men, driven by fear, go to many a refuge, to mountains and forests, to groves and sacred trees. But that is not a safe refuge, that is not the best refuge; a man is not delivered from all pains after having gone to that refuge.

He who takes refuge with Buddha, the Law, and the Church; he who, with clear understanding, sees the four holy truths: pain, the origin of pain, the destruction of pain, and the eightfold holy way that leads to the quieting of pain;—that is the safe refuge, that is the best refuge; having gone to that refuge, a man is delivered from all pain.

A supernatural person, a Buddha, is not easily found: he is not born everywhere. Wherever such a sage is born, that race prospers.

Happy is the arising of the Awakened, happy is the teaching of the True Law, happy is peace in the church, happy is the devotion of those who are at peace.

He who pays homage to those who deserve homage, whether the awakened, Buddha, or their disciples, those who have overcome the host of evils, and crossed the flood of sorrow, he who pays homage to such as have found deliverance and know no fear, his merit can never be measured by anyone.

Happiness

We live happily indeed, not hating those who hate us! among men who hate us we dwell free from hatred! We live happily indeed, free from ailments among the ailing! among men who are ailing let us dwell free from ailments!

We live happily indeed, free from greed among greedy! among men who are greedy let us dwell free from greed!

We live happily indeed! happily indeed, though we call nothing our own! We shall be like the bright gods, feeding on happiness!

Victory breeds hatred, for the conquered is unhappy. He who has given up both victory and defeat, he, the contented, is happy.

There is no fire like passion, there is no losing throw like hatred; there is no pain like this body; there is no happiness higher than rest.

Hunger is the worst of diseases, the elements of the body greatest evil; if one knows this truly, that is Nirvana, the highest happiness.

Health is the greatest of gifts, contentedness the best riches; trust is the best of relationships, Nirvana the highest happiness.

He who has tasted the sweetness of solitude and tranquillity, is free from fear and free from sin, while he tastes the sweetness of drinking in the law.

The sight of the Arya is good, to live with them is always happiness; if a man does not see fools, he will be truly happy.

He who walks in the company of fools suffers a long way; company with fools, as with an enemy, is always painful; company with the wise is pleasure, like meeting with kinsfolk.

Therefore, one ought to follow the wise, the intelligent, the learned, the much enduring, the dutiful, the elect; one ought to follow such a good and wise man, as the moon follows the path of the stars.

Pleasure

He who gives himself to vanity, and does not give himself to meditation, forgetting the real aim of life and grasping at pleasure, will in time envy him who has exerted himself meditation.

Let no man ever cling to what is pleasant, or to what is unpleasant. Not to see what is pleasant is pain, and it is pain to see what is unpleasant.

Let, therefore, no man love anything; loss of the beloved is evil. Those who love nothing, and hate nothing, have no fetters.

From pleasure comes grief, from pleasure comes fear; he who is free from pleasure knows neither grief nor fear.

From affection comes grief, from affection comes fear; he who is free from affection knows neither grief nor fear.

From lust comes grief, from lust comes fear; he who is free from lust knows neither grief nor fear.

From love comes grief, from love comes fear; he who is free from love knows neither grief nor fear.

From greed comes grief, from greed comes fear; he who is free from greed knows neither grief nor fear.

He who possesses virtue and intelligence, who is just speaks the truth, and does what is his own business, him the world will hold dear.

He in whom a desire for the Ineffable (Nirvana) has sprung up, who in his mind is satisfied, and whose thoughts are not bewildered by love, he is called Urdhvasrotas, carried upwards by the stream.

Kinsmen, friends, and lovers salute a man who has been long away, and returns safe from afar.

In like manner his good works receive him who has done good, and has gone from this world to the other;—as kinsmen receive a friend on his return.

Anger

Let a man leave anger, let him forsake pride, let him overcome bondage! No sufferings befall the man who is not attached to name and form, and who calls nothing his own.

He who holds back rising anger like a rolling chariot, him I call a real driver; other people are but holding the reins.

Let a man overcome anger by love, let him overcome evil by good; let him overcome the greedy by liberality, the liar by truth!

Speak the truth, do not yield to anger; give, if thou art asked O for little; by these three steps thou wilt go near the gods.

The sages who injure nobody, and who always control their body, they will go to the unchangeable place, Nirvana, where, if they have gone, they will suffer no more.

Those who are ever watchful, who study day and night, and who strive after Nirvana, their passions will come to an end.

This is an old saying, O Atula, this is not as if of today:

"They blame him who sits silent, they blame him who speaks much, they also blame him who says little; there is no one on earth who is not blamed."

There never was, there never will be, nor is there now, a man who is always blamed, or a man who is always praised.

But he whom those who discriminated praise continually day after day, as without blemish, wise, rich in knowledge and virtue, who would dare to blame him, like a coin made of gold from the Jambu river? Even the gods praise him, he is praised even by Brahman.

Beware of bodily anger, and control thy body! Leave the sins of the body, and with thy body practise virtue!

Beware of the anger of the tongue, and control thy tongue! Leave the sins of the tongue, and practise virtue with thy tongue!

Beware of the anger of the mind, and control thy mind! Leave the sins of the mind, and practise virtue with thy mind.

The wise who control their body, who control their tongue, the wise who control their mind, are indeed well controlled.

Impurity

Thou art now like a sear leaf, the messengers of Yama have come near to thee; thou standest at the door of thy departure, and thou hast no provision for thy journey.

Make thyself an island, work hard, be wise! When thy impurities are blown away, and thou art free frorn guilt, thy wilt enter into the heavenly world of the Arya.

Thy life has come to an end, thou art come near to death, Yama, there is no resting-place for thee on the road, and thou hast no provision for thy journey.

Make thyself an island, work hard, be wise! When thy impurities are blown away, and thou art free from guilt, thou wilt not enter again into birth and decay.

Let a wise man blow off the impurities of himself, as a smith blows off the impurities of silver, one by one, little by little, and from time to time.

As the impurity which springs from the iron, when it springs from it, destroys it; thus do a transgressor's own works lead him to the evil path.

The taint of prayers is non-repetition; the taint of houses, non-repair; the taint of complexion is sloth; the taint of a watchman, alertlessness.

Bad conduct is the taint of woman, niggardliness the taint of a benefactor; tainted are all evil ways, in this world and in the next.

But there is a taint worse than all taints—ignorance is the greatest taint. O mendicants! throw off that taint, and become taintless!

Life is easy to live for a man who is without shame: a crow hero, a mischief-maker, an insulting, bold, and wretched fellow.

But life is hard to live for a modest man, who always looks for what is pure, who is disinterested, quiet, spotless, and intelligent.

He who destroys life, who speaks untruth, who in the world takes what is not given him, who goes to another man's wife; and the man who gives himself to drinking intoxicating liquors, he, even in this world, digs up his root.

O man, know this, that the unrestrained are in a bad state; take care that greediness and vice do not bring thee to grief for a long time!

The world gives according to their faith or according to their pleasure: if a man frets about the food and the drink given to others, he will find no rest either by day or by night.

He in whom that feeling is destroyed, and taken out with the very root, finds rest by day and by night.

There is no fire like passion, there is no shark like hatred, there is no snare like folly, there is no torrent like greed.

The fault of others is easily perceived, but that of one's self is difficult to perceive; a man winnows his neighbour's faults like chaff, but his own fault he hides, as a cheat hides the bad die from the player.

If a man looks after the faults of others, and is always inclined to be offended, his own passions will grow, and he is far from the destruction of passions.

There is no path through the air, a man is not a Samana outwardly. The world delights in vanity, the Tathagatas are free from vanity.

There is no path through the air, a man is not a Samana outwardly. No creatures are eternal; but the awakened Buddha are never shaken.

The Just

A man is not just if he carries a matter by violence; no, he who distinguishes both right and wrong, who is learned and guides others, not by violence, but by the same law, being a guardian of the law and intelligent, he is called just.

A man is not learned because he talks much; he who is patient, free from hatred and fear, he is called learned.

A man is not a supporter of the law because he talks much; even if a man has learnt little, but sees the law bodily, he is a supporter of the law, a man who never neglects the law.

A man is not an elder because his head is gray; his age may be ripe, but he is called "Old-in-vain."

He in whom there is truth, virtue, pity, restraint, moderation, he who is free from impurity and is wise, he is called an elder.

An envious, stingy, dishonest man does not become respectable by means of much talking only, or by the beauty of his complexion.

He in whom all this is destroyed, and taken out with the very root, he, when freed from hatred, is called respectable.

Not by tonsure does an undisciplined man who speaks falsehood become a Samana; can a man be a Samana who is still held captive by desire and greediness?

He who always quiets the evil, whether small or large he is called a Samana, a quiet man, because he has quieted all evil.

A man is not a Bhikshu simply because he asks others for alms; he who adopts the whole law is a Bhikshu not he who only begs.

He who is above good and evil, who is chaste, who with care passes through the world, he indeed is called a Bhikshu.

A man is not a Muni because he observes silence if he is foolish and ignorant; but the wise who, as with the balance, chooses the good and avoids evil, he is a Muni, and is a Muni thereby; he who in this world weighs both sides is called a Muni.

A man is not an Arya because he injures living creatures; because he has pity on all living creatures, therefore is a man called Arya.

Not only by discipline and vows, not only by much learning, not by entering into a trance, not by sleeping alone, do I earn the happiness of release which no worldling can know. O Bhikshu, he who has obtained the extinction of desires has obtained confidence.

The Way

The best of ways is the eightfold; the best of truths the four words; the best of virtues passionlessness; the best of men he who has eyes to see.

This is the way, there is no other that leads to the purifying of intelligence. Go on this path! This is the confusion of Mara, the tempter.

If you go on this way, you will make an end of pain! The way preached by me, when I had understood the removal of the thorns in the flesh.

You yourself must make an effort. The Tathagatas are only preachers. The thoughtful who enter the way are freed from the bondage of Mara.

"All created things perish," he who knows and sees this becomes passive in pain; this is the way to purity.

"All created things are grief and pain," he who knows and sees this becomes passive in pain; this is the way that leads to purity.

"All forms are unreal," he who knows and sees this becomes passive in pain; this is the way that leads to purity.

He who does not rouse himself when it is time to rise, who, though young and strong, is full of sloth, whose will and thought are weak, that lazy and idle man never finds the way to knowledge.

Watching his speech, well restrained in mind, let a man never commit any wrong with his body! Let a man but keep these three roads of action clear, and he will achieve the way which is taught by the wise.

Through zeal knowledge is gained, through lack of zeal knowledge is lost; let a man who knows this double path of gain and loss thus place himself that knowledge may grow.

Cut down the whole forest of desires, not a tree only! Danger comes out of the forest of desires. When you have cut down both the forest of desires and its undergrowth, then, Bhikshus, you will be rid of the forest and of desires!

So long as the desire of man towards women, even the smallest, is not destroyed, so long is his mind in bondage, as the calf that drinks milk is to its mother.

Cut out the love of self, like an autumn lotus, with thy hand! Cherish the road of peace. Nirvana has been shown by Sugata (Buddha).

"Here I shall dwell in the rain, here in winter and summer," thus the fool meditates, and does not think of death.

Death comes and carries off that man, honoured for his children and flocks, his mind distracted, as a carries court off a sleeping village.

Sons are no help, nor a father, nor relations; there is no help from kinsfolk for one whom death has seized.

A wise and well-behaved man who knows the meaning of this should quickly clear the way that leads to Nirvana.

Miscellaneous

If by leaving a small pleasure one sees a great pleasure, let a wise man leave the small pleasure, and look to the great.

He who, by causing pain to others, wishes to obtain pleasure for himself, he, entangled in the bonds of hatred, will never be free from hatred.

What ought to be done is neglected, what ought not to be done is done; the desires of unruly, thoughtless people are always increasing.

But they whose whole watchfulness is always directed to their body, who do not follow what ought not to be done, and who steadfastly do what ought to be done, the desires of such watchful and wise people will come to an end.

A true Brahmin goes scathless, though he have killed father and mother, and two valiant kings, though he has destroyed a kingdom with all its subjects.

A true Brahmin goes scathless, though he have killed father and mother, and two holy kings, and an eminent man besides.

The disciples of Gotama are always well awake, and their thoughts day and night are always set on Buddha.

The disciples of Gotama are always well awake, and their thoughts day and night are always set on the law.

The disciples of Gotama are always well awake, and their thoughts day and night are always set on the church.

The disciples of Gotama are always well awake, and thoughts day and night are always set on their body.

The disciples of Gotama are always well awake, and their thoughts day and night always delight in compassion.

The disciples of Gotama are always well awake, and their thoughts day and night always delight in meditation.

It is hard to leave the world to become a friar, it is hard to enjoy the world; hard is the monastery, painful are the houses; painful it is to dwell with equals to share everything in common, and the itinerant mendicant is beset with pain. Therefore let no man be an itinerant mendicant, and he will not be beset with pain.

A man full of faith, if endowed with virtue and glory, is respected, whatever place he may choose.

Good people shine from afar, like the snowy mountains; bad people are not seen, like arrows shot by night.

Sitting alone, lying down alone, walking alone without ceasing, and alone subduing himself, let a man be happy near the edge of a forest.

The Bhikshu

Restraint in the eye is good, good is restraint in the ear, in the nose restraint is good, good is restraint in the tongue.

In the body restraint is good, good is restraint in speech, in thought restraint is good, good is restraint in all things. A Bhikshu, restrained in all things, is freed from all pain.

He who controls his hand, he who controls his feet, he who controls his speech, he who is well controlled, he who delights inwardly, who is collected, who is solitary and content, him they call Bhikshu.

The Bhikshu who controls his mouth, who speaks wisely and calmly, who teaches the meaning and the law, his word is sweet.

He who dwells in the law, delights in the law, meditates on the law, recollects the law: that Bhikshu will never fall away from the true law.

Let him not despise what he has received, nor ever envy others: a mendicant who envies others does not obtain peace of mind.

A Bhikshu who, though he receives little, does not despise what he has received, even the gods will praise him, if his life is pure, and if he is not slothful.

He who never identifies himself with name and form, and does not grieve over what is no more, he indeed is called a Bhikshu.

The Bhikshu who behaves with kindness, who is happy in the doctrine of Buddha, will reach the quiet place, Nirvana happiness arising from the cessation of natural inclinations.

O Bhikshu, empty this boat! if emptied, it will go quickly; having cut off passion and hatred, thou wilt go to Nirvana.

Cut off the five fetters, leave the five, rise above the fire. A Bhikshu, who has escaped from the five fetters, he is called Oghatinna—"saved from the flood."

Meditate, O Bhikshu, and be not heedless! Do not direct thy thought to what gives pleasure, that thou mayest not for thy heedlessness have to swallow the iron ball in hell, and that thou mayest not cry out when burning, "This is pain."

Without knowledge there is no meditation, without meditation there is no knowledge: he who has knowledge and meditation is near unto Nirvana.

A Bhikshu who has entered his empty house, and whose mind is tranquil, feels a more than human delight when he sees the law clearly.

As soon as he has considered the origin and destruction of the elements of the body, he finds happiness and joy which belong to those who know the immortal Nirvana.

And this is the beginning here for a wise Bhikshu: watchfulness over the senses, contentedness, restraint under the law; keep noble friends whose life is pure, and who are not slothful.

Let him live in charity, let him be perfect in his duties; then in the fulness of delight he will make an end of suffering.

As the Vassika plant sheds its withered flowers, men should shed passion and hatred, O ye Bhikshus!

The Bhikshu whose body and tongue and mind are quieted, who is collected, and has rejected the baits of the world, he is called quiet.

Rouse thyself by thyself, examine thyself by thyself, thus self-protected and attentive wilt thou live happily, O Bhikshu!

For self is the lord of self, self is the refuge of self; therefore curb thyself as the merchant curbs a noble horse.

The Bhikshu, full of delight, who is happy in the doctrine of Buddha will reach the quiet place, Nirvana, happiness consisting in the cessation of natural inclinations.

He who, even as a young Bhikshu, applies himself the doctrine of Buddha, brightens up this world, like the moon when free from clouds.

The Brahmin

Stop the stream valiantly, drive away the desires, O Brahmin! When you have understood the destruction of all that was made, you will understand that which was not made.

If the Brahmin has reached the other shore in both laws in restraint and contemplation, all bonds vanish from he who has obtained knowledge.

He for whom there is neither the hither nor the further shore, nor both, him, the fearless and unshackled, I call indeed a Brahmin.

He who is thoughtful, blameless, settled, dutiful, without passions, and who has attained the highest end, him I call indeed a Brahmin.

The sun is bright by day, the moon shines by night, the warrior is bright in his armour, the Brahmin is bright in his meditation; but Buddha, the Awakened, is bright splendour day and night.

Because a man is rid of evil, therefore he is called Brahmin; because he walks quietly, therefore he is called Samana; because he has sent away his own impurities, therefore he is called a pilgrim.

No one should attack a Brahmin, but no Brahmin, if attacked, should let himself fly at his aggressor! Woe to him who strikes a Brahmin, more woe to him who flies at his aggressor!

It advantages a Brahmin not a little if he holds his mind back from the pleasures of life; the more all wish to injure has vanished, the more all pain will cease.

Him I call indeed a Brahmin who does not offend by body, word, or thought, and is controlled on these three points.

He from whom he may learn the law, as taught by the Well-awakened Buddha, let him worship assiduously, as the Brahmin worships the sacrificial fire.

A man does not become a Brahmin by his plaited hair, by his family, or by birth; in whom there is truth and righteousness, he is blessed, he is a Brahmin.

What is the use of plaited hair, a fool! what of the raiment of goat-skins? Within thee there is ravening, but the outside thou makest clean.

The man who wears dirty raiments, who is emaciated and covered with veins, who meditates alone in the forest, him I call indeed a Brahmin.

I do not call a man a Brahmin because of his origin or of his mother. He is indeed arrogant, and he is wealthy: but the poor, who is free from all attachments, him I call indeed a Brahmin.

Him I call indeed a Brahmin who, after cutting all fetters, never trembles, is free from bonds and unshackled.

Him I call indeed a Brahmin who, after cutting the strap and the thong, the rope with all that pertains to it, has destroyed all obstacles, and is awakened.

Him I call indeed a Brahmin who, though he has committed no offence, endures reproach, stripes, and bonds: who has endurance for his force, and strength for his army.

Him I call indeed a Brahmin who is free from anger, dutiful, virtuous, without appetites, who is subdued, and has received his last body.

Him I call indeed a Brahmin who does not cling to sensual pleasures, like water on a lotus leaf, like a mustard seed on the point of a needle.

Him I call indeed a Brahmin who, even here, knows the end of his own suffering, has put down his burden, and is unshackled.

Him I call indeed a Brahmin whose knowledge is deep, who possesses wisdom, who knows the right way and the wrong, and has attained the highest end.

Him I call indeed a Brahmin who keeps aloof both from laymen and from mendicants, who frequents no houses, and has but few desires.

Him I call indeed a Brahmin who without hurting any creatures, whether feeble or strong, does not kill nor cause slaughter.

Him I call indeed a Brahmin who is tolerant with the intolerant, mild with the violent, and free from greed among the greedy.

Him I call indeed a Brahmin from whom anger and hatred, pride and hypocrisy have dropped like a mustard seed from the point of a needle.

Him I call indeed a Brahmin who utters true speech, instructive and free from harshness, so that he offend no one.

Him I call indeed a Brahmin who takes nothing in the world that is not given him, be it long or short, small or large, good or bad.

Him I call indeed a Brahmin who fosters no desires for this world or for the next, has no inclinations, and is unshackled.

Him I call indeed a Brahmin who has no interests, and when he has understood the truth, does not say How, how? and who has reached the depth of the Immortal.

Him I call indeed a Brahmin who in this world has risen above both ties, good and evil, who is free from grief, from sin, and from impurity.

Him I call indeed a Brahmin who is bright like the moon, pure, serene, undisturbed, and in whom all gayety is extinct.

Him I call indeed a Brahmin who has traversed this miry road, the impassable world, difficult to pass, and its vanity, who has gone through, and reached the other shore is thoughtful, steadfast, free from doubts, free from attachment, and content.

Him I call indeed a Brahmin who in this world, having abandoned all desires, travels about without a home, and in whom all concupiscence is extinct.

Him I call indeed a Brahmin who, having abandoned all longings, travels about without a home, and in whom all covetousness is extinct.

Him I call indeed a Brahmin who, after leaving all bondage to men, has risen above all bondage to the gods, and is free from all and every bondage.

Him I call indeed a Brahmin who has left what gives pleasure and what gives pain, who is cold, and free from all germs of renewed life: the hero who has conquered all the worlds.

Him I call indeed a Brahmin who knows the destruction and the return of beings everywhere, who is free from boildage, welfaring, Sugata, and awakened, Buddha.

Him I call indeed a Brahmin whose path the gods do not know, nor Gandharvas, nor men, whose passions are extinct, and who is an Arhat.

Him I call indeed a Brahmin who calls nothing his own, whether it be before, behind, or between; who is poor, and free from the love of the world.

Him I call indeed a Brahmin, the manly, the noble, the hero, the great sage, the conqueror, the indifferent, the accomplished, the awakened.

Him I call indeed a Brahmin who knows his former abodes, who sees heaven and hell, has reached the end of births, is perfect in knowledge, a sage, and whose perfections are all perfect.

PRAJNA PARAMITA HRIDAYA SUTRA

The Heart of Perfect Wisdom

Adoration to the Omniscient!

This I heard: At one time the Bhagavat (Lord Buddha) dwelt as Rajagriha, on the hill Gridhrakuta, together with large number of Bhikshus and a large number of Bodhisattvas.

At that time the Bhagavat was absorbed in a meditation, called Gambhirava-sambodha. And at the same time the great Bodhisattva Aryavalokiteshvara, performing his study in the deep Prajna-paramita, thought thus: 'There are the five Skandhas, and those he considered as something by nature empty.'

Then the venerable Sariputra, through Buddha's power, thus spoke to the Bodhisattva Aryavalokiteshvara: 'If the son or daughter of a family wishes to perform the study in the deep Prajna-paramita, how is he to be taught?'

On this the great Bodhisattva Aryavalokiteshvara thus spoke to the venerable Sariputra: 'If the son or daughter of a family wishes to perform the study in the deep Prajna-paramita, he must think thus:

'There are five Skandhas, and these he considered as by their nature empty. Form is emptiness, and emptiness indeed is form. Emptiness is not different from form, form is not different from emptiness. What is form that is emptiness, what is emptiness that is form. Thus perception, name conception, and knowledge also are emptiness. Thus, O Sariputra, all things have the character of emptiness, they have no beginning, no end, they are faultless and not faultless, they are not imperfect and not perfect. Therefore, O Sariputra, here in this emptiness there is no form, no perception, no name, no concept, no knowledge. No eye, ear, nose, tongue, body, and mind. No form, sound, smell, taste, touch, and objects. There is no eye, etc., till we come to 'there is no mind, no objects, no mind knowledge. There is no knowledge, no ignorance, no destruction of ignorance,' till we come to 'there is no decay and death, no destruction of decay and death; there are not the Four Truths, viz., that there is pain, origin of pain, stoppage of pain, and the path to it. There is no knowledge, no obtaining, no not-obtaining of Nirvana. Therefore, O Sariputra, as there is no obtaining of Nirvana, a man who has approached the Prajna-paramita of the Bodhisattvas, dwells for a time enveloped in consciousness. But when the envelopment of consciousness has been annihilated, then he becomes free of all fear, beyond the reach of change, enjoying final Nirvana.

'All Buddhas of the past, present, and future, after approaching the Prajna-paramita, have awoken to the highest perfect knowledge.

'Therefore we ought to know the great verse of the Prajna-paramita, the verse of the great wisdom, the unsur—passed verse, the verse which appeases all pain—it is truth, because it is not false—the verse proclaimed in the Prajna-paramita.

"O wisdom, gone, gone, gone to the other, shore, landed at the other shore, Svaha!"

'Thus, O Sariputra, should a Bodhisattva teach in the study of the deep Prajna-paramita.'

Then when the Bhagavat had risen from that meditation, he gave his approval to the venerbale Bodhisattva

Avalokitesvara, saying: 'Well done, well done, noble son! So it is, noble son. So indeed must this study of the deep Prajna-paramita be peformed. As it has been described by thee, it is applauded by Arhat Tathagatas.'

Thus spoke Bhagavat with joyful mind. And the venerable Sariputra, and the honourable Bodhisattva Avalokitesvara, and the whole assembly, and the world of gods, men, demons, and fairies praised the speech of the Bhagavat.

'ENQUIRE FREELY'

The Blessed One addressed the brethren, and said: 'It may be, brethren, that there may be doubt or misgiving in the mind of some brother as to the Buddha, or the truth, or the path, or the way. Enquire, brethren, freely. Do not have to reproach yourselves afterwards with the thought "Our teacher was face to face with us, and we could not bring ourselves to enquire of the Blessed One when we were face to face with him."

And when he had thus spoken the brethren were silent.

And again the second and the third time the Blessed One addressed the brethren, and said: 'It may be, brethren, that there may be doubt or misgiving in the mind of some brother as to the Buddha, or the truth, or the path, or the way. Enquire, brethren, freely. Do not have to reproach yourselves afterwards with the thought, "Our teacher was face to face with us, and we could not bring ourselves to enquire of the Blessed One when we were face to face with him."

And even the third time the brethren were silent.

Then the Blessed One addressed the brethren, and said: 'It may be, brethren, that you put no questions out of reverence for the teacher. Let one friend communicate to another.'

And when he had thus spoken the brethren were silent.

And the venerable Ananda said to the Blessed One: 'How wonderful a thing is it, Lord, and how marvellous! Verily, I believe that in this whole assembly of the brethren there is not one brother who has any doubt or misgiving as to the Buddha, or the truth, or the path, or the way!'

'It is out of the fulness of faith that thou hast spoken, Ananda! But, Ananda, the Tathagata knows for certain that in this whole assembly of the brethren there is not one brother who has any doubt or misgiving as to the Buddha, or the truth, or the path, or the way! For even the most backward, Ananda, of all these five hundred brethren has become converted, and is no longer liable to be born in a state of suffering, and is assured of final salvation.'

The Last Word

Then the Blessed One addressed the brethren, and said 'Behold now, brethren, I exhort you, saying, "Decay is inherent in all component things! Work out your salvation with diligence!'"

This was the last word of the Tathagata!

5.

Judaism

First Revealed Religion
Good life, Severe God

RELIGION OF 'THE CHOSEN PEOPLE'

Judaism is the religion of the Jews, the first of Abraham's three organised religions. Abraham is regarded as the father of the peoples, who lived in, now Iraq, about 4000 years ago. Moon was worshipped in that city, and God is said to have inspired him to leave it and live in a land which will be shown to him. He did so and gave birth to a son, Isaac, in his old age.

God was called YHWH (Jehova) who wanted to be worshipped alone, to which Abraham agreed. This developed the idea of Monotheism, the oneness of an invisible God, along with the Brotherhood of Man. God demanded absolute obedience to his will and his orders for the welfare of mankind. The first five chapters of the Old Testament of the Bible are known as Torah (the law, way of life) which declares that man was made by God out of the dust, and he became alive when God breathed his spirit into his body.

Human sacrifice was prevalent in those days, and God ordered Abraham to sacrifice his son, but just as he was about to fulfil it, an angel appeared and prevented him from doing so. This indicated that the practice was now stopped.

Abraham travelled to Egypt and Cannan with his men to live in the land promised by God through Isaac, who here got married to Rebekah and had two sons. One of them, Jacob, changed his name to Israel at the behest of God one night. The word means 'May God Rule'. Since then the followers of Abraham came to be called Israelites or the Children of Israel.

Jacob had 12 sons, one of whom was named Joseph. He was the favourite of his father, for which reason, some of his brothers tried to kill him. But he was somehow saved and sold into slavery to persons going to Egypt. He had the faculty of interpreting dreams, which so much impressed the ruling Pharaoh, that he gave him a very senior position in his kingdom. During this period, his parents and brothers came to Egypt and joined him.

The Israelites lived happily in Egypt for many centuries. But later on, the Pharaohs started treating them cruelly, and made them slaves. All their male children were ordered to be killed as soon as they were born; but one, Moses, was saved by a clever strategem played by his mother, who put the child in a basket and placed it in the river Nile to flow with the current. The king's daughter had no son of her own, and was bathing beside the river. She saw the basket and took the child home. He was brought up in a royal manner.

When he grew up, he realised that his people were most unhappy, so he decided to revolt, and leave the country with them. He did so many times, buit failed, to counter which God started punishing the Egyptians with plagues, fires, etc. After the tenth plague, the Pharaoh finally agreed to let them leave. They all gathered, collected their belongings and left in a great hurry, afraid that in case the king again changed his mind.

This is known as the famous Exodus of ancient history. The king did soon change his mind, he sent his army after them, but, it is said, that a miracle happened: the waters of the Red Sea parted, letting the people cross to the other side safely.

God YHWH had taken the Hebrews as 'the chosen people', leading them to the new promised land. But the land was nowhere to settle down. They wandered in barren spaces for forty long years, facing great sufferings. It was the leadership of Moses that kept them alive, and did not let them lose hope. It was at Mount Sinai that God gave him the Ten Commandments inscribed on two stones. These were as follows:

I am the LORD thy God, who brought thee out of the land of Egypt, out of the house of bondage.

Thou shalt have no other gods before Me. Thou shalt not take the name of the LORD thy God in vain.

Remember the Sabbath day, to keep it holy.

Six days shalt thou labour, and do all thy work; but the seventh day is a Sabbath unto the LORD thy God, in it thou shalt not do any manner of work, thou, in six days the LORD made. heaven and earth, the sea and all that in them is, and rested on the seventh day; wherefore the LORD blessed the Sabbath day, and hallowed it.

Honour thy father and thy mother, that thy days may be long upon the land which the LORD thy God giveth thee.

Thou shalt not murder.

Thou shalt not commit adultery.

Thou shalt not steal.

Thou shalt not bear false witness against thy neighbour.

Thou shalt not covet thy neighbour's house; thou shalt not covet thy neighbour's wife nor his manservant, nor his maid—servant, nor his ox, nor his ass, nor anything that is thy neighbour's.

• • •

Finally, they reached Canaan. The 12 sons of Jacofb gave rise to 12 tribes, and were governed by many prophets for a long time, the last being Samuel (about 1100 B.C.). Then they decided to have a king, and selected Saul as the first. He was followed by David, the harpist of king Saul. He was very brave and had killed the giant Goliath when as a boy he was challenged for a combat. He was an able ruler, who made Jerusalem as his capital, and also composed the prayers called Psalms sung by the Jews. His son Solomon built the temple and composed the wisdom of Proverbs. After him, the tribes divided—the 10 northern tribes became Israel and the southern two, Judah—the word 'Jew' emerged out of this name.

After two centuries the northern kingdom was destroyed by the Assyrians. The tribes had to disperse, one does not know who went where, and they are known as the 'Lost Tribes of Israel'. Some of them might have come to India, a land where every outsider was welcome. People in some parts of Kashmir are called as Bene-Israel.

More than a century later the southern kingdom of Judah was invaded by the Babylonians and most of the Jews were taken away. The temple was destroyed. A few years later the Persian king Cyrus attacked Palestine and conquered it; he permitted the Jews to return to Jerusalem and also rebuild the temple.

In the 2nd century B.C. the land was again invaded by Antiochus, and after some time recovered by a group of Jews, but again they were conquered by a Persian king. The Romans under Pompey attacked in 63 B.C. and destroyed the temple a few years later, in 70 B.C. This was the greatest blow and the Jews had to disperse—now for a very long time, almost two millennia. In 1948 the British diplomacy made it possible for them to return to their homeland once again—which is the new Israel. This happened chiefly because they had to suffer the devil Hitler's concentration camps treatment given to them in Germany during his reign in that country. Some six million Jews were eliminated in Europe.

The strange story of 'the chosen people' is not very heart-warming, and does not let anyone further trust the God's promises and powers of providing safety and security, either, yet, human nature being what it is—or is not—life does not seem to change towards better ideals. In present day Israel they are facing Palestenian onslaught from all sides.

The Laws of Torah

We may now have a bird's eye-view of their beliefs and ritual as well as other practices, which are not less interesting.

Judaism holds that there is one God who has created the universe, and human beings, and is all powerful. He has given mankind a divine law known as Torah, which has to be followed in its entirety. There are 613 precepts in the Torah, 248 of which are positive and 365 negative. This number is carefully spun in the threads of the prayer shawl which helps them in remembering their obligations. These are God's will and binding on the believing Jew. By practising these a day will come when the kingdom of God will be estabblished on the earth. A Messiah will arrive to announce this, who will be a man, a descendant from the house of David. The Jews will have to play the central role in this program, since it was revealed to them by God through Moses at Mount Sinai.

All people are created equal, and each person has his dignity because he was created by God in his image. One has therefore to love and respect everyone else. Moreover, the poor, sick or orphan, widow and such others have to be helped.

People are free and have the ability to understand the difference between good and evil. **The world in which they live, is full of bounties and one should enjoy these with his fellow-men. There is no need to reject and run away from life, become a monk and try to attain salvation,** which can be achieved in the world itself.

Judaism believes in the immortality of the soul and resurrection of the dead, but one should give good care to the body and soul in life itself rather than doing so over there. There are pictures of heaven where good Jews are sitting studying Torah, wearing crowns on their head, with God around. The following prayer is read every morning:

These are the things, the fruits of which a man enjoys in this world, while the stock remains for him for the world to come: honouring father and mother, the practice of charity, timely

attendance at the house of study morning and evening, hospitality of wayfarers, visiting the sick, dowering the bride, attending the dead to the grave, devotion in prayer, and making peace between man and his fellow: but the study of Torah leads to them all.
(Mishnah)

The welfare of family is more important because on it depends the welfare of the individual, as well as the society in its totality. **A loving and peaceful relationship among the members of the family is therefore a must, and the home is equally important, even more than their place of worship,** the synagogue; parents are required to set high moral standards to guide and influence their children.

The life of a Jew is planned since his birth. A male child is circumcised on the eighth day itself, to initiate him into the religion. God himself is said to have ordered Abraham to do so with his son Ishmael. It is the first covenant and the prayer says that the child may commit himself to Torah, to marriage, and to good deeds. The boy is given his name on this day. The girls have a separate naming ceremony. At the age of five or six the boy is sent to the religious school attached to the local synagogue, and later to other schools. Boys are considered adults at the age of thirteen years and the girls at twelve. They are now responsible and have to follow the Torah rules; in case of infringement, they are punished. They are now called Bar-onshin, which means the 'son of punishment'. A ceremony is held, and the boy reads the Torah in the synagogue. For girls there is a separate ceremony.

Now comes marriage, which is regarded as very important. The first commandment in the Torah says: 'Bear fruit and multiply.' Marriage is necessary for personal happiness as well as running the life-system. **Celibacy is unnatural and should not be undertaken by a Jew**. A Jew mother's child is a Jew, who can marry another Jew, provided he or she is unmarried, and cousins or uncle and niece were allowed to marry. Marriage was a legal contract which two willing persons could sign in the presence of witnesses. The groom usually puts a ring to the bride's finger, saying, 'You are now married to me by this ring according to the law of Moses and Israel.' They then drink wine together and the groom breaks a glass to indicate the destruction of the temple. A document is signed to give certain property rights to the bride in case the husband dies first or divorces her.

Divorce is allowed in jewish marriages. But they are taken as a last resort, and the woman can marry someone else if she so desires.

After death one's body is washed and covered in a white cloth. It is buried, and not cremated, as soon as possible, and mourned for seven days. Prayers are held every evening, after which they visit the synagogue. For another eleven months some practices are performed, and a stone is put to the grave in the cemetry. Prayers are said every year and graves are visited.

Judaism believes that **direct communication with God is possible and desirable**, through meditation, pleas, confession, supplication and thanksgiving. Various kinds of prayers are therefore available which can be said at home or in the synagogue. Every day three services are a must: in the morning, afternoon and evening, which have to be led by a professional. At the end of most religious services, 13 articles of the creed are chanted as follows:

Magnified and praised be the living God;
He is one.
He has neither bodily form nor substance.
His existence has no beginning.
He is the lord of the universe.
He gave his gifts to his prophets.
Moses was his special prophet.
He gave us all the Law of Truth.
God's Law is unchangeable.
He knows our secret thoughts.
He is kind to those who love him but punishes evil.
He will give us salvation in the end.
He will revive the dead.

There are special prayers for sabbath and holy days.

In the beginning prayers and sacrifices were offered at the temple, but after its destruction, synagogues were developed. They are simple structures, where Torah and other holy books are kept, but there are no idols or statues. Social and educational activities are also carried out there. While in the synagogue, the Jews cover their head to show respect.

The dietary rules are very exact and strict; meat of animals that do not have cloven hoofs and do not chew the cud—such as the pig—is prohibited; and of fish that have neither scales nor fins. Blood should be drained out of animals before eating and cooking them. All meat should be ritually cleaned before eating—called **Kasher**—by a healthy animal slaughtered in a special way. Meat and milk should not be taken together, and the pots should also be kept separate.

Charity is also a must and a part of one's income should be used for this purpose.

Several of these practices were followed by Islam in later years.

Thus Judaism limited itself chiefly to the details of the Law described in the Torah and their fulfilment by their people. The Bible is full of God's utterances in which he threatens the wrongdoers of severe punishment and dire consequences, death in most cases. It gives a very nasty colour to the essentially good religion, and the jealous and wrathful nature of God most unbecoming; and has been criticised by quite a few world-renowned thinkers. This added to the severe persecution they had to face wherever they lived in the West, should have made and did make their lives miserable. They were made to live in what came to be known as 'Ghettos' everywhere, and prevented to participate in most general activities.

Because of their living in diaspora most of the years, the Jews were divided into a few groups, the most important being Sepheradi and Ashkenazis, the former being those following

Spanish-Portuguese practices and the latter being descendants of Russian, Central European and Western groups. The oriental Jewery belongs to the first group. The Ashkenazis are generally divided into three groups: Orthodox, Conservative and Reformers. The third is changing with the times; the use of Hebrew has been replaced by English and other local languages, the rituals have been curtailed drastically, and Torah rules have been simplified according to the needs.

Jews have been living in India for almost 2000 years, though in quite small numbers; contrary to the treatment they were given in other countries, they were welcomed and given honour and respect due to guests generally. Their numbers in the early 1940s were about 30 thousand, but now they would be around 5 thousand only. Many of them have migrated to the U.S. and Israel after its formation. They fall into three categories, Bene Israel, Cochinis and Baghdadi, and they follow the Sepharadi kind of practices. Some of them are said to have arrived in India 23 centuries ago as traders, which had started during Solomon's times.

Judaism has been the first among revealed religions of the world. The Old Testament of the Bible is chiefly devoted to the Jews who practised this God-given religion. He is present throughout, speaking and ordering his followers as to how they should behave in order to please him, otherwise they would incur severe penalties. Absolute obedience is what he demands from them. He is given several names, such as Shadai, Eloah, Yah, Adonai and Elohim, in addition to YHWH, which was more common, though difficult to pronounce—so in later years it was simplified to Jehova. It is interesting to note that in the Vedas also—perhaps in Atharva Veda—it finds mention as 'Yahva' whose followers are said to have lived in these parts.

A modern American lady who has earned reputation for healing with God's direct help, Vianna Stibel—her therapy is known as Theta Healing—has surmised that the real God stays far above the skies, in the 7th plane, and those living in the 4th and 5th planes may be exploiting human beings living on the

3rd plane, by projecting themselves as God. An interesting idea indeed, which needs further exploration!

In later years, Jew thinkers started questioning the premises of Judaism, saying that only Reason can be the basis of any such thing—which resulted in certain corrections and adjustments. Certain philosophical schools also developed.

God appeared to Moses on Mount Sinai, and since the Jews were moving at the time, for his worship a Tabernacle was made. It was a tentlike construction which was carried along with them. After they came to Jerusalem, a temple was made. Moses' elder brother Aaron was the first priest. It was here that sacrifices of animals and various kinds of offerings were made to atone for the sins committed by them or for thanksgiving. The temple was destroyed, and remade several times, and after final diaspora in 70 A.D., the system of synagogues was started. God sent his messengers, called prophets, to guide and lead them in the correct practice of religion, and there have been 4-5 major prophets and a dozen junior ones. The word for prophet in Hebrew is 'Navi', which, with a little change, came to be spoken as 'Nabi', popular in Islam.

All prophets were human beings, whose mystical experiences readied them for their Job. The Bible has separate books devoted to their activities. The system of God and their prophets was special to religions of this particular land and their people. There is mention in religious books that many more persons wandered in cities trying to behave like prophets, but people rejected most as mad men and even attacked them. But Moses was a genuine leader of his deeply troubled community and tried his best to help them settie and lead peaceful and useful lives. He not only, perhaps, devised the system, but gave it solemnity, sanction and strength by forming and shaping the process as a covenant, with no less a person than God, the Most Mighty.

LORD-GIVEN LAWS

Moses said to his people, "Obey all the laws that I am teaching you, and you will live, and occupy the land which the Lord, the God of your ancestors, is giving you. Do not add anything to what I command you, and do not take anything away. Obey the commands of the Lord your God that I have given you. You yourselves saw what the Lord did at Mount Peot. He destroyed everyone who worshipped Baal there, but those of you who were faithful to the Lord your God are still alive today.

"No other nation, no matter how great, has a god who is so near when they need him as the Lord our God is to us. He answers us whenever we call for help. No other nation, no matter how great, has laws so just as those that I have taught you. Be on your guard! Make certain that—you do not forget, as long as you live, what you have seen with your own eyes. Tell your children and your grandchildren about the day you stood in the presence of the Lord your God at Mount Sinai, when he said to me, 'Assemble the people. I want them to hear what I have to say, so that they will learn to obey me as long as they live and so that they will teach their children to do the same.'

"Tell them how the Lord spoke to you from the fire, how you heard him speaking but did not see him in any form at all. He told you what you must do to keep the covenant he made with you—you must obey the Ten Commandments, which he wrote on two stone tablets.

"For your own good, then, make certain that you **do not sin by making for yourselves an idol in any form at all**—whether man or woman, animal or bird, reptile or fish. Do not be tempted to worship and serve what you see in the sky—the sun, the moon, and the stars. The Lord your God has given these to all other peoples for them to worship. But you are the people he rescued from Egypt, that blazing furnace. He brought you out to make you his own people, as you are today.

"Even when you have been in the land a long time and have children, do not sin by making for yourselves an idol in any form at all. This is evil in the Lord's sight, and it will make him angry. I call heaven and earth as witnesses against you today that, if you disobey me, you will soon disappear from the land. The Lord will scatter you among other nations, where only a few of you will survive. There you will serve gods made by human hands, gods of wood and stone, gods that cannot see or hear, eat or smell. There you will look for the Lord your God, and if you search for him with all your heart, you will find him. When you are in trouble and all those things happen to you, then you will finally turn to the Lord and obey him. He is a merciful God.

"Search the past, the time before you were born, all the way back to the time when God created man on the earth. Search the entire earth. Has anything as great as this ever happened before? Has anyone ever heard of anything like this? Have any people ever lived after hearing a god speak to them from a fire, as you have? Has any god ever dared to go and take a people from another nation and make them his own, as the Lord your God did for you in Egypt? Before your very eyes he used his great power and strength; he brought plagues and war, worked miracles and wonders, and caused terrifying things to happen. The Lord has shown you this to prove to you that he alone is God and that there is no other.

"The Lord did not love you and choose you because you outnumbered other peoples; you were the smallest nation on earth. But the Lord loved you and wanted to keep the promise that he made to your ancestors. That is why he saved you by his great might and set you free from slavery to the king of Egypt."

The One Place for Worship

"Here are the laws that you are to obey as long as you live in the land at the Lord, the God of your ancestors, is giving you. Listen to them! In the land that you are taking, destroy the places where the people worship their gods on high mountains, on hills, and under green trees.

"Do not worship the Lord your God in the way that these people worship their gods. Out of the territory of all your tribes the Lord will choose the one place where the people are to come into his presence and worship him. There you are to offer your sacrifices that are to be burnt and your other sacrifices, your tithes and your offerings, the gifts that you promise to the Lord, your freewill offerings, and the first-born of your cattle and sheep. There, in the presence of the Lord your God, who has blessed you, you and your families will eat and enjoy the good things that you have worked for. Be joyful there in his presence, together with your children, your servants, and the Levites who live in your towns; remember that Levites will have no land of their own.

"But you are free to kill and eat your animals wherever you live. You may eat as many as the Lord gives you. All of you, whether ritually clean or unclean, may eat them, just as you would eat the meat of deer or antelope. But you must not use their blood as food; you must pour it out on the ground like water. Nothing that you offer to the Lord is to be eaten in the places where you live: neither the tithes of your corn, your wine, or your olive-oil, nor the first-born of your cattle and sheep, the gifts that you promise to the Lord as your freewill offerings, or any other offerings. You and your children, together with your servants and the Levites who live in your towns, are to eat these offerings only in the presence of the Lord your God.

"When the Lord your God enlarges your territory, as he has promised, you may eat meat whenever you wish. If the one place of worship is too far away, then, whenever you wish, you may kill any of the cattle or sheep that the Lord has given you, and you may eat the meat at home, as I have told you. Anyone, ritually clean or unclean, may eat that meat, just as he would eat the meat of deer or antelope. **Only do not eat meat with blood still in it, for the life is in the blood**, and you must not eat the life with the meat. Do not use the blood for food; instead pour it out on the ground like water.

"You are the people of the Lord your God. So when you mourn for the dead, don't gash yourselves or shave the front of your head, as other people do. You belong to the Lord your God; he has chosen you to be his own people from among all the peoples who live on earth.

"Do not eat anything that the Lord has declared unclean. You may eat these animals: cattle, sheep, goats, deer, wild sheep, wild goats, or antelopes—any animals that have divided hoofs and that also chew the cud. **But no animals may be eaten unless they have divided hoofs and also chew the cud**. You may not eat camels, rabbits, or rock-badgers. They must be considered unclean; they chew the cud but do not have divided hoofs. **Do not eat pigs**. They must be considered unclean; they have divided hoofs but do not chew the cud. Do not eat any of these animals or even touch their dead bodies.

"You may eat any kind of fish that has fins and scales, but anything living in the water that does not have fins and scales may not be eaten; it must be considered unclean.

"You may eat any clean bird. But these are the kinds of birds you are not to eat: eagles, owls, hawks, falcons; buzzards, vultures, crows, ostriches, sea-gulls, storks, herons, pelicans, cormorants, hoopoes, and bats.

"All winged insects are unclean; do not eat them. You may eat any clean insect.

"Do not eat any animal that dies a natural death. You may let the foreigners who live among you eat it, or you may sell it to other foreigners. But you belong to the Lord your God; you are his people. Do not cook a young sheep or goat in its mother's milk."

The Law ot the Tithe

"Set aside **a tithe—a tenth of all that your fields produce** each year. Then go to the one place where the Lord your God has chosen to be worshipped; and there in his presence eat the tithes of your corn, wine, and olive-oil, the first-born of your cattle and sheep. Do this so that you may learn to honour Lord your God always. If the place of worship is too far from your home for you to carry there the tithe of the produce that the Lord has blessed you with, then do this: Sell your produce and take the money with you to the one place of worship. Spend it on whatever you want—beef, lamb, wine, beer—and there, in the presence of the Lord your God, you and your families are to eat and enjoy yourselves."

The Seventh Year

"At the end of **every seventh year you are to cancel the debts of those who owe you money**. This is how it is to be done. Everyone who has lent money to a fellow-Israelite is to cancel the debt; he must not try to collect the money; the Lord himself has declared the debt cancelled. You may collect what a foreigner owes you, but you must not collect what any of your own people owe you.

"If in any of the town in the land that the Lord your God is giving you there **is a fellow-Israelite in need, then do not be selfish and refuse to help him**. Instead, be generous and lend him as much as he needs. Do not refuse to lend him something, just because the year when debts are cancelled is near. Do not let such an evil thought enter your mind. If you refuse to make the loan, he will cry out to the Lord against you, and you will be held guilty. Give to him freely and unselfishly, and the Lord will bless you in everything you do. There will always be some Israelites who are poor and in need and so I command you to be generous to them."

The Treatment of Slaves

"If a fellow-Israelite, man or woman, sells himself to you as a slave, you are to **release him after he has served you for six years**. When the seventh year comes, you must let him go free. When you set him free, do not send him away emptyhanded. Give to him generously from what the Lord has blessed you with—sheep, corn, and wine. Remember that you were slaves in Egypt and the Lord your God set you free; that is why I am now giving you this command.

"But your slave may not want to leave; he may love you and your family and be content to stay. Then take him to the door of your house and there pierce his ear; he will then be your slave for life. Treat your female slave in the same way."

The Passover

"Honour the Lord your God by celebrating Passover in the month of Abib; it was on a night in that month that he rescued you from Egypt. Go to the one place of worship and slaughter there one of your sheep or cattle for the Passover meal to honour the Lord your God. When you eat this meal, do not eat bread prepared with yeast. **For seven days you are to eat bread prepared without yeast, as you did when you had to leave Egypt** in such a hurry. Eat this bread—it will be called the bread of suffering."

The Harvest Festival

"Count seven weeks from the time that you begin to harvest the corn, and then celebrate the Harvest Festival, to honour the Lord your God, by bringing him a freewill offering in proportion to the blessing he has given you."

The Festival of Shelters

"After you have threshed all your corn and pressed all your grapes, celebrate the Festival of Shelters for seven days.

"All the men of your nation are to come to worship the Lord three times a year at the one place of worship: at Passover,

Harvest Festival, and the Festival of Shelters. Each man is to bring gift as he is able, in proportion to the blessings that the Lord your God has given him."

The Administration and Justice

"Appoint judges and other officials in every town that the Lord your God gives you. These men are to judge the people impartially. **They are not to be unjust or show partiality in their judgements; and they are not to accept bribes**, for gifts blind the eyes even of wise and honest men, and cause them to give wrong decision. Always be fair and just.

"Do not sacrifice to the Lord your God cattle or sheep that have any defects; the Lord hates this.

"Suppose you bear that in one of your towns some man or woman has **sinned against the Lord and broken his convenant worshipping and serving other god**. If you hear such a report, then investigate it thoroughly. If it is true that this evil thing has happened in Israel, then **take that person outside the town and stone him to death**. However, he may be put to death only if two or more witnesses testify against him; he is not to be put to death if there is only one witness."

Instructions Concerning a King

"After you have taken possession of the land that the Lord your God is going to give you and have settled there, then you will decide you need a king like all the nations round you. Make sure that the man you choose to be king is the one whom the Lord has chosen. He must be one of your own people; do not make a foreigner your king. The king is not to have a large number of horses for his army.

"When he becomes king, he is to have a copy of the book of God's laws and teachings made from the original copy kept by the levitical priests. He is to keep this book near him and read from it all his life."

The Share of the Priests

"The priestly tribe of Levi is not to receive any share of land in Israel; instead, **they are to live on the offerings and other**

sacrifices given to the Lord. They are to own no land, as the other tribes do; their share is the privilege of being the Lord's priests, as the Lord has promised.

"Whenever cattle or sheep are sacrificed, the priests are to be given the shoulder, the jaw, and the stomach. They are to receive the first share of the corn, wine, olive-oil, and wool."

Warning Against Pagan Practices

"When you come into the land that the Lord your God is giving you, don't follow the disgusting practices of the nations that are there. **Don't sacrifice your children in the fires on your altars**; and don't let your people practise divination or look for omens or use spells or charms, and don't let them consult the spirits of the dead."

The Promise to Send a Prophet

Then Moses said, "In the land you are about to occupy, people follow the advice of those who practise divination and look for omens, but the Lord your God does not allow you to do this. Instead, he will send you a prophet like me from among your own people, and you are to obey him.

"I will tell him what to say, and he will tell the people everything I command. He will speak of in my name, and will punish anyone who refuses to obey him. But if any prophet dares to speak a message in my name when I did not command him to do, he must die for it."

Concerning Witnesses

"One witness is not enough to convict a man of a crime; **at least two witnesses are necessary to prove that a man is guilty**. If one man tries to harm another by falsely accusing him of a crime, both are to go to the one place of worship and be judged by the priests and judges who are then in office. The judges will investigate the case thoroughly; and if the man has made a false accusation against his fellow-Israelite, he is to receive the punishment the accused man would have received.

In this way you will get rid of this evil. Then everyone else will hear what happened; they will be afraid, and no one will ever again do such an evil thing."

Concerning Women Prisoners of War

"When the Lord your God gives you victory in battle and you take prisoners, **you may see among them a beautiful woman that you like and want to marry**. Take her to your home, where she will shave her head, cut her fingernails, and change her clothes. She is to stay in your home and mourn for her parents for a month; after that, you may marry her. Later, if you no longer want her, you are to let her go free. Since you forced her to have intercourse with you, **you cannot treat her as a slave and sell her**."

Concerning the First Son's Inheritance

"Suppose a man has two wives and they both bear him sons, but the first son is not the child of his favourlte wife. When the man decides how he is going to divide his property among his children, he is not to show partiality to the son of his favourite wife by giving him the share that belongs to the first-born son. He is to give a double share of his possessions to his first son, even though he is not the son of his favourlte wife. A man must acknowledge his first son and give him the share he is legally entitled to."

Various Laws

"If you see a fellow-Israelite's cow, or sheep running loose, do not ignore it; take it back to him. But if its owner lives a long way off or if you don't know who owns it, then take it home with you. When its owner comes looking for it, give it to him. Do the same thing if you find a donkey, a piece of clothing, or anything else that your fellow-Israelite may have lost.

"Women are not to wear men's clothing, and men are not to wear women's clothing; the Lord your God hates people who do such things.

"If you happen to find a bird's nest in a tree or on the ground with the mother bird sitting either on the eggs or with her young, you are not to take the mother bird, you may take the young birds, but you must let the mother bird go, so that you will live a long and p osperous life.

"Do not plant any crop in the same field as your grapevines; if you do, you are forbidden to use either the grapes or the produce of the other crop.

"Do not hitch an ox and a donkey together for ploughing.

"Do not wear cloth made by weaving wool and linen together.

"Sew tassels on the four corners of your clothes."

Sexual Laws

"Suppose a man marries a girl and later he decides he does'nt wanther, so he makes up false charges against her, accusing her of not being a virgin when they got married.

"If this happens, the girl's parents are to take the blood-stained wedding sheet that proves the girl was a virgin, and they are to show it in court to the town leaders. Then the town leaders are to take the husband and beat him. They are also to fine him a hundred pieces of silver and give the money to the girl's father, because the man has brought disgrace on an Israelite girl. Moreover, she will continue to be his wife and he can never divorce her as long as he lives.

"But if the charge is true and there is no proof that the girl was a virgin, then they are to take her out to the entrance of her father's house, where the men of her city are to stone her to death.

"If a man is caught having intercourse with another man's wife, both of them are to be put to death. In this way you will get rid of this evil.

"Suppose **a man out in the countryside rapes a girl who is engaged to someone else. Then only the man is to be put to death**; nothing is to be done to the girl.

"Suppose a man is caught raping a girl who is not engaged. He is to pay the girl's father the bride price of fifty pieces of silver, and she is to become his wife, because he forced her to have intercourse with him. He can never divorce her as long as he lives.

"No Israelite, man or woman, is to become a temple-prostitute. Also no money earned in this way may be brought into the house of the Lord your God in fulfilment of a vow. **The Lord hates temple-prostitutes**.

"When you lend money or food or anything else to a fellow-Israelite, do not charge him interest. You may charge interest on what you lend to a foreigner, but not on what you lend to a fellow-Israelite. Obey this rule, and the Lord will bless everything you do in the land that you are going to occupy.

"When you walk along a path in someone else's vineyard, **you may eat all the grapes you want, but you must not carry any away in a container**. When you walk along a path in someone else's cornfield, you may eat all the corn you can pull off with your hands, but you must not cut any corn with a sickle."

Divorce and Remarriage

"Suppose a man marries a woman and later decides that he doesn't want her, because he finds something about her that he doesn't like. So he writes out divorce papers, gives them to her, and sends her away from his home. Then suppose she marries another man, and he also decides that he doesn't want her, so he also writes out divorce papers, gives them to her, and sends her away from his home. Or suppose her second husband dies. In either case, her first husband is not to marry her again; he is to consider her defiled.

"When you lend a man something, you are not to take as security his millstones used for grinding his corn. This would take away the family's means of preparing food to keep alive.

"Whoever kidnaps a fellow-Israelite and makes him his slave or sells him into slavery is to be put to death.

"**Do not cheat a poor and needy hired servant**, whether he is a fellow-Israelite or a foreigner living in one of your towns.

Each day before sunset pay him for that day's work; he needs the money and has counted on getting it. If you do not pay him, he will cry out against you to the LORD, and you will be guilty of sin.

"When you gather your crops and fail to bring in some of the corn that you have cut, do not go back for it; it is to be left for the foreigners, orphans, and widows.

When you have picked your ollves once, do not go back and get those that are left; they are for the foreigners, orphans, and widows.

"Suppose two Israelites go to court to settie a dispute, and one is declared innocent and the other guilty. If the guilty man is **sentenced to be beaten the judge is to make him lie face downwards and have him whipped**. The number of lashes will depend on the crime he has committed. He may be given as many as **forty lashes, but no more**; more than that would humiliate him publicly."

Duty to a Dead Brother

"If two brothers live on the same property and one of them dies, leaving no son then his widow is not to be married to someone outside the family; it is the duty of the dead man's brother to marry her. The first son that they have will be considered the son of the dead man, so tbat his family line will continue in Israel. But if the dead man's brother does not want to marry her, she is to go before: the town leaders and say, 'My husband's brother will not do his duty; he refuses to give his brother a descendant among the people of Israel. Then the town leaders are to summon him and speak to him. If he still refuses to marry her, **brother's widow is to go up to him in the presence of the town leaders, take off one of the sandals, spit in his face**, and say, 'This is what happens to the man who refuses to give his brother a descendant.' His family will be known in Israel as 'the family of the man who had his sandal pulled off.'

"Do not cheat when you use weights and measures. **Use true and honest weights and measures**, so that you may live a long time in the land that the Lord your God is giving you. The Lord hates people who cheat."

Harvest Offerings

"After you have occupied the land that the Lord your God is giving you and have settled there, each of you must place in a basket the first part of each crop that you harvest and you must take it with you to the one place of worship. Go to the priest in charge at that time and say to him, 'I acknowledge to the Lord my God that I have entered the land that he promised our ancestors to give us.'

"Then set the basket down in the Lord's presence and worship there. Be grateful for the good things that the Lord your God has given you and your family; and let the Levites and the foreigners who live among you join in the celebration.

"Every third year give the tithe—**a tenth of you crops—to the Levites, the foreigners, the orphans, and the widows**, so that in every community they will have need to eat."

Then Moses together with the levitical priests, said to all the people of Israel, "Give me your attention, people of Israel, and listen to me. Today you have become the people of the Lord your God; so obey him and keep all his laws that I am giving you today."

THE SONG OF MOSES

"Earth and sky, hear my words,
listen closely to what I say.
My teaching will fall like drops of rain
and form on the earth like dew.
My words will fall like showers on young plants,
like gentle rain on tender grass.
I will praise the name of the Lord,
and his people will tell of his greatness.

"The Lord is your mighty defender,
perfect and just in all his ways;
Your God is faithful and true;
he does what is right and fair.
But you are unfaithful unworthy to be his people,
a sinful and deceitful nation;
Is this the way you should treat the Lord,
you foolish, senseless people?
He is your father, your Creator,
he made you into a nation.

"Think of the past, of the time long ago;
ask your fathers to tell you what happened,
ask the old men to tell of the past.
The Most High assigned nations their lands;
he determined where peoples should live.
He assigned to each nation a god,
but Jacob's descendants he chose for himself.

"He found them wandering through the desert,
a desolate, wind-swept wilderness.
He protected them and cared for them,
as he would protect himself.
Like an eagle teaching its young to fly,
catchting them safely on its spreading wings,
the Lord kept Israel from falling.
The Lord alone led his people.
without the help of a foreign god.

He let them rule the highlands;
and they ate what grew in the fields.
They found wild honey among the rocks;
their olive-trees flourished in stony ground.
Their cows and goats gave plenty of milk;
they had the best sheep, goats, and cattle,
the finest wheat, and the choicest wine.

"The Lord's people grew rich, but rebellious;
they were fat and stuffed with food.
They abandoned God their Creator
and rejected their mighty saviour.

Their idolatry made the Lord jealous;
 the evil they did made him angry. .
They sacrificed to gods that are not real,
 new gods their ancestors had never known,
 gods that Israel had never obeyed,
They forgot their God, their mighty saviour,
 the one who had given them life.
"When the Lord saw this, he was angry
 and rejected his sons and daughters.
'I will no longer help them,' he said;
 'then I will see what happens to them,
 those stubborn, unfaithful people.
With their idols they have made me angry,
 jealous with their so-called gods,
 gods that are really not gods.
So I will use a so-called nation to make them angry;
 I will make them jealous with a nation of fools.
My anger will flame up like fire
 and burn everything on earth.
It will reach to the world below
 and consume the roots of the mountains.

" '**I will bring on them endless disasters**
 and use all my arrows against them.
They will die from hunger and fever;
 they will die from terrible diseases.
I will send wild animals to attack them,
 and poisonous snakes to bite them.
War will bring death in the streets;
 terrors will strike in the homes.
Young men and young women will die;
 neither babies nor old men will be spared.

'I would have destroyed them completely,
so that no one would remember them.
But I could not let their enemies boast
that they had defeated my people,
when it was I myself who had crushed them.'
Israel is a nation without sense;
they have no wisdom at all.
They fail to see why they were defeated;
they cannot understand what happened.
Why were a thousand defeated by one,
and ten thousand by only two?
The Lord, their God, had abandoned them;
their mighty God had given them up.
Their enemies know that their own gods are weak,
not mighty like Israel's God.
Their enemies, corrupt as Sodom and Gomorrah,
are like vines that bear bitter and poisonous grapes,
like wine made from the venom of snakes.

"The Lord remembers what their enemies have done;
he waits for the right time to punish them;
The Lord will take revenge and punish them;
the time will come when they will fall;
the day of their doom is near.
The Lord will rescue his people
when he sees that their strength is gone.
He will have mercy on those who serve him
when he sees how helpless they are.
Then the Lord will ask his people,
'Where are those mighty gods you trusted?

You fed them with the fat of your sacrifices
    and offered them wine to drink.
Let them come and help you now;
    let them run to your rescue.
" **'I, and I alone, am God;**
    no other god is real.
I kill and I give life, I wound and I heal,
    and no one can oppose what I do.
As surely as I am the living God,
    I raise my hand and I vow
that I will sharpen my flashing sword
    and see that justice is done.
I will take revenge on my enemies
    and punish those who hate me.
My arrows will drip with their blood,
    and my sword will kill all who oppose me.
I will spare no one who fights against me;
    even the wounded and prisoners will die.'

"Nations, you must praise the Lord's people–
    he punishes all who kill them.
He takes revenge on his enemies
    and forgives the sins of his people."

PSALMS

1.

1. Blessed is the man that walketh not in the counsel of the ungodly, nor standeth in the way of sinners, nor sitteth in the seat of the scornful.
2. But he delights in the law of the Lord; and in his law doth he meditate day and night.
3. And he shall be like a tree planted by the rivers of water, that bringeth forth his fruit in his season; his leaf also shall not wither; and whatsoever he doeth shall prosper.
4. The ungodly are not so; but are like the chaff which the wind driveth away.
5. Therefore the ungodly shall not stand in the judgement, nor sinners in the congregation of the righteous.
6. For the Lord knoweth the way of the rightenous; but the way of the ungodly shall perish.

2.

1. O Lord our Lord; how excellent is thy name in all the earth! who has set thy glory above the heavens.

2. Out of the mouth of babes and suckling hast thou obtained strength because of thine enemies, that thou mightest still the enemy and the avenger.
3. When I consider thy heavens, the moon and thy fingers, the moon and the stars, which thou hast ordained;
4. What is man that thou art mindful of him? and the son of man, that thou visitest him?
5. For thou hast made him a little lower than the angels, and hast crowned him with glory and honour.
6. Thou madest him to have dominion over the works of thy hands; though hast put all things under his feet.
7. All sheep and oxen, yea, and the beasts of the field;
8. The fowl of the air, and the fish of the sea, and whatsoever passeth through the paths of the seas.
9. O Lord our Lord, how excellent is thy name in all the earth!

3.

1. How long wilt thou forget me, O Lord? for ever? how long wilt thou hide thy face from me?
2. How long shall I take counsel in my soul, having sorrow in my heart daily? how long shall mine enemy be exalted over me?
3. Consider and hear me, O Lord my God: lighten mine eyes, lest I sleep the sleep of death;
4. Lest mine enemy say, I have prevalled against him; and those that trouble me rejoice when I am moved.
5. But I have trusted in thy mercy; my heart shall rejoice in thy salvation.
6. I will sing unto the Lord, because he hath dealt bountifully with me.

4.

1. The fool hath said in his heart, There is no God. They are corrupt, they have done abominable works, there is none that doeth good.

2. The Lord looked down from heaven upon the children of men, to see if there were any that did understand, and seek God.
3. They are all gone aside, they are all together become filthy; there is none that doeth good, no, not one.
4. Have all the workers of iniquity no knowledge? who eat bread, and call not upon the Lord.
5. There were they in great fear; for God is in the generation of the righteous.
6. Ye have shamed the counsel of the poor because the Lord is his refuse.
7. On that the salvation of Israel were come out of Zion! when the Lord bringeth back the captivity of his people, Jacob shall rejoice, and Israel shall be glad.

5.

1. The heavens declare the glory of God; and the firmament sheweth his handiwork.
2. Day unto day uttereth speech, and night unto night sheweth knowledge.
3. There is no speech nor language, where their voice is not heard.
4. Their line is gone out through all the earth, and their words to the end of the world. In them hath he set a tabernacle for the sun.
5. Which is as a bridegroom coming out of his chamber, and rejoiceth as a strong man to run a race.
6. His going forth is from the end of the heaven and his circuit unto the ends of it: and there is nothing hid from the heat thereof.
7. The law of the Lord is perfect, converting the soul: the testimony of the Lord is sure, making wise the simple.
8. The statutes of the Lord are right, rejoicing the heart: the commandment of the Lord is pure, enlightening the eyes.

9. The fear of the Lord is clean, enduring for ever: the judgements of the Lord are true and righteous altogether.
10. More to be desired are they than gold, yea, than much fine gold: sweeter also than honey and the honeycomb.
11. Moreover by them is thy servant warned: and in keeping of them there is great reward.
12. Who can understand his errors? cleanse thou me from secret faults.
13. Keep back thy servant also from presumptuous sins; let them not have dominion over me; then shall I be upright, and I shall be innocent from the great transgression.
14. Let the words of my mouth, and the meditation of my heart, be acceptable in thy sight, O Lord, my strength, and my redeemer.

PROVERBS

1. A good name is rather to be chosen than great riches, and loving favour rather than silver and gold.
2. The rich and poor meet together; the Lord is the maker of them all.
3. A prudent man foreseeth the evil, and hideth in himself: but the simple pass on, and are punished.
4. By humility and the fear of the Lord are riches, and honour, and life.
5. Thorns and snares are in the way of the froward: he that doth keep his soul shall be far from them.
6. Train up a child in the way he sbould go; and when he is old, he will not depart from it.
7. The rich ruleth over the poor, and the borrower is servant to the lender.
8. He that soweth iniquity shall reap vanity: and the rod of his anger shall fail.
9. He that hath a bountiful eye shall be blessed; for he giveth of his bread to the poor.
10. Cast out the scorner, and contention shall go out; yea, strife and reproach shall cease.

11. He that loveth pureness of heart, for the grace of his lips the king shall be his friend.
12. The eyes of the Lord preserve knowledge, and he overthroweth t ıe words of the transgressor.
13. The slotl ıful man saith: There is a lion without, I shall be slain in the streets.
14. The mouth of strange women is a deep pit: he that is abhorred of the Lord shall fall therein.
15. Foolishness is bound in the heart of a child; but the rod of correction shall drive it far from him.
16. He that oppresseth the poor to increase his riches, and he that giveth to the rich, shall surely come to want.
17. Rob not the poor, because he is poor: neither oppress the afflicted in the gate.
18. For the Lord will plead their cause, and spoil the soul of those that spoiled them.
19. Make no friendship with an angry man; and with a furious man thou shalt not go:
20. Lest thou learn his ways, and get a snare to thy soul.
21. Be not thou one of them that strike hands, or of them that are sureties for debts.
22. If thou hast nothing to pay, why should he take away thy bed from under thee?
23. Remove not the ancient landmark, which thy fathers have set.
24. Seest thou a man diligent in his business? he shall stand before kings; he shall not stand before mean men.
25. When thou sittest to eat with a ruler, consider diligently what is before thee:
26. And put a knife to thy throat, if thou be a man given to appetite.
27. Be not desirous of his dainties: for they are deceitful meat.
28. Labour not to be rich: cease from thine own wisdom.

29. Wilt thou set thine eyes upon that which is not? for riches certainly will make themselves wings; and they fly away as an eagle toward heaven.
30. Eat thou not the bread of him that hath an evil eye, neither desire thou his dainty meats:
31. For as he thinketh in his heart, so is he: Eat and, drink, saith he to thee; but his heart is not with thee.
32. The morsel which thou hast eaten shalt thou vomit up, and lose thy sweet words.
33. Speak not in the ears of a fool: for he will despise the wisdom of thy words.
34. Remove not the old landmark; and enter not into the fields of the fatherless:
35. For their redeemer is mighty; he shall plead their cause with thee.
36. Apply thine heart unto instruction, and thine ears to the words of knowledge.
37. Withhold not correction from the child: for if thou beatest him with the rod, he shall not die.
38. Thou shalt beat him with the rod, and shalt deliver his soul from hell.
39. My son, if thine heart be wise, my heart shall rejoice, even mine.
40. Yea, my reins shall rejoice, when thy lips speak right things.
41. Let not thine heart envy sinners: but be thou in the fear of the Lord all the day long.
42. For surely there is an end; and thine expectation shall not be cut off.
43. Hear thou, my son, and be wise, and guide thine heart the way.
44. Be not among wine-bibbers; among riotous eaters of flesh:

45. For the drunkard and the glutton shall come to poverty: and drowsiness shall clothe a man with rags.
46. Hearken unto thy father that begat thee, and despise not thy mother when she is old.
47. Buy the truth, and sell it not; also wisdom, and instruction, and understanding.
48. The father of the righteous shall greatly rejoice: and he that begetteth a wise child shall have joy of him.
49. Thy father and thy mother shall be glad, and she that bore thee shall rejoice.
50. My son, give me thine heart, and let thine eyes observe my ways.
51. For a whore is a deep ditch; and a strange woman is a narrow pit.
52. She also lieth in wait as for a prey, and increaseth the transgressors among men.
53. Be not thou envious against evil men, neither desire to be with them.
54. For their heart studieth destruction, and their lips talk of mischief.
55. Through wisdom is an house builded; and by understsnding it is established:
56. And by knowledge shall the chambers be filled with all precious and pleasant riches.
57. A wise man is strong; yea, a man of knowledge increaseth strength.
58. For by wise counsel thou shalt make thy war: and in multitude of counsellors there is safety.
59. Wisdom is too high for a fool: he openeth not his mouth in the gate.
60. He that deviseth to do evil shall be called a mischievous person.

61. The thought of foolishness is sin: and the scorner is an abomination to men.
62. If thou faint in the day of adversity, thy strength is small.
63. If thou forbear to deliver them that are drawn unto death, and those that are ready to be slain;
64. If thou sayest, Behold, we knew it not; doth not he that pondereth the heart consider it? and he that keepeth thy soul, doth not he know it? and shall not he render to every man according to his works?
65. My son, eat thou honey, because it is good; and the honeycomb, which is sweet to thy taste:
66. So shall the knowledge of wisdom be unto thy soul: when thou hast found it, then there shall be a reward, and thy expectation shall not be cut off.
67. Lay not wait, O wicked man, against the dwelling of the righteous; spoil not his resting place:
68. For a just man falleth seven times, and riseth up again: but the wicked shall fall into mischief.
69. Rejoice not when thine enemy falleth, and let not thine heart be glad when he stumbleth:
70. Lest the Lord see it, and it displease him, and he turn away his wrath from him.
71. Fret not thyself because of evil men, neither be thou envious at the wicked.

6.

Christianity

Modern Worldwide Religion

SERVICE-CENTRED RELIGION

Christianity is and has been the most widely spread as well as one if the oldest religion in the world, which was born out of the death, that too on the horrific cross—a most unusual start for a divine phenomenon—taken as a supreme sacrifice on behalf of humanity as a whole for their sins to please God living in the skies. An interesting belief and explanation, which authorised the religion to recruit followers who, in return for accepting Jesus as their saviour, will not be required to be punished for their sins, and offered salvation right away.

Sin has been associated with human existence according to Christian basic ideology, which has its origin in the creation story by God of the universe in Judaism. According to the Book of Genesis, God created everything including man and woman, and prohibited them from eating the forbidden fruit from the garden of heaven, which they did, and thus disobeyed God. It was his Original Sin, which follows him throughout—and the only solution to which is death. For this reason everyone stands damned in the eyes of God. Now, by becoming a Christian, people are saved once and for all by the sacrifice of Jesus on the cross. The simple act of conversion redeems a person and he attains salvation.

Christianity is the direct outcome of Judaism, started by a Jew himself, Jesus, who, in an effort to purify the older religion, which had degenerated to a great extent with the passage of time, lost his life to a well planned and executed conspiracy of the establishment. According to the accepted scripture, he fell down, died, but was resurrected after three days—which radically changed the attitude of people regarding his person—he was taken as the Son of God, and one of his erstwhile enemies named Paul, who saw him while travelling on the road to Damuscus, took upon himself his cause as a mission, devoting his whole life to the new religion. (Ruchira Gupta in her article in 'Outlook', 25. Nov. 13, informs that the road where this happened, is still known as 'Street Called Straight'.) He then spread it in neighbouring countries by sending preachers, starting and establishing churches wherever possible, writing long and short letters to them—which form a major part of the New Testament, the second part of the Bible, related exclusively to Christianity.

Jesus is said to have departed after forty days, but the religion emerging and developing around his name—which had now acquired an additional name, or title, Christ, which meant 'anointed' as well as 'Messiah,' already promised by earlier prophets, to save the community and offer salvation to all who believed in him. But since he himself did not stay to work, which was chiefly and entirely guided by Paul—who had never interacted with Jesus, his own ideas and thoughts were put forward and promoted under the banner of the new religion. These were; 'divine incarnation, vicarious atonement, the abrogation of the law, and the doctrine of the basically sinful nature of man.'

The concept of sin helped the religion not only to take its root in human psyche because of the fear element associated with it, which seemed plausible to the simple men and women, but it also promoted its fast spread everywhere—because easy salvation was promised to everyone who would accept its membership—again, because Jesus had offered sacrifice on their behalf. (The selection from the New Testament presented later in this chapter, entitled " 'Jesus' Sacrifice" describes the details of Jesus' dialogue with God himself—in very clear terms—though this kind of event sounds very surprising, even unbelievable.) The fourth Lateran Council of 1215 A.D. reported that 'people believed that the only defence against the fiends which would assail their souls when they passed out of the body at death was the sacrament of the body and blood of Christ and that infants dying unbaptised went straight to hell.'

•••

Jesus was born in the province of Galilee in north Israel, which was then ruled by the Romans. He was of humble origin, and when he was born, his mother Mary was a virgin. He was brought up in Nazareth, a small town in the province, and baptised by John the Baptist, who is said to have declared that in him a messiah had arrived. The Bible does not tell much about his youth, and presents him with his mission at age 30. He announced to the people that 'The time had come and the Kingdom of God is near. Turn away from your sins and deliver the Good News,.' It was quite striking and the listeners were attracted to him.

A new research by the American scholar Reza Aslam, who has written 'Zealot: The Life and Times of Jesus of Nazareth,' says that there were many Jews in Jesus' times who were gathering followers, performing miracles, and getting killed by Romans, but only Jesus was called a messiah. It was because of the uniqueness of his message. It sound new, hopeful and urgent. The meaning of 'Kingdom of God' was not clear, but it filled people with some kind of inner joy. It was not a moral code or law—too many of which had to be observed in Judaism, but an extension of man's relationship with God himself. Despite its vagueness and uncertainty, it was certainly Great Good News.

Jesus made disciples, most of whom belonged to the lower classes, and performed miracles which helped in the increase of his followers in a big way. He healed the sick and served the poor and downtrodden, alongwith opposing and scolding the priests whenever he found them misbehaving; on one occasion he took a whip and threw them out of the temple of God. His acts outraged the esablishment no end and the powerful politicians mounted their opposition to get rid of him. Attempts were made on his life and a case was filed against him. He was captured and nailed on the cross. He suffered great agony for three hours, but he prayed: 'Father, forgive them for they do not know what they are doing...Into your hands I commit my spirit.' He was 33 at this time.

After his resurrection, the scene took a new turn. He was taken as the promised messenger of God, Messiah, and the new edition of Judaism started taking shape. In the early stages the practices of the synagogues were followed, and the group itself was regarded as a new sect of the old religion. Many of his followers wrote his life-story, out of which the four by Mathew, Mark, Lucas and John were included in the New Testament, the Christian part of the Bible.

The four gospels comprise a little less than a half of the body of the Testament, after which the story of the birth and growth of the Christian sect is related in the chapter entitled. 'The Acts of the Apostles.' Then follow letters—called Epistles—of Paul, Peter, James, etc., to Churches in various cities and individuals working for the movement, The largest number of these, as also the longest, are by Paul—whose conversion from an enemy to a follower is described in interesting detail in 'Acts'—who also undertakes several journeys to Greece and Italy for the purpose.

At this point it would be interesting to know that our own Swami Vivekanand has noted in his reminiscences that when, he was returning to India after his visit to England and Germany, he in a dream saw St. Paul while their ship was passing the island of Crete in the Mediterranean. St. Paul told him that this is the place from where Christianity was promoted to the West. Startled, he woke up and enquired about the place they were passing through.

The zeal of Paul is apparent in these pages of the Bible, though earlier, as noted in 'Acts' he had 'tried' to destroy the

Church; going from house to house, he dragged out the believers, both men and women, and threw them into jail...kept up his violent threats of murder against the followers of the Lord. He went to the High Priest and asked for letters of introduction to the synagogues in Damuscus, so that if he should find there any followers of the way of the Lord, he would be able to arrest them, both men and women, and bring them back to Jerusalem.

Saul Meets Jesus

But while on the Damuscus Road...'Suddenly a light from the sky flashed round him. He fell to the ground and heard a voice saying to him," Saul! Saul! (his name at the time) why do you persecute me?

"Who are you, Lord?" he asked.

"I am Jesus, whom you persecute", the voice said. "But get up and go into the city, where you will be told what you must do."

"The men who were travelling with Saul had stopped, not saying a word; they heard the voice but could not see anyone. Saul got up from the ground and opened his eyes but could not see a thing. So they took him by the hand and led him into Damuscus. For three days he was not able to see, and during that time he could not eat or drink anything."

Poor Saul—or Paul! Then Christ himself sent a person to him, who cured him of the blindness. Saul went straight to the synagogue and began to preach that Jesus was the Son of God... All who heard him were amazed. ... But Saul's preaching became even more powerful and his proofs that 'Jesus was the Messiah were so convincing that the Jews who lived in Damuscus could not answer him.'

Yet they did not believe him and planned to kill him. So '...one night Saul's followers took him down through an opening in the wall, lowering him in a basket.' He returned to Jerusalem and here also he was given the same treatment. To convince the apostles he '... went all over Jerusalem, preaching boldly in the name of the Lord.' Yet noone believed him and planned to kill him. Some of them took pity on the new convert and sent him away to Tarsus, etc., etc.

No wonder, he became the most effective and successful promoter and organiser of the new religion known as Christianity. Had he not been there Christ's religion would also have fizzled out like—as noted in 'Acts' itself—the religions of 'Thendas and Judas. The former claimed to be somebody great, and about four hundred men had joined him. But he was killed, all his followers were scattered and his movement died out'... The latter 'Judas the Galilean appeared during the time of the census; he drew a crowd after him, but he also was killed and all his followers were scattered.'

But 'Saul, also named Paul, exerted himself utmost, preached and made conversions, performed miracles and healed the sick, went to prison and was beaten black and blue. Then the officials tore the clothes off Paul and Silas and ordered them to be whipped. After a severe beating, they were sent to jail, and the jailor was ordered to lock up them tight. Upon receiving this order, the jailor threw them into the inner cell and fastened their feet between heavy blocks of wood.'

Saul alias Paul was a rich and educated person, so his efforts brought better results, To him goes the credit of taking the message to Greece and Rome, where he is believed to have died as the result of persecution. Peter was also martyred here, whose story is generally known. In course of time, St. Peter's Church became the glorious centre of worldwide Christian religion, which continues till day.

A notable idea is the basic condition for those who joined the community: the requirement that 'they will subscribe their earnings to its coffers which will be distributed to the poor according to their needs.' It was quite strict in the beginning because those who lied and paid only a part of it, were punished: a case or two are noted where the liers are killed—they die, but how, is not clear. 'The group of believers was one in mind and heart. No one said that any of his belongings was his own, but they all shared with one another everything they had. With great power the apostles gave witness to the resurrection of Jesus and God poured rich blessings on them all. There was noone in the group who was in need. Those who owned fields and houses would sell them, bring the money received from sale and hand it over to the apostles, and the money was distributed to each one according to his need.'

Immediately thereafter is related the story of Ananias and his wife Sapphira, who sold some property that belonged to them but...'kept a part of the money for himself and gave the rest to the apostles. Peter scolded him severely and said: "Before you sold the property, it belonged to you and after you sold it, the money was not yours. Why, then, did you decide to do such a thing? You have lied not to men, but to God!" As soon as Ananias heard it, he fell down dead, and all who heard about it, were terrified. The young men came in, wrapped his body, carried him out, and buried him.'

After this, Peter takes his wife to task: about three hours later, his wife, not knowing what had happened, came to him. Peter asked her, "Tell me, was this the full amount you and your husband received for your property."

"Yes," she answered, "The full amount."

'So Peter said to her, "Why did you and your husband decide to put the Lord's spirit to the test? The men who buried your husband, are now at the door, and they will carry you out, too." At once she fell down at his feet and died. The young men came in and saw that she was dead so they carried her out and buried her beside her husband. The whole Church and those who heard about it, were terrified.'

Terrified, indeed!—not pleased,—and who will not be at such severe as well as extra instant punishment? Like Good News, a Good and Great Idea, but improperly applied—for which reason, it could not take root. This early Christian Socialism also seems to have died almost similarly instantly like Ananias and Sapphira did.

•••

The celebrated historian Gibbon, in his study of the decline of the Roman empire, devotes a few chapters to the spread of Christianity in Rome, and underlines the central importance of zeal in the fast growth—albeit through enormous sufferings—of their cult in those regions. They were very hard—even stubborn, in their attitudes,—perhaps the basic Jewish trait which tended to survive—not soften—by the mildness of Jesus' behaviour—in the second phase of religious transformation. The Romans were relatively much tolerant as compared to them from the start itself, when Pilate did not find any punishable guilt in Jesus but was forced to send him to the cross bar by the Jews themselves; but their uncompromising refusal to accept the Roman state system as well as religion, brought upon them the persecution they had to face in the first three centuries in Rome and their kingdom. With the result that many of them were martyred, they had to go underground and function secretly to keep themselves alive.

But since suffering being a strongly emotional element, which, unrelated to the rightness or the falseness of the issue involved, influences the people in an disproportionately large way, the Roman people started being christianised, and ultimately, arrived the day when their king Constantine himself declared it as the state religion. The battle was won and the sun rose on the fortunes of the new religion—which continues to shine in almost the whole world till this day.

The last chapter of New Testament entilled 'Revelation,' is a strange, non-normal vision-after-vision presentation of the future, when this life will come to an end and a new Godly life will be born—which leaves the reader wondering if this could really happen. A Bible-editor condones this by saying that though 'they would have remained a mystery to all other...they are presented in a symbolic language that would have been understood by Christians of that day.' Though there are differences of opinion regarding the details of interpreting of the book, the central theme is clear: through Christ the Lord God will finally and totally defeat all his enemies, including

Satan, and will reward his faithful people with the blessings of a new heaven and a new earth when this victory is complete.'

Fine! But since the 'Revealation' to John in those early ages, much water has flown, but the influence of the idea of life's total destruction and rebirth remains alive in modern reasonably scientific times, resulting in funny and untrue announcements. The present writer has noted at least three public notices pasted on walls—in Connaught Place, New Delhi, where we had our offices, and elsewhere, and appearing in newspapers, that the world will come its end on date..., though nothing ever happened. Later in one case in newspapers it appeared that some Koreans killed themselves on that date. I once found such notices on posters, which gave the address also of the promoter Church group, a house in Lajpat Nagar-2, close to a cinema hall. I visited the housc, but found no one to talk to.

• • •

Roman emperor Constantine declared in 312 A.D. Christianity as the state religion. He was himself baptised on his death bed, and he started the construction of majestic churches, which got immense fillip in later times, resulting in richly decorated magnificent buildings spread over large spaces. On the other hand, the tradition of monasticism alongwith celibacy also started because of the martyrs who inspired piety and sacredness among the followers. Constantine also declared Sunday as a holiday, when public services were performed. He punished those who did not accept the religion. In 325 A.D. he called a council in Alexandria to discuss the divinity of Jesus Christ and other religious matters.

In course of time, the Church was divided into two, Eastern and Western, and the divinity of Jesus was not finally decided. In 415 the Council held at Chalcedom declared that it was a Trinity that ruled the religion, that of God, Christ and the Holy Spirit, and that Jesus is God's son. These controversies and interpretations continued till the middle ages. The Eastern Church regarded the Western as uncultured and barbarian. The Pope was regarded as superior and controlled the temporal matters also of the kingdoms under his authority. The religion had spread all over Europe. In 800 A.D. a Holy Roman Empire was established under Charlesmagne. In 1054 A.D. the Roman Church separated from the Constantinople-based Eastern church, which called itself Orthodox. This division was more political than doctrinal.

The Western church was acquiring great riches which resulted in its demoralisation. Salvation started being sold on payment of money, and the Popes had illicit relations with many. Discontent arose and in the sixteenth century, a process of Reformation started, which developed in successive centuries. Martin Luther gave rise to a protest movement, which was supported by Calvin, Zwingli and Melanchton, and resulted in a separate Church named Protestant. In course of time Henry VIII of England also separated from Rome, though he did so for a personal reason: he wanted to divorce his wife which the Pope did not permit. The Protestant version replaced Roman Catholic in various countries, supported by Calvin's Puritan and Presbetarian versions. In England Queen Elizabeth established her own Church, named Anglican, which was closer to the Protestant variety.

Thus a number of Churches came into existence, a majority being against the original Roman Church. The Bible was translated into French, German and English languages which helped in the spread of the original ideology of the religion. The opposition of the Roman Church resulted in persecution, much resented by the public in general. A monk named St. Zavier started his own variety known as Jesuit, which he himself propagated in Eastern lands upto Japan. This as well as other new sects made special efforts to spread in foreign lands, in which they succeeded in a big way. No other religion in the world seems to have done so, using modern facilities for the purpose. In India, they came with the British and followed them wherever they went, conquering new regions. They opened schools, spread English education, started presses and publishing, gave shape to indigenous languages like Hindi and others by translating the Bible into many of them. But they did not succeed in converting the upper classes of the Hindus to Christianity because, as many of their scholars themselves said, the Hindu religion and philosophy was far superior to theirs; they themselves studied this literature and started a strong tradition of translating and publishing these materials in English. This opened new branches of learning, such as Linguistics and cultural studies which went on to prove that Sanskrit was somewhere at the roots of English and other European languages, which also influenced history in its social and other aspects. Christianity in India did make some converts but they were limited to the lower classes because of economic reasons.

Christianity in India has taken a leading role in running educational institutions, hospitals and other services which are open to everyone without any kind of distinction. They were copied by Arya Samaj, Sanatan Dharma, Brahmo and Prarthana Samajas in various parts of the country. The credit of Shanti Niketan, started by Rabindra Nath Tagore, goes to Brahmo ideology; his father Maharshi Debendra Nath was a Brahmo leader. Raja Rammohan Roy and Keshab Chandra Sen were influenced by Christianity, and tried to reshape Hinduism with its new ideas, and started the Brahmo Samaj, the first reformist body started in India in those times. Then Swami Vivekanand also designed his Ramakrishna Mission on the same pattern, though he did not support the idea of freedom from the British—like Tagore in later times—which was activated by his British disciple Sister Nivedita.

Despite its unsatisfactory origins and conflict-ridden journey through two millennia, Christian religion in its totality has done well in serving the society and helping the backward communities to shed superstition and modernise themselves. They have also been relatively tolerant to others and made efforts to change themselves according to circumstances. Though, with the spread of education—a lot of credit for which goes to them only—their influence in the West is diminishing, yet they have to work in countries of Africa, and to some extent in Latin America, which has now captured the high position of Pope himself; and the new Pope Francis has from day one started working in right earnest. Good luck to him!

THE LIFE OF JESUS

God sent the angel Gabriel to a town in Galilee named Nazareth. He had a message for a girl promised in marriage to a man named Joseph, who was a descendant of King David. The girl's name was Mary. The angel came to her and said, "Peace be with you! God has been gracious to you. You will become pregnant and give birth to a son, and you will name him Jesus. He will be great and will be called the Son of the Most High God."

Mary said to the angel, "I am a virgin. How, then, can this be?"

The angel answered, "The Holy Spirit will come on you, and God's power will rest upon you. For this reason he will be Son of God. There is nothing that God cannot do."

"I am the Lord's servant," said Mary, "may it happen to me as you have said."

Mary's Song of Praise

Mary said,

"My heart praises the Lord; my soul is glad because of God my Saviour, for he has remembered me, his lowly servant!

From now on all people will call me happy,

because of the great things the Mighty God has done for me.

His name is holy;

from one generation to another he shows mercy to those who honour him.

He has stretched out his mighty arm and scattered the proud with all their plans.

He has brought down mighty kings from their thrones and lifted up the lowly.

He has filled the hungry with good things, and sent the rich away with empty hands.

He has kept the promise he made to our ancestors, and has come to the help of his servant Israel.

He has remembered to show mercy to Abraham and to all his descendants for ever!"

The Birth of Jesus

At that time the Emperor Augustus ordered a census to be taken throughout the Roman Empire. When this first census took place, Quirinius was the governor of Syria. Everyone, then, went to register himself, each to his own town.

Joseph went from the town of Nazareth in Galilee to the town of Bethlehem in Judaea, the birthplace of King David. Joseph went there because he was a descendant of David. He went to register with Mary, who was promised in marriage to him. She was pregnant, and while they were in Bethlehem, the time came for her to have her baby. She gave birth to her first son, wrapped him in strips of cloth and laid him in a manger—there was no room for them to stay in the inn.

The Shepherds and the Angels

There were some shepherds in that part of the country who were spending the night in the fields. An angel of the Lord appeared to them, and the glory of the Lord shone over them. They were terribly afraid, but the angel said to them, "Don't be afraid! I am here with good news for you, which will bring great joy to all the people. This very day in David's town our Saviour was born—Christ the Lord. You will find a baby wrapped in strips of cloth and lying in a manger."

So they hurried off and found Mary and Joseph and saw the baby lying in the manger.

The shepherds went back, singing praises to God for all they had heard and seen; it had been just as the angel had told them.

Jesus Is Named

A week later, when the time came for the baby to be circumcised, he was named Jesus, the name which the angel had given him before he had been conceived.

The time came for Joseph and Mary to perform the ceremony of purification, as the Law of Moses commanded. So they took the child to Jerusalem to present him to the Lord, as it is written in the law of the Lord.

When Joseph and Mary had finished doing all that was required by the law of the Lord, they returned to their home town of Nazareth in Galilee. The child grew and became strong; he was full of wisdom, and God's blessings were upon him.

The Boy Jesus in the Temple

Every year the parents of Jesus went to Jerusalem for the Passover festival. When Jesus was twelve years old, they went to the festival as usual. When the festival was over, they started back home, but the boy Jesus stayed in Jerusalem. His parents did not know this; they thought that he was with the group, so they travelled a whole day and then started looking for him among their relatives and friends. They did not find him, so they went back to Jerusalem looking for him. On the third day they found him in the Temple, sitting with the Jewish teachers, listening to them and asking questions. All who heard him were amazed at his intelligent answers. His parents were astonished when they saw him, and his mother said to him. "My son, why have you done this to us? Your father and I have been terribly worried trying to find you."

He answered them, "Why did you have to look for me? Didn't you know that I had to be in my Father's house?" But they did not understand his answer.

So Jesus went back with them to Nazareth, where he was obedient to them. His mother treasured all these things in her heart. Jesus grew both in body and in wisdom, gaining favour with God and men.

The Preaching of John the Baptist

It was the fifteenth year of the rule of the Emperor Tiberius; Pontius Pilate was governor of Judaea, Herod was ruler of Galilee. At that time the word of God came to John son of Zechariah in the desert. So John went throughout the whole territory of the River Jordan, preaching, "Turn away from your sins and be baptized, and God will forgive your sins."

Crowds of people came out to John to be baptized by him. John said to all of them, "I baptize you with water, but someone is coming who is much greater than I am. I am not good enough even to untie his sandals. He will baptize you with the Holy Spirit and fire."

In many different ways John preached the Good News to the people and urged them to change their ways. After all the people had been baptized, Jesus also was baptized. While he was praying, heaven was opened, and the Holy Spirit came down upon him in bodily form like a dove. And a voice came from heaven, "You are my own dear Son. I am pleased with you."

When Jesus began his work, he was about thirty years old. He was the son, so people thought, of Joseph the son of Adam, the son of God.

The Temptation of Jesus

Jesus returned from Jordan full of the Holy Spirit and was led by the Spirit into the desert, where he was tempted by the Devil for forty days; in all that time he ate nothing, so that he was hungry when it was over. The Devil said to him, "If you are God's Son, order this stone to turn into bread."

But Jesus answered, "The scripture says, 'Man cannot live on bread alone.'"

Then the Devil took him up and showed him in a second all the kingdoms of the world. "I will give you all this power and all this wealth," the Devil told him, "It has all been handed over to me, and I can give it to anyone I choose. All this will be yours, then, if you worship me."

Jesus answered,"The scripture says, 'Worship the Lord your God and serve only him.'"

When the Devil finished tempting Jesus in every way, he left him for a while. Then Jesus returned to Galilee, and the power of the Holy Spirit was with him. The news about him spread throughout all that territory. He taught in the synagogues and was praised by everyone.

A Man with Evil Spirit

Jesus went to Capernaum, a town in Galilee, where he taught the, people on the Sabbath. They were all amazed at the way he taught, because he spoke with authority. In the synagogue was a man who had the spirit of an evil demon in him; he screamed out in a loud voice, "Ah! What do you want with us, Jesus of Nazareth? Are you here to destroy us? I know who you are: you are God's holy messenger!"

Jesus ordered the spirit, "Be quiet and come out of the man!" The demon threw the man down in front of them and went out of him without doing him any harm.

Jesus left the synagogue and went to Simon's house. Simon's mother-in-law was sick with a high fever, and they spoke to Jesus about her. He went and stood at her bedside and ordered the fever to leave her. The fever left her, and she got up at once and began to wait on them.

After sunset all who had friends who were sick with various diseases brought them to Jesus; he placed his hands on every one of them and healed them all. Demons also went out from many people, screaming, "You are the Son of in God!"

At daybreak Jesus left the town and went off to a lonely place. The people started looking for him, and when they found him, they tried to keep him from leaving. But he said to them, "I must preach the Good News about the Kingdom of God in other towns also, because that is what God sent me to do."

So he preached in the synagogues throughout the country.

Jesus Calls the First Disciples

One day Jesus was standing on the shore of Lake Gennesaret while the people pushed their way up to him to listen to the word of God. He saw two boats pulled up on the beach; the fishermen had left them and were washing the nets. Jesus got into one of the boats—it belonged to Simon—and asked him to push off a little from the shore. He said to Simon, "Push the boat out further to the deep water, and you and your partners let down your nets for a catch."

"Master," Simon answered, "we worked hard all night long and caught nothing. But if you say so, I will let down the nets." They let them down and caught such a large number of fish that the nets were about to break. So they motioned to their partners in the other boat to come and help them. They came and filled both boats so full of fish that the boats were about to sink. Simon Peter and the others with him were all amazed at the large number of fish they had caught. The same was true of Simon's partners, James and John, the sons of Zebedee. Jesus said to Simon, "Don't be afraid; from now on you will be catching men."

They pulled the boats up on the beach, left everything, and followed Jesus.

After this Jesus went out and saw a tax collector named Levi, sitting in his office. Jesus said to him, "Follow me." Levi got up, left everything, and followed him. Then Levi had a big feast in his house for Jesus, and among the guests was a large number of tax collectors and other people. Some Pharisees and some teachers of the Law who belonged to their group complained to Jesus. "Why do you eat and drink with tax collectors and other outcasts?" they asked.

Jesus answered them, "People who are well do not need a doctor, but only those who are sick. I have not come to call respectable people to repent, but outcasts."

Jesus Chooses the Twelve Apostles

Jesus went up a hill to pray and spent the whole night there praying to God. When day came, he called his disciples to him and chose twelve of them, whom he named apostles: Simon (whom he named Peter) and his brother Andrew; James and John, Philip and Bartholomew, Matthew and Thomas, James son of Alphaeus, and Simon (who was called the Patriot). Judas son of James, and Judas Iscariot, who became the traitor.

The Messengers from John the Baptist

When John's disciples told him about all these things, he called two of them and sent them to the Lord to ask him, 'Are you the one John said was going to come, Or should we expect someone else?"

When they came to Jesus, they said, "John the Baptist sent us to ask if you Jesus are the one he said was going to come, or if we should expect someone else."

At that very time Jesus cured many people of their sicknesses, diseases, and evil spirits, and gave sight to many blind people. He answered John's messengers. "Go back and tell John what you have seen and heard: the blind can see, the lame can walk, those who suffer from dreaded skin-diseases are made clean, the deaf can hear, the dead are raised to life, and the Good News is preached to the poor. How happy are those who have no doubts about me!"

Women Who Accomparnied Jesus

Some time later Jesus travelled through towns and villages, preaching the Good News about the Kingdom of God. The twelve disciples went with him, and so did some women who had been healed of evil spirits and diseases: Mary (who was called Magdalene), from whom seven demons had been driven out; Joanna, whose husband Chuza was an officer in Herod's court; and Busanna, and many other women who used their own resources to help Jesus and his disciples.

Jesus' Mother and Brothers

Jesus' mother and brothers came to him, but were unable to join him because of the crowd. Someone said to Jesus, "Your mother and brothers are standing outside and want to see you."

Jesus said to them all, "My mother and brothers are those who hear the word of God and obey it."

Jesus Sends Out the Twelve Disciples

Jesus called the twelve disciples together and gave them power and authority to drive out all demons and to cure diseases. Then he sent them out to preach the Kingdom of God and to heal the sick, after saying to them, "Take nothing with you for the journey: no stick, no beggar's bag, no food, no money, not even an extra shirt. Wherever you are welcomed, stay in the same house until you leave that town; wherever people don't welcome you, leave that town and shake the dust off your feet as a warning to them."

The disciples left and travelled through all the villages, preaching the Good News and healing people everywhere.

When Herod, the ruler of Galilee, heard about all the things that were happening, he was very confused, because some people were saying that John the Baptist had come back to life. Others were saying that Elijah had appeared, and still others that one of the prophets of long ago had come back to life. Herod said, "I had John's head cut off; but who is this man I hear these things about?" And he kept trying to see Jesus.

One day when Jesus was praying alone, the disciples came to him. "Who do the crowds say I am?" he asked them.

"Some say that you are John the Baptist," they answered. "Others say that you are Elijah, while others say that one of the prophets of long ago has come back to life."

"What about you?" he asked them. "Who do you say I am?"

Peter answered, "You are God's Messiah."

Jesus Speaks about His Suffering and Death

Then Jesus gave them strict orders not to tell this to anyone. He also said to them, "The Son of Man must suffer much and be rejected by the elders, the chief priests, and the teachers of the Law. He will be put to death, but three days later he will be raised to life."

And he said to them all, "If anyone wants to come with me, he must forget self, take up his cross every day, and follow me. For whoever wants to save his own life will lose it, but whoever loses his life for my sake will save it."

About a week after he had said these things, Jesus took Peter, John, and James with him and went up a hill to pray. While he was praying, his face changed its appearance, and his clothes became dazzling white. Suddenly two men were seen talking with him. They were Moses and Elijah, who appeared in heavenly glory and talked with Jesus about the way in which he would soon fulfil God's purpose by dying in Jerusalem.

A man said to Jesus. "I wil follow you wherever you go."

Jesus said to him. "Foxes have holes. and birds have nests. but the Son of Man has nowhere to lie down and rest." He said to another man. "Follow me."

But that man said. "Sir, first let me go back and bury my father."

Jesus answered, "Let the dead bury their own dead. You go and proclaim the Kingdom of God."

Another man said, "I will follow you, sir; but first let me go and say good-bye to my family."

Jesus said to him, "Anyone who starts to plough and then keeps looking back is of no use to the Kingdom of God."

Jesus Sends Out the Seventy-two

After this the Lord chose another seventy-two men and sent them out two by two, to go ahead of him to every town and place where he himself was about to go. He said to them, "There is a large harvest, but few workers to gather it in. Pray to the owner of the harvest that he will send out workers to gather in his harvest. Go! I am sending you like lambs among wolves. Don't take a purse or a beggar's bag or shoes; don't stop to greet anyone on the road. Whenever you go into a house, first say, 'Peace be with this house.' If a peace-loving man lives there, let your greeting of peace remain on him; if not, take back your greeting of peace. Stay in that same house, eating and drinking whatever they offer you. But whenever you go into a town and are not welcomed, go out in the streets and say, 'Even the dust from your town that sticks to our feet we wipe off against you. But remember that the Kingdom of God has come near you.'

Jesus Accuses the Pharisees

When Jesus finished speaking, a Pharisee invited him to eat with him; he went in and sat down to eat. The Pharisee was surprised when he noticed that Jesus had not washed before eating. So the Lord said to him, "Now then, you Pharisees clean the outside of your cup and plate, but inside you are full of violence and evil. Fools! Did not God, who made the outside, also make the inside? But give what is in your cups and plates to the poor, and everything will be ritually clean for you.

"How terrible for you Pharisees! You give God a tenth of the seasoning herbs, such as mint and rue and all the other herbs, but you neglect justice and love for God. These you should practise, without neglecting the others."

One of the teachers of the Law said to him, "Teacher, when you say this, you insult us, too!"

Jesus answered; "How terrible also for you teachers of the Law! You put loads on people's backs which are hard to carry, but you yourselves will not stretch out a finger to help them carry those loads. How terrible for you! You make fine tombs for the prophets—the very prophets your ancestors murdered.

"For this reason the Wisdom of God said, 'I will send them prophets and messengers; they will kill some of them and persecute others.' So the people of this time will be punished for the murder of all the prophets killed since the creation of the world, from the murder of Abel to the murder of Zechariah, who was killed between the altar and the Holy Place. Yes, I tell you, the people of this time will be punished for them all!"

When Jesus left that place, the teachers of the Law and the Pharisees began to criticize him bitterly.

Whom to Fear

Jesus said: "I tell you, my friends, do not be afraid of those who kill the body but cannot afterwards do anything worse, I will show you whom to fear; **fear God, who, after killing, has the authority to throw into hell**. Believe me, he is the one you must fear!

"Aren't five sparrows sold for two pennies? Yet not one sparrow is forgotten by God. Even the hairs of your head have all been counted. So do not be afraid, you are worth much more than many sparrows!

"And so **I tell you not to worry about the food you need to stay alive or about the clothes you need for your body.** Life is much more important than food, and the body much more important than clothes. Look at the crows: they don't sow seeds or gather a harvest; they don't store rooms or barns; God feeds them! You are worth so much more than birds!

"So don't be all upset, always concerned about what you will eat and drink. **Your Father knows that you need these things**. Instead, be concerned with his Kingdom, and **he will provide you with these things**."

Riches in Heaven

"Do not be afraid, little flock, for our Father is pleased to give you the kingdom. Sell all your belongings and give the money to the poor. Provide for yourselves purses that don't wear out, and save your riches in heaven, where they will never decrease, because no thief can get to them, and no moth can destroy them."

Jesus went through towns and villages, teaching the people and making his way towards Jerusalem. Someone asked him, "Sir, will just a few people be saved?"

Jesus answered them, **"Do your best to go in through the narrow door**; because many people will surely try to go in but will not be able. The master of the house will get up and close the door.

"How you will cry and grind your teeth when you see Abraham, Isaac, and Jacob, and all the prophets in the Kingdom of God, while you are thrown out! People will come from the east and the west, from the north and the south, and sit down at the feast in the Kingdom of God. Then those who are now last will be first, and those who are now first will be last."

Jesus' Love for Jerusalem

At that same time some Pharisees came to Jesus and said to him, "You must get out of here and go somewere else, because Herod wants to kill you."

Jesus answered them, "Go and tell that fox: 'I am driving out demons and performing cures today and tomorrow, and on the third day I shall finish my work. Yet I must be on my way today, tomorrow, and the next day; it is not right for a prophet to be killed anywhere except in Jerusalem.

"Jerusalem, Jerusalem! You kill the prophets, you stone the messengers God has sent you! How many times have I wanted to put my arms round all your people, just as a hen gathers her chicks under her wings, but you would not let me! And so your Temple will be abandoned. I assure you that you will not see me until the time comes when you say, 'God bless him who comes in the name of the Lord.'"

"There was once a rich man who dressed in the most expensive clothes and lived in great luxury every day. There was also a poor man named Lazarus, covered with sores, who used to be brought to the rich man's door, hoping to eat the bits of food that fell from the rich man's table. Even the dogs would come and lick his sores.

"The poor man died and was carried by the angels to sit beside Abraham at the feast in heaven. The rich man died and was buried, and in Hades, where he was in great pain; he looked up and saw Abraham, far away with Lazarus at his side. So he called out, 'Father Abraham! Take pity on me, and send Lazarus to dip his finger in some water and cool my tongue, because I am in great pain in this fire!'

"But Abraham said, 'Remember, my son, that in your lifetime you were given all the good things, while Lazarus got all the bad things. But now he is enjoying himself here, while you are in pain. Besides all that, there is a deep pit lying between us, so that those who want to cross over from here to you cannot do so, nor can anyone cross over to us from where you are.' "

When he came near Jerusalem, at the place where the road went down the Mount of Olives, the large crowd of his disciples began to thank God and praise him in loud voices for all the great things that they had seen. "God bless the king who comes in the name of the Lord! Peace in heaven and glory to God!"

Jesus Goes to the Temple

Then Jesus went into the Temple and began to drive out the merchants, saying to them, "It is written in the Scriptures that God said, 'My Temple will be called a house of prayer.' But you have turned it into a hideout for thieves!"

Every day Jesus taught in the Temple. The chief priest, the teachers of the Law, and the leaders of the people wanted to kill him, but they could not find a way to do it, because all the people kept listening to him, not wanting to miss a single word.

As all the people listened to him, Jesus said to his disciples, "Be on your guard against the teachers of the Law, who like to walk about in their long robes and love to be greeted with respect in the market-place; who choose the reserved seats in the synagogues and the best places at feasts; who take advantage of widows and rob them of their homes, and then make a show of saying long prayers! Their punishment will be all the worse!"

The Plot against Jesus

The time was near for the Festival of Unleavened Bread, which is called the Passover. The chief priests and the teachers of the Law were afraid of the people, and so they were trying to find a way of putting Jesus to death secretly.

Then Satan entered Judas, called Iscariot, who was one of the twelve disciples. So Judas went off and spoke with the chief priests and the officers of the temple guard about how he could betray Jesus to them. They were pleased and offered to pay him money. Judas agreed to it and started looking for a good chance to hand Jesus over to them without the people knowing about it.

The day came during the Festival of Unleavened Bread when the lambs for the Passover meal were to be killed. Jesus sent off Peter and John with these instructions: "Go and get the Passover meal ready for us to eat."

The Lord's Supper

When the hour came, Jesus took his place at the table with the apostles. He said to them, "I have wanted so much to eat this Passover meal with you before I suffer!"

Then Jesus took a cup, gave thanks to God, and said, "Take this and share it among yourselves. I tell you that from now on I will not drink this wine until the Kingdom of God comes."

Then **he took a piece of bread, gave thanks to God, broke it, and gave it to them, saying, "This is my body, which is given for you**. Do this in memory of me." In the same way, **he gave them the cup after the supper, saying, "This cup is**

God's new covenant sealed with my blood, which is poured out for you."

Jesus left the city and went, as he usually did, to the Mount of Olives; and the disciples went with him. When he arrived at the place, he said to them, "Pray that you will not fall into temptation."

Then he went off from them about the distance of a stone's throw and down and prayed. "Father," he said, "if you will, take this cup of suffering away from me. **Not my will, however, but your will be done**." An angel from heaven appeared to him and strengthened him.

The Arrest of Jesus

Jesus was still speaking when a crowd arrived, led by Judas, one of the twelve disciples. He came up to Jesus to kiss him. But Jesus said, "Judas, is it with a kiss that you betray the Son of Man?"

When the disciples who were with Jesus saw what was going to happen, they asked, "Shall we use our swords, Lord?" And one of them struck the High Priest's slave and cut off his right ear.

But Jesus said, "Enough of this!" He touched the man's ear and healed him.

Then Jesus said to the chief priests and the officers of the temple guard and the elders who had come there to get him, "Did you have to come with swords and clubs, as though I were an outlaw? I was with you in the Temple every day, and you did not try to arrest me. But this is your hour to act, when the power of darkness rules."

They arrested Jesus and took him away into the house of the High Priest; and Peter followed at a distance. A fire had been lit in the centre of the courtyard, and Peter joined those who were sitting round it. When one of the servant-girls saw him sitting there at the fire, she looked straight at him and said, "This man too was with Jesus!"

But Peter denied it, "Woman, I don't even know him!"

The men who were guarding Jesus mocked him and beat him. They blindfolded him and asked him, "Who hit you? Guess!" And they said many other insulting things to him.

Jesus is Brought before the Council

When day came, the elders, the chief priests, and the teachers of the Law met together, and Jesus was brought before the Council. "Tell us," they said, "are you the Messiah?"

He answered, "If I tell you, you will not believe me; and if I ask you a question, you will not answer. **But from now on the Son of Man will be seated on the right of Almighty God**."

They all said, "Are you, then, the Son of God?"

He answered them, "You say that I am."

The whole group rose up and took Jesus before Pilate, where they began to accuse him: "We caught this man misleading our people, telling them not to pay taxes to the Emperor and claiming that he himself is the Messiah and king."

Pilate asked him, "Are you the king of the Jews?"

"So you say," answered Jesus.

Then Pilate said to the chief priests and the crowds, "I find no reason to condemn this man."

But they insisted even more strongly, "With his teaching he is starting a riot among the people all through Judaea. He began in Galilee and now has come here."

Jesus is Sent to Herod

When Pilate heard this, he asked, "Is this man a Galilean?" When he learnt that Jesus was from the region ruled by Herod, he sent him to Herod, who was also in Jerusalem at that time. Herod was very pleased when he saw Jesus, because he had heard about him and had been wanting to see him for a long time. He was hoping to see Jesus perform some miracle. So Herod asked Jesus many questions, but Jesus made no answer. The chief priests and the teachers of the Law stepped forward and made strong accusations against Jesus. Herod and his soldiers mocked Jesus and treated him with contempt; then they put a fine robe on him and sent him back to Pilate.

Jesus is Sentenced to Death

Pilate called together the chief priests, the leaders, and the people, and said to them, "You brought this man to me and said that he was misleading the people. Now, I have examined him here in your presence, and have not found him guilty of any of the crimes you accuse him of. Nor did Herod find him guilty, for he sent him back to us. There is nothing this man has done to deserve death. So I will have him whipped and let him go."

The whole crowd cried out, "Kill him!"

Pilate wanted to set Jesus free, so he appealed to the crowd again. But they shouted back, "Crucify him! Crucify him!."

Pilate said to them the third time. "But what crime has he committed? I cannot find anything he has done to deserve death! I will have him whipped and set him free."

But they kept on shouting at the top of their voices that Jesus should be crucified, and finally their shouting succeeded. So Pilate passed the sentence on Jesus that they were asking for.

A large crowd of people followed him; among them were some women who were weeping and wailing for him. Two other men, both of them criminals, were also led out to be put to death with Jesus. **When they came to the place called "The Skull," they crucified Jesus there,and the two criminals, one on his right and the other on his left. Jesus said, "Forgive them, Father! They don't know what they are doing."**

The people stood there watching while the Jewish leaders jeered at him: "He saved others; let him save himself if he is the Messiah whom God has chosen! "

One of the criminals hanging there hurled insults at him: "Aren't you the Messiah? Save yourself and us!"

The other one, however, rebuked him, saying "Don't you fear God? You received the same sentence he did. Ours, however, is only right, because we are getting what we deserve for what we did; but he has done no wrong." And he said to Jesus, "Remember me, Jesus, when you come as King!"

Jesus said to him, "I promise you that today you will be in Paradise with me."

The Death of Jesus

It was about twelve o'clock when the sun stopped shining and darkness covered the whole country until three o'clock; and the curtain hanging in the Temple was torn in two. Jesus cried out in a loud voice. **"Father! In your hands I place my spirit!" He said this and died.**

The army officer saw what had happened, and he praised God, saying, "Certainly he was a good man!"

The Burial of Jesus

There was a man named Joseph from Arimathea, a town in Judaea. He was a good and honourable man, who was waiting for the coming of the Kingdom of God. Although he was a member of the Council, he had not agreed with their decision and action. He went into the presence of Pilate and asked for the body of Jesus. Then **he took the body down, wrapped it in a linen sheet, and placed it in a tomb which had been dug out of solid rock** and which had never been used. It was Friday, and the Sabbath was about to begin.

The women who had followed Jesus from Galilee went with Joseph and saw the tomb and how Jesus' body was placed in it. Then they went back home and prepared the spices and perfumes for the body.

The Resurrection

Very early on Sunday morning the women went to the tomb, carrying the spices they had prepared. They found the stone rolled away from the entrance to the tomb, so they went in;

but they did not find the body of the Lord Jesus. They stood there puzzled about this, when suddenly two men in bright shining clothes stood by them. Full of fear, the women bowed down to the ground, as the men said to them, "**Why are you looking among the dead for one who is alive? He is not here; he has been raised**. Remember what he said to you while he was in Galilee; 'The Son of Man must be handed over to sinful men, be crucified, and three days later rise to life.'"

Then the women remembered his words, returned from the tomb, and told all these things to the eleven disciples and all the rest. The women were Mary Magdalene, Joanna, and Mary the mother of James; they and the other women with them told these things to the apostles. But the apostles thought that what the women said was nonsense, and they did not believe them. But **Peter got up and ran to the tomb; he bent down and saw the linen wrappings but nothing else**. Then he went back home amazed at what had happened.

The Walk to Emmaus

On that same day two of Jesus' followers were going to a village named Emmaus, about eleven kilometres from Jerusalem, and they were talking to each other about all the things that had happened. As they talked and discussed, **Jesus himself drew near and walked along with them**; they saw him, but somehow did not recognize him. Jesus said to them. "What are you talking about to each other, as you walk along?"

They stood still, with sad faces. One of them, named Cleopas, asked him, "Are you the only visitor in Jerusalem who doesn't know the things that have been happening there these last few days?"

"What things?" he asked.

"The things that happened to Jesus of Nazareth," they answered.

Jesus said to them, "How foolish you are, to believe everything the prophets said!"

As they came near the village to which they were going, Jesus acted as if he were going farther; but they held to him back, saying, "Stay with us; the day is almost over and it is getting dark." So he went in to stay with them. He sat down to eat with them, took the bread, and said the blessing; **then he broke the bread and gave it to them. Then their eyes were opened and they recognized him, but he disappeared from their sight**.

They got up at once and went back to Jerusalem, where they found the eleven disciples gathered together with the others and saying, "The Lord is risen indeed! He has appeared to Simon!"

Jesus Appears to His Disciples

While the two were telling them this, **suddenly the Lord himself stood among them and said to them, "Peace be with you!"**

They were terrified, thinking that they were seeing a ghost. But he said to them, "Why are you alarmed? Why are these doubts coming up in your minds? **Look at my hands and my feet, and see that it is I myself**. Feel me, and you will know, for a ghost doesn't have flesh and bones, as you can see I have."

He said this and showed them his hands and his feet. They still could not believe, they were so full of joy and wonder; so he asked them, "Have you anything here to eat?" **They gave him a piece of cooked fish, which he took and ate in their presence**.

Then he opened their minds to understand the Scriptures, and said to them, "This is what is written: the Messiah must suffer and must rise from death three days later, and in his name the message about repentance and the forgiveness of sins must be preached to all nations, beginning in Jerusalem."

Jesus Is Taken Up to Heaven

Then he led them out of the city as far as Bethany, where he raised his hands and blessed them. As he was blessing them, he departed from them and was taken up to heaven.

CONCEPTS AND BELIEFS

The Trinity

The mystery we call God has revealed himself to humankind as a Trinity of Persons—the Father, the Son, and the Holy Spirit. Upon it are based all other teachings of the Church. In the Bible there is frequent mention of the Father, the Son, and the Holy Spirit. But if there is only one God, how can this be?

In the unity of the Godhead there are three Persons distinct from one another. The Father is God, the Son is God, and the Holy Spirit is God, and yet there is but one God. We speak of the Father as Creator of all that is, of the Son, the Word of God, as our Saviour, and of the Holy Spirit 'poured into our hearts'—as our Sanctifier. God is Father means to believe that you are his son or daughter; that God your Father accepts and loves you; that God has created you as a lovable human being.

God is saving Word means to believe that you are a listener; that your response to God's Word, to his gospel which frees you to choose union with God and brotherhood with your neighbour. God is Spirit means to believe that you are meant to live a sanctifying life sharing in God's own nature.

Jesus Christ

The second Person of the Trinity became a man, Jesus Christ. His mother was Mary of Nazareth, daughter of Joachim and Anne. Joseph, Mary's husband, was like a father to Jesus. Jesus' true Father is God; he had no human father.

Conceived in Mary's womb by the power of the Holy Spirit, Jesus was born in Bethlehem of Judea, probably between 6 and 4 B.C. He died on Calvary (outside of old Jerusalem) as a relatively young man, most likely in his early thirties. 'He has both a divine nature and a human nature. His divinity does not overwhelm with his humanity—and vice versa. He experienced the death that all human beings experience, but during his dying, at his death, and after his death, he remained God. After his death, Jesus descended to the dead.' He rose from the dead on Easter morning. He is living with his Father and the Spirit—and in our midst. He is both, God's connect to human beings and our path to God. Jesus is the saving presence of God in the world.

Jesus comes to you, in his Word—when the Word of God is preached to you or when you read the Scriptures,with attentive reverence. **He is also present to you in the seven sacraments—especially in the Eucharist**. Another way you meet him is in other people–whatever you do for your brothers.

Jesus is the key, the centre and the purpose of man's needs. In the words of Saint Paul, "Many are the promises of God, their Yes is in him."

The Holy Spirit

God is present to all of creation. "In him we live and move and have our being." And there is another personal presence of God within those who love him. Jesus himself speaks of it in the Gospel of John, where he says: "Whoever loves me will keep my word, and my Father will love him, and we will come to him and dwell with him."

This special presence of the Trinity is properly ascribed to the Holy Spirit, as Saint Paul says, "The love of God has been poured out into our hearts through the Holy Spirit." **The Holy Spirit is silently working to transform you**. Its gifts are: wisdom, to value the things of heaven understanding the truths of religion, counsel to choose the best approach in serving God, fortitude, knowledge, piety, and fear of the Lord.

Other gifts of the Spirit are called **charisms**, favours granted for the help of others. Nine charisms are: the gifts of speaking with wisdom, speaking with knowledge, faith, healing, miracles, prophecy, discerning of spirits, tongues, and interpreting speeches.

Grace is the presence to you of God's living, dynamic Spirit, as a result of which you live with a new inner life, 'sharing' in the divine nature. Under its influence you live a life of love that builds up **Christ's Body, the Church**.

In this life, your love for God is bound together with your love of others—by God's own commandment, **you are to love your neighbour as yourself**. Increase your love for self by trying to deepening your understanding of those around you by being forgiving and by widening your circle of compassion to embrace all living creatures and nature.

The Church

The life of Jesus, the Word made flesh, was the foundation of the Church. He gathered followers who committed themselves to him. He then chose his inner circle—the Twelve. who were allowed to join his Last Supper with him. They were called **apostles**, whose mission was to be Jesus' representatives.

At the Last Supper he took bread and wine and said: "Take and eat, this is my body: take and drink, this is my blood." The Twelve thus entered into a union of total intimacy with him and with one another, they became one body in Jesus.

Jesus also spoke of the 'new testament'. God was establishing a new relationship for the human beings, a covenant sealed with the blood of Christ himself. The earliest account of the Eucharist, reveals what the Last Supper meant for the future of the Church. Jesus said, "Do this in remembrance of me." The

Last Supper was Jesus' final step before his death in prepanng the Twelve: how they, and their successors through the ages, were to carry out his mission.

The founding of the Church was completed with the sending of the Holy Spirit. The birth of the Church took place on the day of Pentecost: the sending of the Spirit took place publicly, his crucifixion took place in public view. Since then the Church has shown itself to be a divine-human realify—a combination of the Spirit working and the people striving.

Christ is the sacrament of God, the Church is your sacrament, the visible sign of Christ. But **the Church is not a sacrament 'for members only'—it is for the benefit of the faithful and of the whole world**. The Church is the primary visible instrument, through which the Spirit is bringing about the oneness of us all.

The Bible

The Scripture, the Bible, is a collection of books. It contains 73 books. The 46 books of the Old Testament were written between 900 B.C. and 150 B.C. The 27 books of the New Testament were written between 50 and 150 A.D.

The Old Testament made up of historical, didactic and prophetic books, of prophets, who experienced God and were his spokesmen. These books were mostly written in Hebrew. The Old Testament books reveal Israel's insight into the reality of the **God, Yahweh**, the same God whom Jesus, a Jew, called Father.

The New Testament books were written in Greek, and are made up of **gospels (Good News)** and epistles or letters. The first four are the gospels of Matthew, Mark, Luke and John; the first three of these are called Synoptic, because they tell the same story in the same way. The Acts of the Apostles is a sequel to the Gospel of Luke. The fourth Gospel of John fills out the views of Jesus not found in the three Gospels.

Next come the **epistles or letters of Saint Paul**—which were written to meet the needs of various Christian communities. Then come the Catholic epistles concerning matters important to all Christian communities. The final book is the Book of Revelation, a message for Christians, promising Christ's ultimate triumph.

The basic theme of the New Testament is Jesus Christ. **It does not throw enough light on his early years, which new research shows, he passed in India, where he was influenced by Buddhism**. He is also said to have survived crucifixion, after he returned to India, and lived in Kashmir, where he passed away—his grave still exists in the Khanyar locality of Srinagar. A grave of Christ is also said to exist in Japan, which relates another interesting story of his life.

Original Sin

The concept of Original Sin is a special feature of Christian religion. The Book of Genesis depicts this about human beings. Chapters 1 and 2 tell the story of creation, that God created all things, including man and woman, and saw that they were good. But into this good world entered sin. The man, Adam, rejects God and tries to become his equal. As a result of this original sin, he feels alienated from God. He hides. When God confronts him, he blames the woman, Eve, for his sin, and she in turn blames the serpent. Thus the man's guilt has distorted all his relationships.

Chapters 4 to 11 depict the escalation of sin in the world, rippling out from Adam's original sin. In chapter 11 man tries again to become God's equal by building a tower reaching to the heavens. This rejection of God spills over into man's rejection of his fellowman. The result has been division, pain, bloodshed, and death. Excepting Jesus Christ and his mother, Mary, every human being is affected by original sin. But Christ has conquered sin by death and resurrection. This has swallowed up the original sin and its widespread effects.

Then there is personal sin—sin committed whenever we knowingly violate the moral law. But God will forgive any sin if the person is truly sorry.

He must be reconciled to Christ and the Church before he or she receives holy Communion. He can return to God's grace by confession by having perfect sorrow or contrition.

The Sacraments

Baptism: Through immersing in the waters of baptism, one is grafted into the mystery of Christ. In a mysterious way, one dies with him, is buried with him, and rises with him. **As a baptized Christian, one is an adopted brother or sister of Christ**. Both original and personal sins are cleansed away in the waters of baptism. One's baptism into Christ is the beginning of a lifelong vocation.

Many people exercise their calling through parish activities, assisting their priests, serving as distributors of holy Communion, choir leaders, ushers, etc. Some people enter religious orders and become religious Brothers and Sisters. These people dedicate themselves to God by vowing to live the evangelical counsels of poverty, chastity, and obedience.

Confirmation: Confirmation is the sacrament by which those born anew in baptism receive the seal ot the Holy Spirit. It is the sacrament of initiation into the life of adult Christian witness. To perform it the celebrant moistens his thumb with the mixture of olive oil and balsam, and traces the sign of the cross on one's forehead. The celebrant addresses one using his new confirmation name, and says: "Be sealed with the Gift of the Holy Spirit." The Gift being the Spirit himself.

Eucharist: "At the Last Supper, on the night when he was betrayed, Jesu instituted the eucharistic sacrifice of his Body and Blood. This he did to perpetuate the sacrifice of the Cross until he should come again, and so to entrust to the Church a memorial of his death and resurrection.

In eyery Mass, Christ is present, in the person of his priest and under the form of bread and wine. His death becomes a reality, offered as our sacrifice to God in sacramental manner. At Mass we offer Christ, our passover sacrifice, to God ourselves along with him. We then receive the risen Lord, in holy

Communion. We thus enter into the mystery of our salvation—the death and resurrection of Christ. Eating the supper of the Lord, we become one body in him.

The Eucharist can draw you into the compelling love of Christ and set you afire.

Penance: Penance is the sacrament by which we get God's forgiveness for sins committed after baptism. It reconciles us with God and the Church community. The sacrament of penance is a joyful reunion. In penance, Jesus embraces and heals you.

Anointing of the Sick: In serious illness one experiences mortality. He realizes that he is going to die. Because it may lead you to face God in the light of your own death, there is a formal sacrament for this situation: anointing of sick. God thus invites you to commune with him the entire Church asks God and to lighten your sufferings, and bring you salvation.

If one is in danger of death, he should not delay receiving the sacrament. The sacrament helps one to share fully in the cross of Christ.

Matrimony: Jesus made marriage the sacrament of matrimony, giving it a new dimension to the Christian vocation that begins in baptism. A husband and wife are called to love each other in a practical way: by serving each other's personal needs, by communicating their personal thoughts and feelings to each other so their oneness increase. This love is beautifully sexual.

A major purpose of matrimony is the begetting of new life—children. But a couple's love also gives life to other people. Matrimony is much more than a private arrangement between two people. They live a truly sacramental life when they follow the advice given in Ephesians: "Be subordinate to one another out of reverence for Christ."

In the Catholic Church, a couple's union is exclusive (one man with one woman) and indissoluble.

Death and Judgement: In the New Testament the Letter to the Hebrews, says, "It is appointed that human beings die once, and after this the judgement." If your basic love—at the moment of death is the **absolute Good whom we call God,** God remains your eternal possession, called heaven. If it is anything less than God, you experience emptiness, called hell.

The judgement consists in a revelation of your chosen condition—eternal union with God, or alienation.

Purgatory: If you die in the love of God but possess any stains of sin, they are cleansed away in a purifying process called purgatory. These stains are the punishment due to venial or mortal sins already forgiven but for which sufficient penance was not done during one's lifetime. After passing through purgatory, one will be unselfish, capable of perfect love.

The Final Judgement on the last day is expressed in the Creeds of the Church. **On that day all the dead will be raised and be present before God as human beings. Then God will conduct a panoramic judgement of all that humankind did and endured through the long centuries.**

When will that day come? The day has already begun when God says to all living things: "Behold, I make all things new.... They are accomplished. I [am] the Alpha and the Omega, the beginning and the end." (Revelation 21).

Holy Orders

The Church shares in the nature and tasks of Church, including sharing in his priesthood. There is the common priesthood and the special or 'ministerial priesthood' that certain members of the Church receive through the sacrament of holy orders.

Priests receive their priesthood from bishops, who possess the fullness of the sacrament of holy orders. Priests preach his gospel, baptize, heal, forgive sin in penance, act as witness in the matrimony and anointing of the sick and celebrate the Eucharist.

Deacons also have a sharing in the sacrament of holy orders. Conferred by a bishop, it is the first stage in ordination to priesthood, though some may not go on to become priests. They serve the people of God at the direction of priests.

The Ten Commandments

1. You shall honour no other god but me.
2. You shall not misuse the name of the Lord your God.
3. Remember to keep holy the Sabbath.
4. Honour your father and your mother.
5. You shall not kill.
6. You shall not commit adultery.
7. You shali not steal.
8. You shall not bear false witness against your neighbour.
9. You shall not covet your neighbour's wife.
10. You shall not covet your neighbour's goods.

Confession

Confessing at least once a year is a general rule, but if no grave sin has been committed in that time, is not obligatory. It is a personal encounter with Jesus Christ represented by the priest in the confessional room. The penitent admits to God that he or she has sinned, expresses sorrow, accepts a penance prayer, acts of self-denial or service to others, and resolves to do better in the future.

The following new form, though preferable, is optional:

Father greets you kindly.

You respond and then make and say the Sign of the Cross.

Father invites you to have confidence in God.

You answer, "Amen."

Father may recite some short selection from the Bible.

You introduce yourself—Not by name—and tell how long it has been since your last confession. You then tell your sins.

Father will give you the necessary advice and answer your questions. He assigns a penance and you make an Act of Contrition. Father then places his hands on our head and prays:

"God, the Father of mercies, through the death and resurrection of his Son has reconciled the world to himself and sent the Holy Spirit among us for the forgiveness of sins; through the ministry of the Church may God give you pardon and peace, and I absolve you from your sins in the name of the Father, and of the Son, and of the Holy Spirit."

You answer, "Amen."

Father then says, "Give thanks to the Lord, for he is good."

You answer, "His mercy endures for ever."

Father then dismisses you in these words, "The Lord has freed you from your sins. Go in peace."

PRAYERS

Sign of the Cross

In the name of the Father, and of the Son, and of the Holy Spirit. Amen. (Said at the beginning and end of prayers.)

Our Father

Our Father, who art in heaven, hallowed be thy name; thy kingdom come; thy will be done on earth as in heaven. Give us this day our daily bread; and forgive us our trespasses as we forgive those who trespass against us; and lead us not into temptation, but deliver us from evil. For the kingdom, the power, and the glory are yours, now and for ever. Amen.

Hail Mary

Hail Mary, full of grace. The Lord is with you. Blessed are you among women, and blessed is the fruit of your womb, Jesus. Holy Mary, Mother of God, pray for us sinners, now and at the hour of our death. Amen.

Prayer of Praise

Glory to the Father, and to the Son, and to the Holy Spirit; as it was in the beginning, is now, and ever shall be world without end. Amen.

Act of Contrition

My God, I am sorry for my sins with all my heart. In choosing to do wrong and failing to do good, I have sinned against you whom I should love above all things. I firmly intend, with your help, to do penance, to sin no more, and to avoid whatever leads me to sin. Our Saviour Jesus Christ suffered and died for us. In his name, my God, have mercy. Amen.

Grace before and Thanksgiving after Meals

Bless us, O Lord, and these your gifts, which we are about to receive from your bounty, through Christ, our Lord. Amen.

We give thanks for all your benefits, almighty God, who lives and reigns forever. May the souls of the faithful departed, through the mercy of God, rest in peace. Amen.

Prayer to Jesus Christ Crucified

Behold, my beloved and good Jesus. I cast myself upon my knees in your sight, and with the most fervent desire of my soul I pray and beseech you to impress upon my heart lively sentiments of faith, hope, and charity, with true repentance for my sins and a most firm desire of amendment; while with deep affection and grief of soul I consider within myself and mentally contemplate your five most precious wounds, having before my eyes that which David the prophet long ago spoke about you, my Jesus: "They have pierced my hands and my feet; I can count all my bones."

Prayer to Christ in the Eucharist

Benediction is a simple act of worship. We begin by contemplating God's presence in our midst. Then the priest makes the Sign of the Cross over us with the host enshrined in the monstrance. Finally, we make our response in words of praise and thanksgiving.

While the congregation sings an opening song, the celebrant removes the host from the tabernacle, places it in a monstrance, and enthrones it on the altar. He incenses the host and a period of silent contemplation or public prayer ensues. Then, after the homily a hymn is sung.

The celebrant then says or sings a prayer such as the following:

Celebrant: Lord Jesus Christ, you gave us the Eucharist as the memorial of your suffering and death. May our worship of this sacrament of your body and blood help us to experience the salvation you won for us and the peace of the kingdom where you live with the Father and the Holy Spirit, one God, for ever and ever.

People: Amen.

The celebrant blesses the people with the host and then returns the Eucharist to the tabernacle. Afterward the people themselves may say or sing an acclamation such as the Divine Praises.

Blessed be God.
Blessed be his holy name.
Blessed be Jesus Christ, true God and true man.
Blessed be the name of Jesus.
Blessed be his most Sacred Heart.
Blessed be his most Precious Blood.
Blessed be Jesus in the most Holy Sacrament of the Altar.
Blessed be the Holy Spirit, the Paraclete.
Blessed be the great Mother of God,
  Mary most holy.
Blessed be her holy and Immaculate
  Conception.
Blessed be her glorious Assumption.
Blessed be the name of Mary,
  Virgin and Mother.
Blessed be Saint Joseph,
  her most chaste spouse.
Blessed be God in his angels and in his saints.

JESUS' SERMON ON THE MOUNT

Blessed are the poor in spirit,
for their's is the kingdom of heaven,

Blessed are those that mourn, for they
shall be comforted.

Blessed are the meek, for they shall
inherit the earth.

Blessed are they which do hunger
and thirst after righteousness,
for they shall be filled.

Blessed are the merciful, for they
shall obtain mercy.

Blessed are the pure in heart, for
they shall see God.

Blessed are the peacemakers, for
they shall be called the children of God.

Blessed are they which are persecuted
for righteousness' sake, for
their's is the kingdom of heaven,

Blessed areye when men shall revile
you, and persecute you, and shall
say all manner of evil against you,
falsely, for my sake.

Rejoice, and be exceeding glad; for great
is your reward in heaven, for so
persecuted they the prophets
which were before you.

TEACHINGS OF JESUS

"You are like salt for all mankind. But if salt loses its saltiness, there is no way to make it salty again. It has become worthless, so it is thrown out and people trample on it.

"You are like light for the whole world. A city built on a hill cannot be hidden. No one lights a lamp and puts it under a bowl; instead he puts it on the lampstand, where it gives light for everyone in the house. In the same way your light must shine before people, so that they will see the good things you do and praise your Father in heaven.

"Do not think that I have come to do away with the Law of Moses and the teachings of the prophets. I have not come to do away with them, but to make their teachings come true. Remember that as long as heaven and earth last, not the least point nor the smallest detail of the Law will be done away with—not until the end of all things. So then, whoever much disobeys even the least important of the commandments and teaches others to do the same, will be least in the Kingdom of heaven. On the other hand, whoever obeys the Law and teaches others to do the same, will be great in the Kingdom of heaven. I tell you, then, that you will be able to enter the Kingdom of heaven only if you are more faithful than the teachers of the Law and the Pharisees in doing what God requires.

Anger

"You have heard that people were told in the past, 'Do not commit murder; anyone who does will be brought to trial.' But now I tell you: whoever is angry with his brother will be brought to trial, whoever calls his brother 'You good for nothing!' will be brought before the Council, and whoever calls his brother a worthless fool will be in danger of going to the fire of hell. So if you are about the fire to offer your gift to God at the altar and there you remember that your brother has something against you, leave your gift there in front of the altar, go at once and make peace with your brother and then come back and offer your gift to God.

"If someone brings a lawsuit again you and takes you to court, settle the dispute with him while there is time, before you get to court. Once you are there, he will hand you over to the judge, who will hand you over to the police and you will be put in jail. There you will stay, I tell you, until you pay the last penny of your fine."

Adultery

"You have heard that it was said: 'Do not commit adultery.' But now I tell you: anyone who looks at a woman and wants to possess her is guilty of committing adultery with her in his heart. So if your right eye causes you to sin take it out and throw it away! It is much better for you to lose a part of your body than to have your whole body thrown into the hell. If your right hand causes you to sin, cut it off and throw it away! It is much better for you to lose one of your limbs than for your whole body to go to hell."

Divorce

"It was also said, 'Anyone who divorces his wife must give her a written notice of divorce.' But now I tell you: if a man divorces his wife, for any cause other than her unfaithfulness, then he is guilty of making her commit adultery if she marries again; and the man who marries her commits adultery also."

Vows

"You have also heard that people were told in the past, 'Do not break your promise, but do what you have vowed to the Lord to do.' But now I tell you: do not use any vow when you make a promise. Do not swear by heaven, for it is God's throne; nor by earth, for it is the resting place for his feet; nor by Jerusalem, for it is the city of the great King. Do not even swear by your head, because you cannot make a single hair white or black. Just say 'Yes' or 'No'—anything else you say comes from the Evil One."

Revenge

"You have heard that it was said, 'An eye for an eye, and a tooth for a tooth.' But now I tell you: do not take revenge on someone who wrongs you. **If anyone slaps you on the right cheek, let him slap your left cheek too**. And if someone takes you to court to sue you for your shirt, let him have your coat as well. And if one of the occupation troops forces you to carry his pack one kilometre, carry it two kilometres. When someone asks you for somethmg, give it to him; **when someone wants to borrow something, lend it to him**."

Love for Enemies

"You have heard that it was said, 'Love your friends, hate your enemies.' But now I tell you: **love your enemies and pray for those who persecute you**, so that you may become the sons of your Father in heaven. For he makes his sun to shine on bad and good people alike, and gives rain to those who do good and to those who do evil. Why should God reward you if you love only the people who love you? Even the tax collectors do that! And if you speak only to your friends, have you done anything out of the ordinary? Even the pagans do that! You must be perfect just as your Father in heaven is perfect!"

Charity

"Make certain you do not perform your religious duties in public so that people will see what you do. If you do these things publicly, you will not have any reward from your Father in heaven.

"So when you give something to a needy person, do not make a big show of it, as the hypocrites do in the houses of worship and on the streets. They do it so that people will praise them. I assure you, they have already been paid in full. But **when you help a needy person, do it in such a way that even your closest friend will not know about it**. Then it will be a private matter. And your Father, who sees what you do in private, will reward you."

Prayer

"When you pray, do not be like the hypocrites! They love to stand up and pray in the houses of worship and on the street corners, so that everyone will see them. I assure you, they have already been paid in full. But when you pray, go to your room, close the door, and pray to your Father, who is unseen. And your Father, who sees what you do in private, will reward you.

"**When you pray, do not use a lot of meaningless words,** as the pagans do, who think that their gods will hear them because their prayers are long. Do not be like them. Your Father already knows what you need before you ask him.

"If you forgive others the wrongs they have done to you, your Father in heaven will also forgive you. But if you do not forgive others, then your Father will not forgive the wrongs you have done."

Fasting

"And **when you fast, do not put on a sad face as the hypocrites do**. They neglect their appearance so that everyone will see that they are fasting. I assure you, they have already been paid in full. When you go without food, wash your face and comb your hair, so that others cannot know that you are fasting—only your Father, who is unseen, will know. And your Father, who sees what you do in private, will reward you."

God and Possessions

"No one can be a slave of two masters; he will hate one and love the other; he will be loyal to one and despise the other. You cannot serve both God and money.

"This is why **I tell you not to be worried about the food and drink you need in order to stay alive**, or about clothes for your body. After all isn't life worth more than food? And isn't the body worth more than clothes? Look at the birds: they do not sow seeds, gather a harvest and put it in barns; yet your Father in heaven takes care of them! Aren't you worth much more than birds? Can any of you live a bit longer by worrying about it?

"And why worry about clothes? Look how the wild flowers grow: they do not work or make clothes for themselves. But I tell you that not even King Solomon with all his wealth had clothes as beautiful as one of these flowers. It is God who clothes the wild grass—grass that is here today and gone tomorrow, burnt up in the oven. Won't he be all the more sure to clothe you? How little faith you have!

"So do not start worrying: 'Where will my food come from? or my drink? or my clothes?' These are the things the pagans are always concerned about. Your Father in heaven knows that you need all these things. Instead, be concerned above everything else with the Kingdom of God and with what he requires of you, and he will provide you with all these other things. So do not worry about tomorrow; it will have enough worries of its own. There is no need to add to the troubles each day brings."

Judging Others

"Do not judge others, so that God will not judge you, for God will judge you in the same way as you judge others, and he will apply to you the same rules you apply to others. Why, then, do you look at the speck in your brother's eye, and pay no attention to the log in your own eye? How dare you say to your brother, 'Please, let me take that speck out of your eye,' when you have a log in your own eye? You hypocrite! First take the log out of your own eye, and then you will be able to see clearly to take the speck out of your brother's eye.

"Do not give what is holy to dogs—they will only turn and attack you; Do not throw your pearls in front of pigs—they will only trample them underfoot."

Ask, Seek, Knock

"**Ask, and you will receive; seek, and you will find; knock, and the door will be opened to you**. For everyone who asks will receive, and anyone who seeks will find, and the door will be opened to him who knocks.

CHRIST'S SACRIFICE

Paul wrote to the Hebrews: "My Christian brothers, who also have been called by God! Think of Jesus, whom God sent to be the High Priest of the faith we profess. He was faithful to God, who chose him to do this work, just as Moses was faithful in his work in God's house.

"Let us hold firmiy to the faith we profess. For we have a great High Priest who has gone into the very presence of God—Jesus, the Son of God. Our High Priest is not one who cannot feel sympathy for our weaknesses. On the contrary, we have a High Priest who was tempted in every way that we are, but did not sin. Let us have confidence, then, and approach God's throne, where there is grace. There we will receive mercy and find grace to help us just when we need it."

Jesus Our High Priest

"We have such a High Priest, who sits at the right of the throne of the Divine Majesty in heaven. He serves as High Priest in the Most Holy Place.

"He went into heaven, where he now appears on our behalf in the presence of God. **The Jewish High Priest goes into the Most Holy Place every year with the blood**

of an animal. But Christ did not go in to offer himself many times, for then he would have had to suffer many times ever since the creation of the world. Instead, now when all ages of time are nearing the end, he has appeared once and for all, to remove sin through the sacrifice of himself. Everyone must die once, and after that be judged by God. In the same manner Christ also was offered in sacrifice once to take away the sins of many. He will appear a second time, not to deal with sin, but to save those who are waiting for him.

The Jewish Law is not a full and faithful model of the real things; it is only a faint outline of the good things to come. The same sacrifices are offered for ever, year after year. How can the Law, then, by means of these sacrifices make perfect the people who come to God.

"For the blood of bulls and goats can never take away sins."

"For this reason, when Christ was about to come into the world, he said to God:

'You do not want sacrifices and
offerings,
but you have prepared a body for me.
You are not pleased with animals burnt
whole on the altar
or with sacrifices to take away sins.
Then I said, **'Here I am,**
to do your will, O God,
just as it is written of me in the book
of the Law.'"

"So God does away with all the old sacrifices and puts the sacrifice of Christ in their place. Because Jesus Christ did what God wanted him to do, we are all purified from sin by the offering that he made of his own body once and for all.

"Christ offered one sacrifice for sins, an offering that is effective for ever, and then he sat down at the right-hand side of God. There he now waits until God puts his enemies as a footstool under his feet. With one sacrifice, then, he has made perfect for ever those who are purified from sin.

"And the Holy Spirit also gives us his witness. First he says, 'This is the covenant that I will make with them in the days to come,' says the Lord:

'I will put my laws in their hearts and write them on their minds.'

And **then he says, 'I will not remember their sins and evil deeds an longer."**

Let Us Come Near to God

"We have, then, my brothers, complete freedom to go into the Most Holy Place by means of the death of Jesus. He opened for us a new way, a living way, through the curtain—that is, through his own body; We have a great priest in charge of the house of God. So let us come near to God with a sincere heart and a sure faith, with hearts that have been purified from a guilty conscience and with bodies washed with clean water.

"There is no longer any sacrifice that will take away sins if we purposely go on sinning after the truth has been made known to us. Instead, all that is left is to wait in fear for the coming Judgement and the fierce fire which will destroy those who oppose God!"

❑ ❑ ❑

7.

Islam

God-given Social System

أفإين مات أو قتل انقلبتم على أعقابكم

ومن ينقلب على عقبيه فلن يضر الله شيئا

وسيجزي الله الشكرين ۝ (سوره آل عمران آيت ١٤٤)

٥ فبما رحمة من الله لنت لهم ولو كنت فظا

غليظ القلب لانفضوا من حولك فاعف عنهم

واستغفر لهم وشاورهم في الأمر فإذا عزمت فتوكل

على الله إن الله يحب المتوكلين ۝ (سوره آل عمران آيت ١٥٩)

٦ وما أرسلنك إلا رحمة للعلمين ۝ (سورة الانبياء آيت ١٠٧)

THE RELIGION OF EQUALITY, DUTIES AND PEACE

"In the name of Allah, the Compassionate, the Merciful. All praise is for Allah, the 'Rabb' of the Worlds. The Compassionate, the Merciful. Master of the Day of Judgment. O'Allah! You alone we worship and You alone we call on for help. O'Allah! Guide us to the right way. The way of those whom You have favoured; not of those who have earned Your wrath, or of those who have lost the way."

—*Al-Fathiha:* 1.1-7

Allah is one and the greatest of all. He is self sufficient master, whom all creatures need. He gave no birth nor was He born. He has given the life and will take it back one day. He is sustainer of all. He is maker of the whole universe. No one is His partner or His companion. None but Allah is worthy of worship. He is for ever and will remain for ever. He is omnipresent and nothing is out of His knowledge.

Islam is a religion which teaches total acceptance and submission to Allah - the Almighty. The word 'Islam' is derived from the Arabic verb 'Aslama' which means to accept, surrender or submit. The follower of Islam is known as 'Muslim'. All Muslims believe that 'none is worthy of worship but Allah; Muhammad (Sallallaahu Alaihi Wasallam) is the messenger of Allah.

Muslims demonstrate Islam by worshiping Allah, following His commands and strictly avoiding polytheism. Thus Islam is a monotheistic religion. Muslims believe in the doctrine that there is only one God that is Allah - the Almighty.

Monotheism has three aspects:

(*a*) Oneness of Allah: to believe that there is only one 'Ilah' (God) for the entire universe Who is its Creator, Organizer, Sustainer and Giver of Security, etc.

(*b*) Oneness of the worship of Allah: to believe that none has the right to be worshiped (e.g.—praying, invoking, asking for help, swearing, offering sacrifice, fasting, pilgrimage) but Allah.

(*c*) Oneness of the names and the qualities of Allah: to believe in the following;

√ We must not name or qualify Allah except by what He or His messenger (S.A.W) has named or qualified Him.

√ None can be named or qualified with the names or qualifications of Allah.

√ We must believe in all the qualities of Allah which Allah has stated in His book - The Holy Qur'an—and mentioned through His messengers.

Universe is defined as all existing things, including the earth and its creatures and all the heavenly bodies.

Qur'anic verses referring to the story of the **creation of earth**, mountains, seasons, skies and heavens are given below.

(*a*) "Ask them: "Do you really deny the One Who created the earth in two periods and do you set up rivals in worship with Him while He is the Rabb of the worlds. He set upon it mountains towering high above its surface, He bestowed blessings upon it and in four periods, provided it with sustenance according to the needs of all those who live in and ask for it. Then He turned towards the sky, which was but smoke. He said to it and to the earth: 'Come forward both of you, willingly or unwillingly,' and they submitted: 'We shall come willing'. So, from this creation, He formed the seven heavens in two periods and to each heaven He ordained its laws. He adorned the lowest heaven with brilliant lamps and made it secure. Such is the design of the All-Mighty, the All-Knowing." (Ha-Mim: 41.9-12)

(*b*) "Surely your Rabb is Allah Who created the heavens and the earth in six Yome (time periods) and is firmly established on the throne of authority. He makes the night cover the day and the day follows the night automatically. He created the sun, the moon and the stars; and made them subservient to His will. Take note: His is the creation, and His is the command. Blessed is Allah, the Rabb of the worlds! Call on your Rabb with humility and in private; for He does not love the transgressors." (AI-A'raf: 7.54-55)

Qur'anic verses referring to **Adam's creation** are as follows:

(*a*) "Note that occasion, when your Rabb said to the angels: I am going to place a vicegerent on earth. The angels said: "Will You place there one who will make mischief and shed blood while we sing Your praises and glorify Your name?" Allah said: "I know what you know not." (Al-Baqara: 2.30)

(*b*) "To Adam We said: Dwell with your wife in Paradise and eat anything you want from its bountiful food from wherever you wish, but do not approach this tree, or you shall both become transgressors." (AI-Baqara: 2.35)

(*c*) Shaitan vowed to mislead Adam and his descendants:

"Indeed We created you, then We fashioned you, then We asked the angels: Prostrate yourselves before Adam.

They all prostrated accordingly except Iblees (Shaitan) who did not join those who prostrated. Allah said: What prevented you from prostrating when he commanded you? He replied: I am better than he; you created me from fire and him from clay. Allah said: Get down from here. You have no right to brag here of your superiority. Get out; henceforth you are of the petty ones. Shaitan requested: "Give me respite till the Day of Resurrection." Allah said: "The respite you requested is hereby granted." Shaitan declared: "Since You let me deviate, now I will lie in ambush for mankind on Your right way. I will come upon them from the front, from the rear, from the right, and from the left, and You will not find most of them to be grateful." Allah said: "Get out from here, you despicable outcast; I will certainly fill hell with you and all of them who follow you."" (Al-A'raf: 7.11-18)

(*d*) Shaitan caused Adam to lose paradise:

"But Shaitan tempted them with the tree to disobey Allah's commandment and caused them to be expelled from Paradise, and We said: "Get out from here, some of you being enemies to others, and there is for you in the earth an abode and provisions for a specified period."" (Al-Baqara: 2.36)

(*e*) Need of Allah's revelations for guidance:

"Get out from here all of you," We said at the time of Adam's departure from Paradise. There will come to you a guidance from Me, those who accept and follow it shall have nothing to fear or to regret. But those who reject and defy Our revelations will be inmates of Hellfire wherein they shall live forever." (Al-Baqara: 2.38-39)

(*f*) "O Prophet, remind mankind about the incident when your Rabb brought into existence the offspring from the loins of Adam and his descendants (virtually each single individual of mankind) and made them testify about themselves. Allah asked them: "Am I not your Rabb?" They all replied: "Yes! We bear witness that You are." This

We did, lest you mankind should say on the Day of Resurrection: "We were not aware of this fact that You are our Rabb and that there will be a Day of Judgement."" (AI-A'raf: 7.172)

There is no **compulsion in Islam**:

(*a*) "There is no compulsion in religion. True guidance has been made clearly distinct from error. Therefore, whoever renounce 'Taghut' (forces of Shaitan) and believes in Allah has grasped the firm hand-hold that will never break. Allah, Whose hand-hold you have grasped, hears all and knows all." (AI-Baqara: 2.256)

(*b*) "If it had been the will of your Rabb that all the people of the world should be believers, all the people of the earth would have believed! Would you then compel mankind against their will to believe? It is not possible for anyone to believe except by the permission of Allah, and He throws filth on those who do not use their common sense. Say: "Look at whatever exists in the heavens and the earth." Signs and warnings do not benefit those people who do not believe. Now are they waiting for evil days like the ones that befell the people who passed away before them? Say: "Wait if you will; I too will wait with you." When such a time comes, We rescue Our Rasools and those who believe—this is Our way; it is but right that We rescue the believers." (Yunus: 10.99-103)

(*c*) "O people of the Book! Let us get together on what is common between us and you: that we shall worship none but Allah; that we shall not associate any partners with Him; that we shall not take from along ourselves any lords beside Allah." If they reject your invitation then tell them: "Bear witness that we are Muslim (who have surrendered to Allah)." (Al-i'Imran: 3.64)

Articles of Faith

The cardinal articles of faith in Islam are as follows:

1. To believe in the oneness of Allah. (Tauheed)
2. To believe in Allah's angels.
3. To believe in the holy books of Allah.
4. To believe in all His prophets and messengers.
5. To believe in the day of Doom, Resurrection and Judgement.
6. To believe in fate, good or bad.

Allah commands affirmation in the following:

(1) Oneness of Allah the almighty and his attributes (adjectives) by depth of the heart

All Muslims (followers of Islam) believe that "none is worthy of Worship but Allah; Muhammad (Sallallaahu Alaihi Wasallam) is the messenger of Allah." Muslims have fundamental faith in Imaan. The literal meaning of Imaan is to believe in someone's words and relying solely on his authority. In religious terms, it implies belief in the unseen and relying solely on the anthority of the messenger of Allah.

(*a*) "O believers! Believe in Allah, His Rasool and the Book which He has revealed to His Rasool and every Book which He previously revealed. He who denies Allah, His angels, His Books, His Rasools and the Laws has gone far astray." (An-Nisaa: 4.136)

(*b*) Allah's attributes and" Ayat-al-Kursi":

"Allah! There is no god but Him: the Living, the Eternal. He neither slumbers nor sleeps. To Him belongs all that is in the Heavens and the Earth. Who can intercede with Him without His permission? He knows what is before them and what is behind them. They cannot gain access to anything out of His knowledge except what He pleases. His throne is more vast than the heavens and the earth, and guarding of these both does not fatigue Him. He is the Exalted, the Supreme." (Al-Baqara: 2.255)

(*e*) Muhammad (pbuh) is the Prophet for the whole of mankind:

"O Muhammad, say: "O mankind! I am the Rasool of Allah towards all of you from He to whom belongs the kingdom of the heavens and the earth. There is no deity but Him. He brings to life and causes to die. Therefore, believe in Allah and His Rasool, the unlettered Prophet (Muhammad) who believes in Allah and His Word. Follow him so that you may be rightly guided."" (Al-A'raf: 7.158)

(2) Allah's angels (Peace be upon them)

Angels are called as 'malaika' in Arabic, 'malakh' in Hebrew, 'Angelos' in Greek while 'Farishte' in Persian and Urdu. Allah created angels which are quite different to mankind. They are spiritual creatures of Allah, made by Noor (light). **They do not have the capacity to think but simply obey the commands of Allah**. They are invisible to us but everything is visible to them. They do not have any gender, thus they do not marry nor have any offspring. They neither feel hungry nor sleepy as their bodies are immaterial but **they can resume any form by the command of Allah**. They have two or more wings without muscles and feathers unlike birds. They are assigned separate duties related to the heavenly bodies and the universe.

The Qur'anic verse referring to the creation of angels (P.B.D.T):

"Praise be to Allah, the Creator of the heavens and the earth Who appoint the angels having two, three and four pairs of wing."

There are four arch angels of Allah which are superior to others, which includes Jibraeel, Mikaeel, Izraeel and Israfeel. (P.B.D.T.)

(1) Jibraeel: His task is to bring Allah's messages, commands and books to the prophets. The message is called as Wahi (revelation). Jibraeel conveyed the Holy Qur'an to Hazrat Muhammad (S.A.W) bit by bit. He used to console and guide the prophets in their sorrows on behalf of Allah.

Qur'anic verse referring to the duties of Jibraeel (Gabriel):

"Surely this word (The Qur'an) is brought by the noble Messenger, possessor of power, having very high rank with the Throne (Allah), who is obeyed in heaven, and is trustworthy." (At-Takwir: 81.19-21)

(2) Mikaeel: His responsibilities include sending rains and provisions to Allah's all creatures. Countless angels work under him to control winds and all water bodies (e.g, mountains, oceans, lakes and rivers).

Qur'anic verse referring to the duties of Mikaeel:

(*a*) "And We send down from the sky Rain charged with blessing and We produce therewith Gardens and Grain for harvests." (Al-Qaf: 50.9)

(*b*) "Each person has been assigned guardian angels before him and behind him, who watch him by the command of Allah. The fact is that Allah never changes the condition of a people until they intend to change it themselves. If Allah wants to afflict a people with misfortune, none can ward it off, nor they can find any protector besides Him." (Ar-Ra'd: 13.11)

(3) Izraeel: His task is to draw souls from the bodies of all the living creatures. Innumerable angels coordinate under his supervision to draw souls of the righteous and evil-doers.

Qur'anic verses referring to the duties of Izraeel:

(*a*) "Say: 'The angel of death (Izra'il) assigned for you will carry off your souls and bring you back to Your Rabb.'" (As-Sajda: 32.11)

(*b*) "By those angels who violently pull out the souls of the wrongdoers, and those who gently draw out the souls of the righteous, and those who glide about swiftly through space, then speed headlong to carry out the commands of Allah, and those who regulate the affairs of the world!" (An-Nazia't: 79.1-5).

(4) Israfeel: His task is to blow the trumpet after which the universe will perish and then again at the time of resurrection.

Qur'anic verses referring to the duties of Israfeel:

(*a*) "On that Day, the Trumpet shall be sounded and shall come forth in multitude." (An-Nabaa: 78.18)

(*b*) "On that Day when the heavens shall burst asunder, with clouds and the angels will be sent down ranks after ranks." (Al-Furqan: 25.25)

(*c*) "The angels will stand all around and eight of them will be carrying the Throne of your Rabb above them." (Al-Haqqa: 69.17)

(*e*) "It is guarded by nineteen guards. We have appointed none but angels as wardens of the fire; and We have made their number a trial for the unbelievers, so that the People of the Book may be convinced and the faith of the true believers may be increased, and that no doubts will be left for the People of the Book and the believers, and that those in whose hearts there is a disease and the disbelievers may say: 'What could Allah mean by this parable?' Thus, Allah leaves to stray whom He wills and guides whom He pleases. No one knows the forces of your Rabb except Himself, and this (Qur'an) is nothing but a reminder to mankind." (Al-Muddaththir: 74.30-31)

The Holy Qur'an

(*i*) The Qur'an was revealed during the month of Ramazaan:

"Surely We have revealed this (Qur'an) in the night of Qadr. And what will make you understand, what the night of Qadr is! The night of Qadr is better than one thousand months. The angels and the Spirit (Gabriel) come down with every decree, by the leave of their Rabb, that night is the night of Peace, till the break of dawn!" (Al-Qadr: 97.1-5)

(*ii*) Al-Qur'an is revealed in the Arabic language:

"We have revealed this Qur'an in the Arabic language so that you (Arabs) may understand. We relate to you the best of stories through this Qur'an by Our revelation to you (O Muhammad), though before this you were one of those who did not know." (Yusuf: 12.2-3)

(*iii*) "On that Day you shall see that every nursing mother will forget her nursing-babe and every pregnant female wIll miscarry, and you will see people as if they are intoxicated, though they will not be drunk: such will be the horror of Allah's chastisement." (Al-Sajda: 32.2

(*iv*) This Quran is the revelation of Allah:

"This Qur'an is not such as could be produced by anyone other than Allah; in fact it is the cor.firmation ot prior revelations (Psalms, Torah, and Gospel) and fully explains the Holy Book (prior scriptures); there is no doubt in this fact that it is (revealed) from the Rabb of the Worlds. Do they say: 'He (the Prophet) has forged it?' Tell them: 'If what you say be true; then produce one Surah like this, you may even call to your aid anyone you want other than Allah.' Nay! They do not believe that which they cannot grasp, for they have not yet seen its prophecy fulfilled. The same way those who passed before them disbelieved. But see what was the end of the wrongdoers! Of these people there are some who will believe in it and some will not; and your Rabb best knows the troublemakers." (Yunus: 10.37-40)

(*v*) Al-Qur'an is a guide for those who are God-conscious:

"This is The Book in which there is no doubt. (Since its Author, Allah, the Creator of this universe, possesses complete knowledge, there is no room for doubt about its contents.) It is a guide for those who are God-conscious, who believe in the Unseen, who establish Salah (five regular daily prayers) and spend in charity out of what We have provided for their sustenance; who believe in this Revelation (The Qur'an) which is sent to you (O Muhammad) and the Revelations which were sent before you (Torah, Psalms, Gospel...) and firmly believe in the Hereafter. They are on True Guidance from their Rabb and they are the ones who will attain salvation." (Al-Baqara: 2.2-5)

(*vi*) "This Qur'an is not such as could be produced by anyone other than Allah; in fact it is the confirmation of prior revelations (Psalms, Torah, and Gospel) and fully explains the Holy Book (prior scriptures); there is no doubt in this fact that it is (revealed) from the Rabb of the Worlds." (Yunus: 10.37)

(*vii*) Al-Qur'an is a mercy, blessing, and cure for the problems of mankind: "O mankind! There has come to you an instruction from your Rabb, a cure for whatever (disease) is in your hearts, a guidance and a blessing for the true believers. Say: 'It is the grace and mercy of Allah (that He has sent this Qur'an), so let the people rejoice over it, for it is better than (the worldly riches) they are collecting.' O Prophet, ask them: "Have you ever considered that out of the sustenance which Allah has given you, I have made some things Halal (lawful) and others Haram (unlawful)? Ask them: 'Did Allah permit you to do so, or do you ascribe a false thing to Allah?'"

Prophets (Anbiyaas) and Messengers (Rasools) (Peace be upon them)

Allah has sent His prophets and messengers to show the path of religion to all the people in different countries at different times. More than a lakh of messengers were sent among which the first was Adam (A.S.) - the father of mankind and the last was Muhammad (S.A.W.).

"Allah chooses His messengers from among the angels and from among the human beings, for surely Allah is All-Hearing, All-Seeing." (Al-Hajj: 22.75)

(*a*) Every nation was sent a Rasool for their guidance:

"Every nation was sent a Rasool. Once their Rasool came, judgement was passed between them with all fairness and they were not wronged in the least. They ask: 'When will this promise be fulfilled, tell us if what you say be true?' Say: 'I have no control over any harm or benefit to myself, except what Allah wills. For every nation there is a deadline: when their deadline comes, it can neither be delayed for even a moment, nor it can be advanced.' Say: 'Have you ever considered that if his scourge fall upon you by night or by day you can do nothing to avert it? What then is there that the criminals wish to hasten? Would you believe it when it actually overtakes you? Then you would beg it to be removed although it had been your own wish to hurry it on.' Then it will be said to the wrongdoers: 'Taste the everlasting punishment! Should you not be rewarded according to your deeds?'" (Yunus: 10.47-52)

(*b*) All Rasools were sent with the same Message, there is no god but Allah, so worship Him alone:

"The fact is that to every Rasool whom We sent before you, We revealed the same Message: 'There is no god but Me, so worship Me Alone.' Inspite of receiving that message, they still say: 'The Beneficent (Allah) has offspring!' Glory be to Him! The angels are but His honored servants. They do not precede Him in speaking and they act according to His commandment. He knows what is before them and what is behind them and they do not intercede except for the one whom He approves, and for fear of Him they tremble. If any of them were to say: 'I am also a deity besides Him,' We would send him to hell, thus shall We reward the wrongdoers." (Al-Anbiyaa: 21.25-29).

Advent of Prophet Muhammad (S.A.W.) was described in Torah and Gospel:

(*a*) "Or lest you say: 'If the Book had been revealed to us, we could have followed its guidance better than them,' a veritable sign has now come to you from your Rabb as a guidance and mercy. Who then is more unjust than the one who denies the revelations of Allah and turns away from them? Very soon those who turn away from Our revelations will face dreadful punishment for their aversion.'" (Al-An'am: 6.157)

(*b*) Allah appointed Muhammad (S.A.W.) as a Rasool:

"All that is in the heavens and earth declares the glory of Allah, the King, the Holy, the Mighty, the Wise. It is He Who has raised among the unlettered people a Rasool of their own, who recites to them His revelations, purifies them, and teaches them were Book and Wisdom, though prior to this they were in gross error, he is also sent for others of them who have not yet joined them (become Muslims). He is the Mighty, the Wise. That is the grace of Allah, which He bestows on whom He pleases. Allah is the Lord of mighty grace." (Al-Jamu'a: 62.1-4)

(*c*) The Life of Rasoolallah (Muhammad S.A.W.) is the best Model:

"You have indeed, in the life of Rasool-Allah, the 'Best Model' for him whose hope is in Allah and the Day of the Hereafter, and who engages himself much in the remembrance of Allah. When the true believers saw the confederate forces they said: 'This is what Allah and His Rasool had promised us: Allah and his Rasool were absolutely true.' This increased them all the more in their faith and their zeal in obedience. Among the believers there are men who have been true to their covenant with Allah: of them he is also sent for others of them who some have completed their vow through sacrificing their lives, and some others are waiting for it, and have not changed their determination in the least. All this happens so that Allah may reward the truthful for their truth and punish the hypocrites or accept their repentance if He wills: for Allah is Forgiving and Merciful." (Al-Ahzab: 33.21-24).

To believe in the day of Doom, Resurrection and Judgement.

"As for the doomsday, it shall come, when the Trumpet will be blown with a single blast and the earth with all its mountains will be lifted up and crushed into pieces with a single stroke. On that day the Great Event will come to pass, heaven shall split asunder, and the day shall seem flimsy. **The angels will stand all around and eight of them will be carrying the Throne of your Rabb above them**. That shall be the day when you will be brought before your Rabb, and none of your secrets shall remain hidden." (Al-Haqqa: 69.13-18)

(1) Everyone has to die: "Every soul shall taste death. You shall receive your full reward for everything which you have striven for, on the Day of Resurrection. Whoever is spared from the fire and is admitted into paradise will have attained the objective of this worldly life; for the life of this world is nothing but an illusory enjoyment." (Al-Imran: 3.185)

(2) There is no escape from death: "Have you reflected on the case of thousands of people (Israelites) who fled their homes for fear of death? Allah said to them: "Die" (gave them death). Then He gave them life again. Surely Allah is bountiful to mankind, but most of the people are ungrateful." (Al-Baqara: 2.243)

There is a life after death: "If you could witness the scene, when they will be made to stand before the hellfire' they will say: 'We wish we could return to earthly life again; then we would not deny the revelations of our Rabb, and we would join the believers!' In fact, they will say this because they had come to know the reality which they were concealing before, As a matter of fact even if they be sent back, they would certainly repeat the same things which they had been forbidden to do. Indeed they are liars. Today they say: 'There is no other life except the life on this earth and we shall never be raised to life again.' If you could witness the scene when they will be brought before their Rabb; He will ask, 'Is this not a reality?' They will say: 'Yes, our Rabb, this is the reality.' He will order: 'Well, then taste the punishment for denying this reality.'" (Al-An'am: 6.27-30)

On the Day of Judgement the Book of Deeds will be laid open and justice will be done with all fairness: "Therefore, worship Allah and be among His thankful servants. They have not recognized the worth of Allah as His worth should be recognized. On the Day of Resurrection the whole earth shall be in His grasp and all the heavens shall be rolled up in His right hand. Glory be to Him! Exalted be He above what thy associate with Him. The Trumpet shall be blown, and all that is in the heavens and the earth shall swoon except those whom Allah will please to exempt. Then the Trumpet will be blown for the second time and behold! They shall all stand up, looking around. The earth will be shining with the light of her Rabb, the Book of record will be laid open, the Prophets and other witnesses will be brought in, and justice shall be done between people with all fairness: none shall be wronged. Every soul will be paid in full according to its deeds, for He knows fully well as to what they did." (Az-Zumar: 39.66-70)

The day of judgement will be equal to fifty thousand years: "A questioner asked you about the punishment which is bound to happen. It is for the disbelievers and there is none to avert it. It will come from Allah, the Owner of the Ways of Ascent. The angels and the Spirit ascend to Him in a Day the measure of which is fifty thousand years. Therefore, endure with graceful patience. They see it (Day of Judgement) to be far-off: but We see it quite near. On that Day, the sky shall become like molten brass and the mountains like tufts of wool; even a close friend will not ask of his friend, though they will see each other. To save himself from the punishment of that Day, the culprit (disbeliever) will wish to give his children, his wife, his brother, his relatives—who gave him shelter—and all that is in the earth, in ransom to save himself. By no means! It will be the fire of hell, eager to pluck out his skull, it will be calling all those who try to escape and turn their back, who collected wealth and withheld it. Indeed, man has been created impatient, when evil befalls him, he becomes despondent; but when blessed with good fortune, he becomes stingy; with the exception of those who offer the Salah (prayer), remain steadfast in their Salah, set aside a due share in their wealth for the beggars and the deprived, accept the truth of the Day of Judgement, dread the punisment of their Rabb—for none is secure from the punishment of their Rabb—and guard their private parts, except from their wives and those whom their right hands possess, for in their case they are not blameworthy. As for those who seek to go beyond this, they are transgressors. Those who keep their trusts and honor their promises, who stand firm in their testimonies and strictly guard their Salah. It is they who shall live with honor in paradise." (Al-Ma'arij: 70.1-35)

The day of judgement will be very difficult especially for those who deny Allah's revelations and oppose His cause:

"When the Trumpet will be sounded, that Day will be a very difficult Day, not easy for the disbelievers. Leave Me and the one (Walid bin Mughirah, a staunch opponent of the Prophet) whom I created, alone. I gave him abundant resources, thriving sons, and made his life smooth and comfortable. Yet he hopes that I shall give him more. By no means! Because he has stubbornly denied Our revelations. Soon I shall make him suffer mounting calamities, surely he pondered and devised a plot. May he perish, how he plotted! Again, may he perish, how he plotted! He looked around, frowned and scowled, then he turned his back in scornful pride and said: 'This is nothing but counterfeited magic, this is nothing but the word of a human being.' Soon I shall cast him into Saqar. What will make you understand, what Saqar is? It is burning fire which leaves nothing and spares none. It shrivels human flesh. It is guarded by nineteen guards. We have appointed none but angels as wardens of the fire; and We have made their number a trial for the unbelievers, so that the People of the Book may be convinced and the faith of the true believers may be increased, and that no doubts will be left for the People of the Book and the believers, and that those in whose hearts there is a disease and the disbelievers may say: 'What could Allah mean by this parable?' Thus, Allah leaves to stray whom He wills and guides whom He pleases. Noone knows the forces of your Rabb except Himself, and this (Qur'an) is nothing but a reminder to mankind." (Al-Muddaththir: 74.8-31)

A scene from the Day of judgement: " They ask you as to what will happen to the mountains. Tell them: 'My Rabb will crush and scatter them like fine dust. He will turn earth into a plain leveled ground, wherein you will not see neither any curve nor crease.—On that Day the people will follow the call of the Caller, no one will dare show any crookedness; there voices hushed before the Beneficent (Allah), and you shall hear nothing but the sound of the marching feet. On that Day, no intercession will avail except the one to whom the Beneficent (Allah) shall grant permission and would like to give him a hearing. He knows what is before them and what is behind them while they do not encompass any knowledge about Him. Their faces shall be humbled before the Ever-living, the Ever-existent (Allah). The one who is carrying the burden of iniquity will be doomed; but the one who is a believer and does good deeds shall fear no tyranny or injustice." (Ta-ha: 20.105-112).

Reward for the right-hand group:

(*i*) "Those of the right hand—happy shall be those on the right hand! They shall be among the thornless trees, clusters of bananas, extended thick shades, constantly flowing water, abundant fruits of unforbidden never ending supply, and will be reclining on high raised couches. We shall create their wives of special creation and make them virgins beloved by nature, equal in age, for those of the right hand." (Al-Waqi'a: 56.27-38)

***(ii)* Food and entertainment for the righteous in paradise:** "As for the righteous, they will be in a secure place; among gardens and springs, dressed in fine silk and rich brocade, sitting face to face. Such shall be their place! And We shall wed them to Hourin-Ayn (damsels with beautiful, big and lustrous eyes). There, in full peace, they shall call for every kind of fruit; and after having prior death in the world, they shall taste death no more; and He (Allah) will protect them from the torment of hell as a grace from your Rabb, and that will be the supreme achievement. Surely We have made this Qur'an easy by revealing in your own language so that they may take heed. If they do not accept the admonition then wait, surely they too are waiting." (Al-Dukhan: 44.51-59)

***(i)* Punishment for the left-hand group:** "Many of them will be from the former and many from the later generations. As for those of the left hand—how unfortunate will be the people of the left hand! They will be in the midst of scorching winds and in boiling water: in the shade of a pitch-black smoke, neither cool nor refreshing. For they lived in comfort before meeting this fate. They persisted in heinous sins and used to say: "When we are dead and turned to dust and bones, shall we then be raised to life again? And our forefathers, too?" Tell them: "Surely those of old and those of present age shall certainly be brought together on an appointed time of a known Day. Then, "O the mistaken rejecters, you shall eat of the Zaqqum tree, and fill your bellies with it; and drink on top of it scalding water; yet you shall drink it like a thirsty camel." Such will be their entertainment on the Day of Reckoning."(Al-Waqi'a: 56.39-56)

***(ii)* Food and drink for the sinners in hell:** "Surely the Zaqqum tree shall be the food of the sinners; it will be like the drags of oil which shall boil in the belly like the boiling of scalding water. A voice will be heard: "Seize him and drag him into the depth of the hell, then pour scalding water over his head, then the voice will say: Taste it; you were such a powerful noble! This is the punishment which you use to doubt."" (Al-Dukhan: 44.43-50)

Individual's fate—good or bad: Good or bad events are due to individual's fate; planned by the Allah to judge the action of the individual in particular circumstances.

Prosperity in this world is not a reward but a respite: "We did send Rasools before you to other nations and afflicted them with suffering and adversities so that they might learn humility. Why did they not humble themselves when the sufferings overtook them? On the contrary, their hearts became hardened and Shaitan made their sinful acts seem fair to them. When they neglected the warning they had received, then, instead of punishment, We opened the gates of every kind of prosperity for them; but just as they were rejoicing in what they were given, We suddenly seized them; lo! They were plunged into despair! Thus We cut off the roots of the wrongdoers. All praises are due to Allah the Rabb of the worlds." (Al-An'am: 642-45).

It is Allah Who gives daughters and sons as He pleases: "To Allah belongs the kingdom of the heavens and the earth. He creates whatever He pleases. He gives daughters to whom He pleases and gives sons to whom He pleases. To some He gives both sons and daughters, and makes barren whom He will; surely He is All- knowledgeable, All-Powerful." (Ash-Shura: 42.49-50)

Five Fundamentals of Islam

The Fundamental Principles of Islam are five in number:

1. **Imaan:** The declaration of 'La ilaha illallah Muhammadur-rasoolullah', which means that there is no God but Allah and Muhammad (S.A.W.) is His prophet.
2. **Salaat:** The observance of obligatory prayers five times a day.
3. **Saum:** The observation of fast during the day time in the month of Ramazaan.
4. **Zakaat:** Distribution of Zakaat (Islamic alms-fee) by rich people among the deserving, amounting to 1/40th in one's possession for a complete year.
5. **Hajj:** The performance of Hajj (pilgrimage) to Mecca at least once in a life time, if circumstances permit.

(1) Imaan (Faith in Allah)

(*a*) Affirmation by heart in Kalemah. To believe that 'none is Worthy of worship but Allah; Mohammad (S.A.W.) is the messenger of Allah'.

"In the name of Allah, the Compassionate, the Merciful. All praise is for Allah, the 'Rabb' of the Worlds. The Compassionate, the Merciful. Master of the Day of Judgement." (Al-Fathiha: 1.1-4).

(*b*) "Allah has the most excellent names (over ninety-nine attributes); call on Him by them; and shun those people who use profanity in His names, such people shall be requited for their misdeeds." (Al-A'raf: 7.180)

(*c*) **Fifteen exclusive attributes of Allah:** "Allah is He, besides Whom there is no god, the Knower of the unseen and the seen. He is the Compassionate, the Merciful. Allah is He, besides Whom there is no god, the King, the Holy, the Giver of peace, the Granter of security, the Guardian, the Almighty, the Irresistible,1he Supreme: Glory be to Allah! He is far above the shirk they commit (by associating other gods with Him). He is Allah, the Creator, the Evolver, the Modeler. His are the most beautiful names. All that is in the heavens and the earth declares His glory, and He is the All-Mighty, the All-Wise." (Al-Hashr: 59.22-24)

(*d*) **Live Islam, die as a Muslim, and be not divided among yourselves:** "O believers! Fear Allah as He should be feared and die not but as true Muslims. All together hold fast the rope of Allah (Faith of Islam) and be not divided among yourselves. Remember Allah's favors upon you when you were enemies; He united your hearts, so by His favor you become brethren; you were at the brink of the fiery pit and He saved you from it. Thus Allah makes His revelation clear to you, so that you may be rightly guided." (Al-i'Imran: 3.102-103)

(2) Salaat (Namaaz)

(*a*) **Order for Wuzu (ablution) and Permission of Tayammum:** "O believers! When you rise up for Salaah (prayer), wash your faces and your hands as far as the elbows, wipe your heads with wet hands and wash your feet to the ankles. If you had an emission of semen, then take a full bath. However, if you are sick or on a journey or you have used the toilet or you had intercourse with your women (your wife) and you do not find any water then resort to Tayammum—find clean soil and rub your faces and hands with it. Allah does not wish to burden you; He only wishes to purify you and to perfect His favor upon you, so that you may be thankful." (Al-Maida: 5.6)

(*b*) **Five times daily Salaat (prayers) and extra prayer called Tahajjud for the Holy Prophet (S.A.W.) and Al-Quran is a healing and mercy for the believers:**

(*i*) "Establish Salah from the decline of the sun till the darkness of the night (Zuhr, Asr, Maghrib and Isha) and read at Fajr (dawn); for the reading at Fajr is witnessed (by the angels). During a part of the night, pray Tahajjud, an additional prayer for you (O Muhammad), very soon your Rabb may exalt you to 'Maqam-e-Mahmood' (a station of great glory)." (Al-Israa: 17.78-79)

(*ii*) "Therefore be patient with what they say. Glorify your Rabb with His praise before sunrise and before sunset, glorify Him during the hours of the night as well as at the ends of the day, so that you may find satisfaction." (Ta-ha: 20.130)

(*iii*) "Therefore, glorify Allah in the evening and in the morning—all praise is due to Him in the heavens and the earth—so glorify Him in the late afternoon and when the day begins to decline." (Ar-Rum: 30.17-18)

(*iv*) "Therefore, O Prophet, bear with them in patience whatever they say, and keep on glorifying your Rabb before sunrise and before sunset. And glorify Him during a part of the night and after the prostration (prayers)." (Qaf: 50.39-40)

(*v*) "Stand in prayers at night, but not the whole night, half of it or a little less, or a little more; and recite the Qur'an with measured tone." (Al-Muzzammil: 73.2-4).

(3) Saum (Roza/Fasting):

Observance of one month's compulsory fasting during day by adults.

(*a*) **Obligation of Fasting:** "O believers! Fasting is prescribed for you as it was prescribed for those before you so that you may learn self-restraint. Fast the prescribed number of days; except if any of you is ill or on a journey, let him fast a similar number of days later. For those who cannot endure it for medical reasons, there is a ransom: the feeding of one poor person for each missed day. But if he feeds more of his own free will, it is better for him. However, if you truly understand the rationale of fasting, it is better for you to fast." (Al-Baqara: 2.183-184).

(*b*) Revelation of the Quran and fasting in the month of Ramazaan: "It is the month of Ramazaan in which the Qur'an was revealed, a guidance for mankind with clear teachings showing the right way and a criterion of truth and falsehood. Therefore, anyone of you who witnesses that month should fast therein, and whoever is ill or upon a journey shall fast a similar number of days later on. Allah intends your well-being and does not want to put you to hardship. He wants you to complete the prescribed period so that you should glorify His Greatness and render thanks to Him for giving you guidance." (Al-Baqara: 2.185).

(*d*) Nights of the Fasting month and Timings of fasting: "It is made lawful for you to approach your wives during the night of the fast; they are an apparel for you and you for them. Allah knows that you were committing dishonesty to your souls. So He has relented towards you and pardoned you. Now, you may approach your wives and seek what Allah has written for you. Eat and drink until the white thread of dawn appears to you distinct from the black thread of night, then complete your fast till nightfall. Do not approach your wives during I'htikaf (retreat in the mosques in last ten days of Ramazaan). These are the limits set by Allah do not ever violate them. Thus Allah makes His revelations clear to mankind so that they may guard themselves against evil." (Al-Baqara: 2.187)

(4) Zakaat:

The word Zakaat covers two meanings. The first relates to purification—that is, purification by means of Zakaat from sins and bad qualities such as greed. The second meaning relates to growth and increase—that is, the giving of Zakaat results in growth and increase in our wealth. Both meanings are referred to in the following verse of the Qur'an:

"Take Sadaqat (this commanded Sadaqat means Zakat-ul-Mall) from their wealth, so that they may thereby be cleansed and purified, and pray for them; for your prayer will give them comfort. Allah hears all and knows all." (At-Tauba: 9.103)

In other words, it's said to be **distribution of compulsory charity among the deserving poor by wealthy people amounting to 1/40th in once possession for a complete year**. Assets that have potential of growth are subject to Zakaat which may be broadly classified as follows;

(*a*) Gold, silver and money.

(*b*) Stock-in-trade.

(*c*) Livestock (goats, sheeps, cows and camels, etc).

(*d*) Agricultural produce.

The agreed amount of Zakaat payable is two and a half percent of;

(*a*) The value of gold and silver if equal to Nisaab (minimum wealth) in weight.

(*b*) Trading stock or its value at the time of obligation of payment of Zakaat, if the stock is equal to Nisaab.

(*c*) Cash on hand if equal to Nisaab.

Qur'anic verses referring to pay Zakaat:

(*a*) "Yet they were commanded nothing but to worship Allah, with their sincere devotion to Him, being True in their faith; to establish Salaah (prayers); and to pay Zakaat (poor-due); and that is the infallible true Religion." (Al-Baiyina: 98.5)

(*b*) "Who will loan to Allah a beautiful loan which Allah will increase manifold? Allah alone can decrease and increase wealth, and to Him you all shall return." (Al-Baqara: 2.245).

Who is eligible for Zakaat?

(*a*) "They ask you what they should spend in charity. Say: 'Whatever you spend with a good heart, give it to parents, relatives, orphans, the helpless, and travelers in need.

Whatever good you do, Allah is aware of it.' (Al-Baqara: 2.215).

(*b*) "O believers, give what is due to your relatives, the needy and the traveler in need. That is best for those who seek the pleasure of Allah and it is they who will attain felicity." (Ar-Rum: 30.38).

(5) Hajj (Pilgrimage to Mecca):

Hajj is a devotional act of pilgrimage performed from the 8th to 12th of the month 'zil-hijja' (12th month of Islamic calendar). All the pilgrims gather in Mecca. They perform the Tawaaf-e-Kaa'ba (seven rounds of Kaa'ba), perform special prayers at Muqam-e-Ibrahim (A.S.). Then they go to perform 'Saee' which is walking between two hills, Safa and Manvah, seven times. Thereafter they go to drink Zam-Zam (holy water). They then go to Mina (which is a few kilometers away from the Kaa'ba) on the 8th of zil-hijja, and then on the 9th, they assemble in the field of Arafaat and pray there. Pilgrims pass the 9th zil-hijja's night at Muzdalfa (another place nearby); they collect pebbles and return back to Mina on 10th morning. They hurl the pebbles on 1st Shaitaan (1st pillar—the symbol of devil), thereafter they perfom the Qur'baani (sacrificing goat or sheep or camet' etc) and celebrate Eid-uz-Zuha festival. Then again on 11th zil-hijja, the pilgrims hurl stones on the 2nd and 3rd Shaitaans (2nd and 3rd pillar). Then on 12th they go for the Tawaaf-e- Ziarat to Mecca. Thus all the five days are for prayers. Thereafter the pilgrims go to Madina, stay there for eight days and perform 40 (8 × 5) farz Salaats at Masjid-e-Nabvi and pay respects to Muhammad's (S.A.W.) grave. Some pilgrims go to Madina first and thereafter to Mecca to perform Hajj so as to accommodate the flow of lakhs of pilgrims visiting for Hajj.

Performance of Hajj once in a life-time is compulsory, if circumstances permit to the wealthy people; that is—if they are in a position both physically and materially to undertake the journey to Mecca and make sufficient provisions for their dependents in their absence.

Importance of the Kaa'ba:

(*a*) "Undoubtedly the first House for the worship of Allah ever built for mankind is the one at Bakka (Makkah), a blessed site and a guidance for all the worlds. In it are clear signs and the Station of Ibrahim (Abraham) where he used to worship. Whoever enters it is safe. Performance of Hajj (pilgrimage) to this House is a duty to Allah for all who can afford the journey to it; and the one who disobeys this commandment should know that Allah is Self-sufficient, beyond the need of anyone from the worlds," (Al-i'Imran: 3.96-97)

(*d*) **Umrah** (pilgrimage to Makkah): "Complete the Hajj (obligatory pilgrimage to Makkah) and the Umrah (optional visit to Makkah) for the sake of Allah. If you are prevented from proceeding then send such offering for sacrifice as you can afford and do not shave your head until the offerings have reached their destination. But if any of you is ill or has an ailment in his scalp which necessitates shaving, he must pay ransom either by fasting or feeding the poor or offering a sacrifice. If in peacetime anyone wants to take the advantage of performing Umrah and Hajj together, he should make an offering which he can afford; but if he lacks the means, let him fast three days during the Hajj and seven days on his return making ten days in all. Thus order is for the one whose household is not in the precincts of the Sacred Mosque.

"Fear Allah and know that Allah is strict in retribution. Hajj is in the well known months. He who undertakes to perform it must abstain from husband-wife relationship, obscene language, and wrangling during Hajj. Whatever good you do, Allah knows it. Take necessary provisions with you for the journey, and piety is the best provision of all. Fear Me, O people endowed with understanding. There is no blame on you if you seek the bounty of your Rabb during this journey. When you return from Arafaat (stop at Muzdalitah and) praise Allah near Mash'ar-il-Haram. Praise Him as He has guided you, for before this you were from the people who had lost the Right Way.

"Then return from where the others return and ask Allah's forgiveness; surely Allah is Forgiving, Merciful. When you have fulfilled your sacred duties, praise Allah as you used to praise your forefathers or with deeper reverence. There are some who say: 'Our Rabb! Give us abundance in this world.' Such people will not have any share in the hereafter. Celebrate the praises of Allah during these appointed days. If anyone hastens to leave Mina after two days or stays there a day longer there is no blame on him provided he spends these days in piety. Fear Allah and remember that you will surely be gathered before Him." (Al-Baqara: 2.196-203)

Rights of People (Haquooqul Ibaad)

Every individual has to attend to the rights of parents, relatives, neighbours, friends and all other creatures. They are also supposed to pass on the same to fellow Muslims in particular and others in general.

Those who treat their parents with kindness shall be rewarded and those who rebuke their parents shall be punished:

"We have enjoined man concerning his parents—his mother carries him in her womb while suffering weakness upon weakness and then weans him for two years. That's why We commanded him: 'Give thanks to Me and to your parents, and keep in mind that, to Me is your final goal.. If they argue with you to commit shirk, of which you have no knowledge, then do not obey them; however you should still treat them kindly in this world, but follow the way of that individual who has turned to Me. After all, to Me is your return; then I will inform you about the reality of all that you have done.'" (Luqman: 31.14-15)

Stand firm for justice:

"We said: 'O Dawood! We have made you a vicegerent on the earth, so rule among the people with justice and do not follow your own desires lest they mislead you from the Way of Allah. As for those who go astray from the Way of Allah, they shall surely have a severe Punishment because of forgetting the Day of Reckoning.'" (Sad: 38.26)

Islam has streamlined the principles for the professionals engaged in households, business communities, cultivators, factories, science and technology. Islamic society is, thus based upon righteousness and mutual help:

"Cooperate with one another in righteousness and piety, and do not cooperate in sin and transgression" (AI-Maida: 5.2)

Islamic society has enunciated many rules like payment by installment allowed to the debtor, if he is in strained circumstances based on the Qur'anic command:

"If the debtor is in a difficulty, grant him time till it is easy for him to repay; but if you waive the sum by way of charity it will be better for you, if you understand it." (Al-Baqara: 2.280)

Prohibition of usury (includes interest also):

(a) "Those who devour usury will not stand except as one whom the Evil One by his touch hath driven to madness. That is because they say: 'Those who live on usury will not rise up before Allah except like those who are driven to madness by the touch of Shaitan. That is because they claim: Trading is no different than usury, but Allah has made trading lawful and usury unlawful. He who has received the admonition from his Rabb and has mended his way may keep his previous gains; Allah will be his judge. Those who turn back (repeat this crime), they shall be the inmates of hellfire wherein they will live for ever. Allah has laid His curse on usury and blessed charity to prosper. Allah does not love any ungrateful sinner." (Al-Baqara: 2.275-276).

Concepts of Banking in Islam:

A developed system of banking can be had under Islamic law, in consonance with the spirit of Islam. The interest-free economy practiced in the early days of Islam is neither capitalistic nor communistic, yet it has the good features of both. It can create a healthy society which blossomed in the past and in which there was no accumulation of wealth in a few hands, no hoarding and no profiteering. Based on the principle of 'neither do harm, nor be harmed', it worked well and guaranteed to the poor their sustenance. Every citizen was provided with means of livelihood, peace and prosperity. This was due to the fact that interest was eliminated from the society for all.

Mankind was of one faith, and God sent prophets bearing good things, and denouncing threats; and sent down with them the scripture in truth, that it might judge between men of that concerning which they disagreed: and none disagreed concerning it, execpt those to whom the same scriptures were delivered, after the declarations of God's will had come unto them, out of envy among themselves. And God directed those who believed, to that truth concerning which they disagreed, by his will: for God directeth whom he pleaseth into the right way. Did ye think ye should enter paradise, when as yet no such thing had happened unto you, as hath happened unto those who have been before you? They suffered calamity and tribulation, and were afflicted; so that the apostle, and they who believed with him said, When will the help of God come? Is not the help of God nigh? They will ask thee what they shall bestow is alms. Answer: The good which ye bestow, let it be given to parents, and kindred, and orphans, and the poor and the stranger. Whatsoever good ye do, God knoweth it.

SELECTION FROM THE HOLY QUR'AN

WOMEN

Marry not women who are idolaters, until they believe; verify a maid-servant who believeth is better than an idolatress, although she please you more. And give not women who believe in marriage to the idolaters, until they believel for verily, a servant who is a true believer, is better than an idolater, though he please you more. They invite into hell fire, but God inviteth unto paradise and pardon through his will, and declareth his signs unto men, that they may remember.

They will ask thee also concerning the courses of women: Answer, They are a pollution: therefore separate yourselves from women in their courses, and go not near them until they be cleansed. But when they are cleansed, go in unto them as God hath commanded you, for God loveth those who repent, and loveth those who are clean. Your wives are your tillage; go in therefore unto your tillage in what manner soever ye will: and do first some act that may be profitable unto your souls; and fear God, and know that ye must meet him; and bear good tidings unto the faithful.

They who vow to abstain their wives, are allowed to wait four months: but if they go back from their vow, verily

God is gracious and merciful; and if they resolve on a diyorce, God is he who heareth and knoweth. The women who are divorced shall wait concerning themselves until they have their courses thrice, and it shall not be lawful for them to conceal that which God hath created in their wombs, if they believe in God and the last day and their husbands will act more justly bring them back at this time, if they desire a reconcillation. The women ought also to behave towards their husbands in like manner as their husbands should behave towards them, according to what is just: but the men ought to have a superiority over them. God is mighty and wise. Ye may divorce your wives twice: and then either retain them with humanity or dismiss them with kindness, but it is not lawful for you to take away anything of what ye have given them, unless both fear that he cannot observe the ordinances of God. And if ye fear that they cannot observe the ordinances of God, it shall be no crime in either of them on account of that for which the life shall redeem herself. These are the ordinances of God; therefore transgress them not; for whoever transgresseth the ordinances of God, they are unjust doers.

But if the husband divorce her a third time, she shall not be lawful for him again, until she marry another husband. But if he also divorce her, it shall be no crime in them, if they return to each other, if they think they can observe the ordinances of God; and these are the ordinances of God: he declareth them to people of understanding. But when ye divorce women, and they have fulfilled their prescribed time, either retain them with humanity, or dismiss them with kindness; and retain them not by violence, so that ye transgress; for he who doth this, surely injureth his own soul. And make not the signs of God a jest: but remember God's favor towards you, and that he hath sent down unto you the book of the Koran, and wisdom, admonishing you thereby; and fear God, and know that God is omniscient.

But when ye have divorced your wives, and they have fulfilled their prescribed time, hinder them not from marrying their husbands, when they have agreed among themselves according to what is honorable. This is given in admonition unto him among you who believeth in God, and the last day. This is most righteous for you, and most pure. God knoweth, but ye know not. Mothers, after they are divorced, shall give suck unto their children two full years, to him who desireth the time of giving suck to be completed; and the father shall be obliged to maintain them and clothe them in the meantime, according to that which shall be reasonable. No person shall be obliged beyond his ability.

In the Name of the Most Merciful God.

O men, fear your Lord, who hath created you out of one man, and out of him created his wife, and from them two hath multiplied many men and women: and fear God by whom ye beseech one another; and respect women who have borne you, for God is watching over you.

And give the orphans when they come to age their substance; and render them not in exchange bad for good: and devour not their substance, by adding it to your substance; for this is a great sin. And if ye fear that ye shall not act with equity towards orphans of the female sex, take in marriage of such other women as please you, two, or three, or four, and not more. But if ye fear that ye cannot act equitably towards so many, marry one only, of the slaves which ye shall have acquired. This will be easier, that ye swerve not from righteousness.

And give women their dowry freely; but if they voluntarily remit unto you any part of it, enjoy it with satisfaction and advantage. And give not unto those who are weak of understanding, the substance which God hath appointed you to preserve for them; but maintain them thereout, and clothe them, and speak kindly unto them.

And examine the orphans until they attain the age of marriage: but if ye perceive they are able to manage their affairs well, deliver their substance unto them; and waste it not extravagantly, or hastily, because they grow up. Let him who is rich abstain entirely from the orphan's estates; and let him who is poor take thereof according to what shall be reasonable.

And then ye deliver their substance unto them, call witnesses thereof in their presence: God taketh sufficient account of your actions. Men ought to have a part of what their parents and kindred leave behind them when they die: and women also ought to have a part of what their parents and kindred leave, whether it be little, or whether it be much; a determinate part is due to them.

And when they who are of kin are present at the dividing of what is left, and also the orphaas, and the poor; distribute unto them some part thereof; and if the estate be too small, at least speak comfortably unto them. And let those fear to abuse orphans, who if, they leave behind them a weak offspring, are solicitous for them: let them therefore fear God, and speak that which is convenient. Surely they who devour the possessions of orphans unjustly, shall swallow down nothing but fire into their bellies, and shall broil in raging flames.

God hath thus commanded you concerning your children. A male shall have as much as the share of two females: but if they be females only, and above two in number, they shall have two-third parts what the deceased shall leave; and if there be but one, she shall have the half. And the parents of the deceased shall have each of them a sixth part of what he shall leave, if he have a child; but if he have no child, and his parents be his heirs, then his mother shall have the third part. And if he have brethren, his mother shall have a sixth part, after the legacies which he shall bequeath, and his debts be paid.

Ye know not whether your parents or your children be of greater use unto you. This is an ordinance from God, and God is knowing and wise. Moreover, ye may claim half of what your wives shall leave, if they have no issue; but if they have issue, then ye shall have the fourth part of what they shall leave, after the legacies which they shall bequeath, and the debts be paid. They also shall have the fourth part of what ye shall leave, in case ye have no issue; but if ye have issue, then they shall have the eighth part of what ye shall leave, after the legacies which ye shall bequeath and your debts be paid.

And if a man or woman's substance be inherited by a distant relation, and he or she have a brother or sister; each of them two shall have a sixth part of the estate. But if there be more than this number, they shall be equal sharers in a third part, after payment of the legacies which shall be bequeathed, and the debts, without prejudice to the heirs. This is an ordinance from God: and God is knowing and gracious.

These are the statutes of God. And whoso obeyeth God and his apostle, God shall lead him into gardens wherein rivers flow, they shall continue therein forever; and this shall be great happiness. But whose disobeyeth God, and his apostle, and transgresseth his statutes, God shall cast him into heltfire; he shall remain therein forever, and he shall suffer a shameful punishment.

If any of your women be guilty of whoredom, produce four witnesses from among you against them, and it they bear witness against them, imprison them in separate apartments until death release them, or God affordeth them a way *to* escape. And if two of you commit the like wickedness, punish them both: but if they repent and amend, let them both alone; for God is easy to be reconciled and merciful.

Verily, repentance will be accepted with God from those who do evil ignorantly, and then repent speedily; unto them will God be turned: for God is knowing and wise. But no repentance shall be accepted from those who do evil until the time when death presenteth itself unto one of them, and he saith, Verily, I repent now; nor unto those who die unbelievers for them have we prepared a grievous punishment.

O true believers, it is not lawful for you to be heirs of women against their will nor to hinder them from marrying others, that ye may take away part of what ye have given them in dowry; unless they have been guilty of a manifest crime, but converse kindly with them. And if ye hate them, it may happen that ye may hate a thing wherein God hath placed much good.

If ye be desirous to exchange a wife for another wife, and we have already given one of them a talent; take not away anything therefrom: will ye take it by slandering her, and doing her manifest injustice? And how can ye take it, since the one of you hath gone in unto the other, and they have received from you a firm covenant?

Marry not women whom your fathers have had to wife (except what is already past): for this is uncleanness, and an abomination, and an evil way. Ye are forbidden to marry your mothers, and your daughters, and your sisters, and your aunts both on the father's and on the mother's side, and your brother's daughters, and your sister's daughters, and your mothers who have given you suck, and your foster-sisters, and your wives' mothers, and your daughters-in-law which are under your tuition, born of your wives unto whom ye have gone in (but if ye have not gone in unto them, it shall be no sin in you to marry them), and the wives of your sons who proceed out of your loins; and ye are also forbidden to take to wife two sisters; except what is already past; for God is gracious and merciful. Ye are also forbidden to take to wife free women who are married, except those women whom your right hands shall possess as slaves.

This is ordained you from God. Whatever is beside this, is allowed you; that ye may with your substance provide wives for yourselves, acting that which is right, and avoiding whoredom. And for the advantage which ye receive from them, give them their reward, according to what is ordained but it shall be no crime in you to make any other agreement along yourselves, after the ordinance shall be complied with; for God is knowing and wise.

Whoso among you hath not means sufficient that he may marry free women, who are believers, let him marry with such of your maid-servants whom your right hands possess, as are true believers; for God well knoweth your faith. Ye are the one from the other; therefore marry them with the consent of their masters; and give them their dower according to justice; such as are modest, not guilty of whoredom, nor entertaining lovers.

And when they are married, if they be guilty of adultery, they shall suffer half the punishment which is appointed for the free women. This is allowed unto him among you, who feareth to sin by marrying free women; but if ye abstain from marrying slaves, it will be better for you; God is gracious and merciful. God is willing to declare these things unto you, and to direct you according to the ordinances of those who have gone before you, and to be merciful unto you. God is knowing and wise.

God desireth to be gracious unto you; but they who follow their lusts, desire that ye should turn aside from the truth with great deviation. God is minded to make his religion light unto you: for man was created weak. O true believers, consume not your wealth among yourselves in vanity; unless there be merchandising among you by mutual consent, neither slay yourselves; for God is merciful towards you; and, whoever doth this maliciously and wickedly, he will surely cast him to be broiled in hellfire; and this is easy with God.

❑ ❑ ❑

8.

Sikhism

Youngest, Militant Religion

—Annie Besant

THE TEN GURUS

Sikhism may be called a double movement. Essentially religious in its beginnings, it was forced by the pressure of circumstances into a militant organization. Most people in thinking of the Sikh think of a gallant warrior, a brave soldier. But we shall err seriously if we look on him as only, or even as fundamentally, a fighter. The movement itself is fundamentally a religious one. It grew up in the midst of Hinduism, having for its ideal the joining together of the Hindus and the Muslims in one league of love to God and service to man. The thought of Guru Nanak, as we find it expressed not only in his words, but far more in his life, was to join together these warring elements of the Indian people on a platform that both could accept.

That platform is *bhakti* or devotion to God. The name Sikh comes from the word '*Sishya*', which means disciple, and thus love to God and to the Teacher is the very basis and root of Sikhism.

In its philosophy it is Hindu, but as a movement it is reformatory in nature, seeking to find under the formalism and the ceremonialism of the time, the life which lay below the form, the essence of the truth that had inspired the ceremonies. In the time of Guru Nanak, as too often in the history of the world, a great religion had grown more and more formal and men were starving on the husk of the grain rather than eating the grain itself.

Guru Nanak sought to find the grain and, in so doing, threw aside to a large extent the husk. He strove to lead men to see the reality of religion, its life, its essence, and to find that life and that essence in love to God and the Guru, in love to men as children of the one God. You might almost sum up in that phrase the very essence of Sikhism.

How he tried to draw together the warring elements around him. How his life was one song of praise and love to God, how he was ever seeking the Supreme and, having found him, strove to teach his fellows how they too, by devotion.

There were ten Gurus, one after the other, in unbroken succession. Guru Nanak (1469-1539) the first, the purest, the saintliest and the noblest of all, the heart and soul of the movement. Guru Angad (1539-1552), of whom there is little to be said, save that he gathered together many of the songs and the teachings of his predecessor and so began the compilation of the Sikh scriptures, the 'Adi Grantha Sahib.' Guru Amar Das (1552-1574), who conferred with the Muslim Emperor, Akbar, on matters of religion; showing how the spirit of Guru Nanak still ruled, and that an attempt was being made to bring about peace between the rival faiths of Hinduism and Islam. Then Guru Ram Das (1574-1581), still on terms of friendship with the liberal-minded and magnanimous Akbar who gives him a piece of land at Amritsar where he dug out the famous tank. The fifth, Guru Arjunmal (1581-1606), the builder of the Golden Temple, which gave the Sikhs a centre, a home, and a rallying place.

The temple is first dedicated to Hari (Hari Mandir it was called), for Guru Nanak ever taught that in the name of Hari lay salvation. Later it became the Darbar Sahib. Now the Sikhs begin to gather round their temple, and to form a definite community. Arjunmal, their religious teacher, becomes the head of the organized religious community gathered at a special spot —the beginning of the Sikh State. His great work is to gather together the teachings of his predecessors, and it is he who compiles the 'Adi Grantha Sahib' from the songs and the teachings of the preceding Gurus, and from the songs of the saints in the Sikh movement.

Now comes the first touch which tells of the future struggle. Jehangir is on the throne of Akbar, less liberal, less magnanimous than his predecessor. His son rebels against him. Guru Arjunmal, apparently without any reason, or for a reason which really was no reason at all, was accused of sympathizing with the rebel son. The root of the accusation appears to have lain in the anger and the jealousy of the powerful minister to whom he had refused his child in marriage; and this minister, stirring up the suspicions of Jehangir against him, induces the Emperor to seize the Guru and imprison him. He dies from the hardships of the imprisonment.

This is the point where the community, which had been purely religious and peaceful, begins to be led by this outrage on its Teacher and Ruler, along the path that will forge it into a great military body. Jehangir is followed by Shah Jahan and later by Aurangzeb, and things grow worse and worse under that fanatical ruler.

The sixth Guru Har Govind (1606-1645), begins to organize his followers to defend themselves. He binds them into a body no longer to join together Hindu and Muslim, but a body apart and separate from both.

The Sikh State is beginning to emerge and now there is warfare and struggle, that does much to weld the Sikhs more and more fIrmly into a fIghting body.

The seventh Guru Har Rai (1645-1661), of whom little is said, is quiet and peaceful, but around him the struggle continues; war, increasing military spirit, until the religious side almost fades into the background save for the inspiration and the binding force it gives.

Then comes, Guru Har Kishan (1661-1664), who is but a child of six years. He dies when he is nine years old, and is followed by the ninth Guru Tegh Bahadur (1664-1675).

His life is very troubled, and he is cruelly murdered by Aurangzeb. He is succeeded by his son, the last and tenth Guru, Govind Singh (1675-1708), who gives to the Sikhs their great military organization, and makes them into the body that under Ranjit Singh, erected the Sikh Empire in the Punjab.

Guru Govind Singh

This tenth Guru, a mere boy, flees for his life after his father's murder, and for some twenty years he remains in retirement, thinking out his mission. Naturally, he broods over his father's murder; naturally he is bitter against his father's enemies; the hatred of the Muslim seems to become almost a duty for the Guru, and therefore for the Sikh. The old friendship has vanished.

For some twenty years, then, he ponders the work that lies before him, thinking over his role as a religious teacher, but still more as a military leader. And at last he is ready for his life's mission. He is determined to separate off the Sikhs from all possibility of confusion with men of any other faith. He calls to him five devoted disciples, and with these five men and himself in the midst he institutes the ceremony of Pahul, a simple, warrior-like initiation. His wife happens to be passing with five kinds of sweetmeats, and he takes a little of each and throws them into some water. He stirs the water with a two-edged dagger; he sprinkles it on the five men and they each drink it. Then they in turn sprinkle him and give him to drink, and **he proclaims them as the Khalsa, the pure, and bids them add to their names the further name of Singh, the lion.**

These are the first initiated disciples, marked out from all others by special signs that every Sikh must carry on his person. The long hair, dividing him from the shaven Hindu; the comb; the two-edged dagger or knife; the steel bangle; the short breeches coming to the knee. These are the five marks—the five K's as they are called, because each begins with a K in the vernacular—which separates every Sikh from all others and which the true Sikhs bear today. Wherever five Sikhs are gathered together, there, he said, would be his spirit, and there the power of initiation. He is to be the last of the Gurus; after him there is to be no other teacher. The power is to lie in the Khalsa to be exercised by the council of its chiefs, the Guru Mata; the authority is in the sacred book which, later, Guru Govind completes.

Now Guru Govind is the warrior chief and the Sikhs flock to his standard. He builds up a great army; his men are known for their marvellous courage, for the way they face great odds in battle, who died as joyfully as other men lived. No wonder that at first they carried all before them; yet, after much struggling, being but a few, after all, amid myriads, we find them beaten back by overwhelming numbers, for these few had set themselves against the mighty Muslim Empire in the North.

Few against a multitude they may be, but they are never discouraged, never disheartened. Their Guru is with them wherever they go, and where he is they are confident. He is beaten back and back, until at last, by a mighty effort, he turns and drives off the troops of the enemy; they pursue him no further. The place where that saving battle was fought is called The Well of Salvation.

It is after this, to encourage his followers, that he gives out the last of the Sikh scriptures, the *Book of the Tenth King*, or Guru, *Daswin Padshahi*, the completion of the 'Adi Grantha Sahib.'

Then comes the end. There is a quarrel with a Pathan over a trifling matter of trade, but the man threatens his life, and the Guru strikes him down. The dead man's sons arrive and he addresses them with kindness and favour. Remembering the murder of his own father, he pities the sons whom he has made fatherless; he takes them into his service and confidence. At last he knows that his time has come. He speaks to one of these young sons, about the duty of revenge, about the slaying of the slayer of the kinsman, and provokes him to strike his own death blow. He saves his killer from the anger of his followers, saying that he has but avenged his father's blood and he must go free. He bids them to follow the Scripture, and to be faithful to the Khalsa, and dies.

After his death there are no more Teachers; and authority now lies with the 'Adi Grantha Sahib,' the council of chiefs, and the Khalsa. This is the whole community of the Sikhs, wherein there was to be no difference of caste, no difference between man and man—all were to be brothers and were to be equal.

Then follows a brilliant story of military struggle and success crowned at last, by the victories of Ranjit Singh (1797-1839), who makes the Punjab practically the Sikh Empire.

After his death in 1839 this empire fell into a sad history of treachery, of betrayal, of brave men deceived and sold, yet struggling on desperately against all. Never was there a more heroic story of gallant men struggling against overwhelming odds. Their own heroism could not save them, and the Punjab passed into the hands of the British troops in 1849.

THE FAITH : GURU NANAK

Let us now pass from that and see what was the faith that gave to Sikhism its binding power, its heroism, its strength. It is the life and the teaching of Guru Nanak, the sweetest of characters and the saintliest of men.

From childhood he had been marked out—as all God's prophets are marked out—as different from his fellows. The story of his childhood is not eventful, but it is strange. He was born into a family of good people of the commonest quality. He was like a young eagle in the nest of a sparrow, the sparrow, did not understand the eagle, and they could not make out what manner of creature it was. Quiet, reserved, silent, wandering away to meditate when other boys were at play, and will not play their games. Neither will he learn as others learn for he wants his teacher to explain the mystic meaning of the letters, and he angers the pandit by asking questions that the good man cannot answer! He must know what is within, he cannot be satisfied with what is without. There is nothing more troublesome to the commonplace man or woman than to be pressed with questions as to realities, and so Nanak, in his childhood, is a great trial to his father.

Surely he must be mad; he sits for hours meditating, he takes no food; surely he must at least have a fever. They bring a doctor to see him. Nanak asks the doctor whether he can cure the diseases of his soul. Or see him when the ceremony of the sacred thread is to be performed. When everything was ready and the Purohit [the family priest] was about to invest him with it, Nanak turned round and enquired: 'Tell me, Panditji, of what use is this thread? What are the duties of the man who is invested with it? Why is it necessary to put it on?'

'Nobody can perform any sacrificial ceremonies without putting it on,' said the Purohit, who was merely a village pandit, and did not know the secret signification of the sacred thread. 'This thread purifies the wearer and entitles him to attend and perform all ceremonies.'

'If a man who has put on this sacred thread,' said Nanak, 'does not change his ways, and leads an impure life, does this thread purify him and help him in any way in the end? Does not he reap the fruit of his actions?'

'I do not know,' replied the Purohit, 'but it is ordained in the Sastras, and we must follow our forefathers. '

'From the cotton of compassion spin out the thread of love; make the knots of abstinence and truth; let your mind put on this thread; it is not broken, nor soiled, nor burned, nor lost. Praised be they who have put this on,' said Nanak.

'You have spoken' well,' said the Purohit, 'but look at all the expense and trouble your father has been put to, see 'all these friends and relations; they will be all disappointed if you won't put this on.'

'I am truly sorry that I cannot oblige you,' said Nanak; 'I cannot put it on, and I will advise you also to think more about the essence of things than the form. Only by true conviction one gains respect, and by praising God and by living truthfully man reaches perfection.'

At last his mother entreated him for her sake not to disappoint her. Then Nanak simply said: 'Mother, I obey.' He took the thread and put it on.

There you have a very characteristic story of this youth with the mark of a Prophet upon him, ever seeking the inner truth through the outer appearances.

As a youth, he is still a most unsatisfactory son to his good father. He will not take up agriculture, he won't have a shop, and he won't travel in commerce. His trade consists in giving money, or rather food, to sannyasis, which his father thinks is highly unsatisfactory, but Nanak thinks that it is the best bargain that can be made. What is to be done with such a young man? His father sends him to his sister and her husband who love him. Then he takes service under a Nawab and serves faithfully and well. But at last he wearies of the world and determines to give up service, to give up the household life into which he has entered, and to wander seeking for God, and for the realization of his love.

There is another characteristic scene. The Nawab sends for the young man, and after a time he comes. The Nawab is angry because he did not come at once.

'I am not now your servant, Nawab Sahab,' was Nanak's reply. 'Now I am a servant of God.'

'Do you believe in one God or many gods?' enquired the Nawab.

'Only in one, indivisible, self-existent: incomprehensible and all-pervading adorable God do I believe,' replied Nanak.

'Then since you believe in one God, and I too believe in one God, your God must be the same as mine; so then if you are a firm believer, come with me to the mosque and offer prayers with us.'

'I am ready,' said Nanak.

His father-in-law was struck dumb with amazement, and he at once left the Court believing that Nanak had embraced Islam.

It was Friday, and as the time for prayer was at hand the Nawab got up and, accompanied by Nanak, proceeded to the mosque. When the Kazi began to repeat the prayer the Nawab and his party began to go through the usual bowing ceremony, but Nanak stood silently still. When the prayer was over the Nawab turned towards Nanak, and indignantly asked: 'Why did you not go through the usual ceremonies? You, are a liar and your pretensions are false. You did not come here to stand like a log.'

'You put your face to the earth,' observed Nanak, 'while your mind was funning wild in the skies: you were thinking of getting horses from Kandahar, not offering prayers; and your priest, Sir, while going automatically through the bowing process, was thinking of the safety of the mare which foaled only the other day. How can I offer prayers with those who go through customary bows and repeat words like a parrot?'

The Nawab acknowledged that he was really thinking of getting horses and all the time he was praying the thought harassed him, but the Kazi was greatly displeased and turning towards Nanak showered a volley of questions.

Again the spirit of the seeker for reality. Nanak now begins his wanderings, singing with a musician Mardana and a friend Bala. In a village, a poor man, Lalu, a carpenter, a man of pure life, welcomes the wandering Sannyasi, gives him his own bed, brings him warm food, and Nanak eats. Next day a rich banker in the town gives a great feast for the Brahmins, and invites Nanak to come and eat with them. Nanak goes, but he will not take the food. Says the host: 'Why don't you take my food?'

'Because,' said Nanak, 'your food is not pure, for you have cooked it for self-glorification; it is a *tamasic* gift and therefore impure.'

'You call my food impure while that of the low caste Lalu is pure? How is that?' asked Rai Bhag contemptuously.

'You treat your guests irreverently and contemptuously,' said Nanak, 'That shows your *tamasic* aims. I ate food cooked by Lalu, for it was cooked with love and brought with reverence, with no desire for repayment. You must learn a lesson from humble Lalu. Your food is full of blood.'

'What proof have you that my food is impure?' demanded Rai Bhag angrily.

Nanak took Rai Bhag's food in one hand while in the other he took the food cooked by Lalu, and, as he squeezed Rai Bhag's food oozed drops of blood but Lalu's oozed milk.

Such was the way in which Guru Nanak taught, the teaching ever bearing on reality and exposing mere show. Men quarrel as to whether he was a Hindu or a Muslim but he was above the distinctions of outer creed; he loved all men and called himself nothing. When he came to die, after seventy years of noble life and priceless teaching, his disciples disputed as to what faith he really belonged; should he be burned as a Hindu, or should he be buried as a Muslim? And as they disputed, one lifted the sheet over the corpse, and the body had disappeared so he was neither burned nor buried!

Such was the spirit of the great Teacher, as shown in his life and conduct, and in the teachings that he left behind him. They show the spirit that moved him—that profound devotion to the Supreme, that love for God that worldly men call madness, that passion and devotion that the saints in every age and in every religion have felt. Philosophically he was a Hindu; his keynot is his hatred of sham.

THE TEACHINGS : GURU-BANI

Let us take his teaching and the teaching of his successors, and see how they taught and the spirit of the teaching. I give here, a large number of extracts from the 'Adi Grantha Sahib', classified under certain headings on which I had asked for specific Sikh teaching.

The 'Adi Granth Sahil' is divided into several parts. *Japji,* or *Guru Mantra,* by Guru Nanak. *Sodur Rehi* Ras by Guru Nanak with additions. *Kirtan Sohila* by Guru Nanak with additions. 31 sections in verse form: Sri Raga, Todi, Tokkari, Majh, Bairan, Kedara, Gauri, Teilang, Bhairo, Asa, Sodhi, Basant, Gujri, Bilawal, Sarang, Deva Gandhari, Gand, Mular, Bihagra, Ram Kali, Kama, Wiad Hans, Nat Narayan, Kalyan, Sorath, Mati Gaura, Parbhati, Dhanasri, Maru, Jai Jaiwanti, Jeit Siri. *Bhog. Bhog ka Banee.*

First as the Supreme. 'Thou art I, I am Thou, Of what kind is the difference?' 'In all the One dwells, the One is contained.' 'He Himself is One, and He Himself is many. He does not die or perish. He neither comes nor goes. Nanak says that He is always contained in all.'

We catch the echo of the Upanishads in more popular language, the deep thought of Hindu philosophy put into a more popular form.

> One Omkara, true Name, Maker, Spirit, fearless, unmalevolent, timeless Form. From no womb, self-

existent, great-bliss or through Guru's favour to be realized. True from before; true from before the ages *yugas* true is and true to be, O Nanak.

—*Japa I*

———

Signless, that none may cross, unreachable or unknowable; no object for the senses untouched by time or action; of unborn essence; from no womb; self-existent; unconditioned; unwavering; may I unto this true verity be sacrifice.

He hath no form, nor colour, nor outline; by the true Word He is to be pointed out. He hath no mother, father, son, nor kindred, nor lust, nor wife, nor clan; untinged by maya untranscended; higher than highest; Thou light of all; Brahm in all vessels hid; His light complete in every vehicle [heart].

By Guru's teaching the adamant portals throw ajar, with fearless gaze fixed firm. Having created beings, He placed over them time [death], and kept all regulation under His control. By Guru's service the true wealth they find; by acting on His word freedom they gain. In a pure vessel heart only Truth may live; rare are they of conduct pure. Essence in the highest Essence merged; Nanak in Thee doth refuge find.

—*Sorath I*

———

I bow down [or glorify] the primal One, Omkara;
Who hath spread out this water, land and sky;
The first Spirit, unmanifest, imperishable;
Whose light illuminates the fourteen lokas;
Abiding in the elephant and the ant alike;
Who knoweth as equal the ruler and pauper;
From form duality; the signless Spirit
Directly knowing; the inner controller of every vessel [heart]

—*Guru*

He Himself, the Formless and the Form; That One without qualities and with qualities; One alone is spoken of, O Nanak. That One alone is many.

—Guru V,Bavanakhhri

———

The Parabrahman, Supreme Lord, cometh not into wombs.

With Thy word createst Thou creation, and after making Thou pervadest it.

Thy form could not be seen, how shall I meditate on Thee?

Thou functionest in all; Thy power showeth this;

Thy love fills treasures which are inexhaustible;

These jewels [of peace, etc.], are priceless.

—Guru V, Var-Maru

———

Countless Avatiiras of Vishnu didst Thou make.

Countless Braluniindas are the abodes of Thy Law;

Countless Mahesvaras are created and absorbed;

Countless Bralunas Thou didst set to fashion the worlds:

So rich is my Lord,

Whose great qualities I cannot speak of in details;

Whom countless mayas attend.

The hearts of countless beings are His resting place;

Countless are the devotees who embrace [lit. or draw close to] Thy limbs personified for worship.

Countless are the devotees who dwell with Hari.

Countless are the kings [lit. Lords of Umbrellas] who pay Thee homage.

Countless Indras standing at Thy portals;

Countless heavens in Thy glance;

Countless Thy priceless Names;

Whose countless resonances sounded forth;
Countless journeys of wondrous action;
Countless Saktis and Sivas obedient to His will;
Countless the beings whom Thou nourishest;
In whose feet are countless Tirthas [sacred places];
Countless pure ones repeat Thy dear name;
Countless worshippers render Thee worship;
Infinite Thy Expanse; there is no second;
Whose pure and spotless glories are countless;
Whose praise is sung by countless Brahma-Rshis;
In the winking of an eye whose creations and absorptions are countless;
Countless Thy qualities that may not be numbered;
Countless wise men declare Thy knowledge;
Countless meditators meditate on Thee;
Countless ascetics perform austerities;
Countless Munis sit in silence;
Unmanifest Lord, imperceptible Master,
Filling all hearts and controlling from within,
Wherever I look Thou dwellest there;
The Guru [or great one] illumined Nanak
[with this knowledge].

—Guru V, Bhairon

———

Who hath no discus, mark, nor class, nor caste, nor sub-caste,
Of whom none can say: 'He hath form, colour, outline or vesture,'
Changeless form shining through Anubhava, direct perception of innermost spiritual consciousness,
Whom we might call the Indra [Lord] of countless Indras, and King of kings.

Three worlds, lords of earth, gods, men, demons and forest grass are saying, *neti, neti* not this; not this.

Who can utter all Thy names? the wise declare Thy functional names alone.

—Guru X Jdpa

———

In every way I said, there was no other, O friend,

He dwells in all the continents and islands

He fills all iokas.

—Guru V] Devagandhari

———

His greatness the Veda doth not know;

Brahma knoweth not His mystery;

Avataras know not His limit;

The supreme Lord, Parabrahm, is boundless.

—Guru V, Ramkali

———

All are made liable to errors, the Maker alone does not err.

—Guru I, Sri Raga

———

And then for worship; every Hindu knows the arati and the way in which light, and one thing after another, are offered in worship to the image of the God. Guru Nanak deprecates the use of images in worship, and in his own arati offers the whole universe in the worship of Brahman, the Supreme,

Space itself Thy salver; the sun and moon Thy lamps;

The starry host thy pearls, O Father.

The fragrant breeze of the Malaya mountains Thy incense;

The wind waving its *chawri* fan over Thee;

All forest vegetation [vegetable kingdom] as flowers, O Light!

What a rejoicing arati or hymn of praise O Destroyer of fear or samsara; the Anahat Sabda [the soundless or unstruck sounc] sounds as Thy kettledrum.

Thousands are Thy eyes; Nay! Nay! Thou hast none;

Thousands are Thy forms; Nay! Nay! Thou hast none;

Thousands are Thy holy feet; Nay! Nay! Thou hast none;

Thou art without nostril [sense of smell] yet Thou hast a thousand nostrils;

This wondrous working of Thine bewilders us,

In everything, O Glory! is Thy Light.

In every one the Light of That Light shines.

In Guru's presence [or by Guru's teaching] shineth forth that Light;

That is rejoicing arati which to Him is pleasing.

Such is his teaching. It breathes the purest spirit of devotion that reaches beyond all forms to the One Formless; a heart is found that feels a greater passion of devotion for the ideal of the One than for any of the forms in which the One manifests Himself. In Guru Nanak there is no denial of the forms in which the Supreme is shown, but he takes the view of the Upanishads, that there is one Brahman, supreme over all, of whom all the gods are but the partial manifestations, of whose beauty the highest forms are but reflections.

When we are asked what it is he teaches as to creation, we find pure Vedantic teaching, that creation is but maya and that by the power of Isvara and maya all things come forth.

By will [order] the fonns come forth.

—Guru I, Japa

One Mother [Maya] united with God gave birth to three acceptable children [disciples];

One of them sends forth samsara, the other provides and the third habitually dissolves.

As it pleaseth Him so He directeth them, according to His will.

He looketh on but is not seen; great is the marvel, hail to Him, hail!

The primal, the unstained, without beginning, the indestructible, in every age assuming the same vesture.

—*Guru I, Japa*

When the Maker causes emanation or expansion,

Then the creation takes up infinite bodies;

Whenever Thou drawest in,

Then all the embodied merge in Thee.

—*Guru X, Chaupai*

There are hundreds of thousands of Akasas and Patalas.

—*Guru I, Japa*

The limits of His creation cannot be known.

—*Guru I, Japa*

This world is the house of the True one, the True one dwells therein.

—*Guru II Asavar*

This world is the temple of Hari, but awful darkness without the Guru.

Those who are led by the mind [lit. mind facing], these blind rustics worship Him as being distinct [lit. another].

—*Guru III, Prabhati*

Here is Siddha's question:
How is the world produced O man, [and] how can pain be destroyed?
Answer of Guru Nanak:
In Egoism the world has its birth, by forgetting the name we suffer.

—Guru I, Sidhgosht

As to the *jiva* he teaches that he is the same in essence with the Supreme, and that by reincarnation and by karma, he can realize himself and know that there is no difference. He speaks of endless births and he repeats that phrase that we find with the Jaina as with the Hindu, that human birth is difficult to gain and that in human birth is liberation to be found.

This *jiva* is not subject to death.

—Guru V, Gauri

———

In the body is mind, in the mind is the True one
That True one merging in uniting with the
True one is absorbed.

—Guru I, Raga Dhanasri

———

The same thing is in the body which is in the Brahmanda;
Whosoever seeks finds.

—Pippa Bhakta Dhanasri

———

Neither caste nor birth is asked; enquire at the House of the True. According to one's actions are caste and birth.

—Guru I, Parbhati

The man who performs good actions,
He is called a Deva in this world:
He who does evil deeds in this world,
Men call him an Asura [demon].

Guru X, Vichitra Natak

———

On karma, the teaching is very clear: Soweth himself, eateth himself.

—*Guru I, Japaji*

——————

In the field of karma he reapeth whatever he soweth.

Guru V, Baramah Majh

——————

Let us not blame anyone,
Whatever we act that we enjoy and suffer;
Karmas are ours, bondage is ours too,
Coming and going is the activity of maya.

—*Guru V*

——————

In many births we became insects and moths;
In many births we became elephants, fish, and deer;
In many births we became birds and serpents;
In many births we were yoked as steeds and bullocks;
Seek the Lord! It is the surer [opportunity] of seeking; after long ages this human body has been attained.'
Many lives have we wandered over mountains.
Many lives have we been miscarried from the womb.
Many lives have we been created as herbage.
We have been made to wander through eighty-four lakhs of wombs.
The association of the good hath let us attain this birth.
Serve thou devotedly, says Hari. This is the Guru's teaching.
If he cast off vanity, falsehood and pride
And die living, then is he accepted in that court [i.e., presence].

—*Guru V, Gauri Rag*

——————

As iron placed on an anvil is beaten into shape,

So is a deluded [or ignorant] soul thrown into wombs and made to wander, [so that] it may bend [or turn to the Right Path].

—*Guru I, Suhi Raga Kafi*

Here is a beautiful description of the Jivan-Mukta:

Who in his mind knows the Lord's will to be for the best,

He is verily called Jivan-Mukta.

To him joy is the same as sorrow.

He is ever blissful; to him there is no separation,

Gold to him is the same as clay.

To him nectar is the same as bitter poison.

Honour and dishonour are the same to him.

The pauper and the king are equal for him.

Whatever is made to happen by the Lord, that same [he considers] fit and proper.

O Nanak, such a man is called a Jivan-Mukta.

—*Guru V, Sukhmani*

And here is a fine poem on the Brahmajñani:

Brahmajñani is ever unstained, like the lotus which is not wetted by water.

Brahmajñani is ever free from fault, or evil, as the sun dries up all things;

Brahmajñani looks upon every one equally, as wind touches the king and pauper alike.

Brahmajñani suffers, endures all equally, as the earth dug by some and smeared with sandal by others.

Such is the quality of Brahmajñani as the burning power of fire is innate.

Brahmajñani is purer than the pure, as impurity touches not water.

In the mind of Brahmajñani shines light, as the sky shines above earth.

To the Brahmajñani friend and foe are equal, Brahmajñani hath no pride.

Brahmajñani is higher than the high, but he thinks himself lower than every one.

Those men become Brahmajñani, O Nanak, whom the Lord Himself makes such.

Brahmajñani is the dust [of the feet] of every one;

Brahmajñani has gathered [or known] the essence of Atma.

Brahmajñani is compassionate to all; no evil cometh from the Brahmajñani.

Brahmajñani always looks upon all equally, on whatever he looks he showers nectar.

Brahmajñani is free from bondage, Brahmajñani's yoga is pure.

Brahmajñani's food is wisdom; O Nanak, the meditation of Brahmajñani is Brahma.

Brahmajñani fixes his hope on the One, Brahmajñani doth never perish.

Brahmajñani is pervaded by humility, Brahmajñani delights in doing good to others.

Brahmajñani is free from activity of the three Gunas, Brahmajñani makes his own mind prisoner.

Whatever befalls a Brahmajñani he considers it good, Divine qualities fructify in a Brahmajñani.

Everything is uplifted along with a Brahmajñani, O Nanak; the whole world repeats the name of the Brahmajñani.

Brahmajñani has one colour [state of the mind, i.e., Love]. The Lord dwells with the Brahmajñani.

Brahmajñani is supported by the name, to the Brahmajñani the Name is his all in all.

Brahmajñani is ever awake in the Real, Brahmajñani relinquishes egoism.

In the heart of Brahmajñani there is the highest bliss; in the Brahmajñani's house there is ever peace.

Brahmajñani dwells in happiness; O Nanak, there is no destruction for the Brahmajñani.

Brahmajñani is the knower of Brahma; Brahmajñani is ever in love with the One.

Brahmajñani is free from anxiety, Brahmajñani's beliefis are pure.

He is Brahmajñani whom the Lord Himself makes such; the glory of the Brahmajñani is great.

A very fortunate person may see a Brahmajñani. We should offer ourselves as a sacrifice for [go round] a Brahmajñani.

Mahesvara, Siva the great Lord, seeks a Brahmajñani, O Nanak.

The Brahmajñani is the Supreme Lord Himself.

The Brahmajñani is a priceless treasure.

Everything is in the heart of Brahmajñani, he who knows the secret of the Brahmajñani.

Let us ever salute the Brahmajñani; we could not pronounce half a letter of the Brahmajñani.

Brahmajñani is the Lord of all; who can measure in speech the Brahmajñani!

Brahmajñani alone knows the Goal of the Brahmajñani.

Of the Brahmajñani there is neither limit nor the other shore. O Nanak, we ever salute the Brahmajñani.

Brahmajñani is the maker of all creation. Brahmajñani is the giver of mukti, yoga and life.

Brahmajñani is the whole Spirit, Purusha, and ordainer.
Brahmajñani is the protector of the unprotected,
Brahmajñani guards every one.
All this is the form of Brahmajñani, Brahmajñani is the Formless Supreme Self Himself.
The splendour or grace of the Brahmajñani befits Brahmajñani alone. Bramajnani is the Treasure of all.

—Guru V, Sukhmani

———

He who causes no fear to others, and fears no one.
Say Nanak! hear O mind, call him Jnani [wise].

—Guru IX

———

Here are some slokas on devotion to the Gurudeva:

O Nanak! know that to be the true Guru who unites [thee] with all, my dear.

—Guru I Sri Raga

———

Every day a hundred times would I sacrifice myself unto my own Guru;
Who transformed me into God, and it did not take him long to do so.

—Guru I, Vara Asli

———

If a hundred moons and a thousand suns were to rise,
And there were so much light, without Guru there would be still awful darkness.

—Guru II, Aslivan

———

Blessed by my true Guru, knower of Rari, Who showed us friend and foe equal in our sight.

—Guru IV, Vara Vadhans

———

Gurudeva is mother, Gurudeva is father, Gurudeva is'the Supreme Lord;

Gurudeva is friend, destroyer of ignorance, Gurudeva is relative and real brother;

Gurudeva is the giver and teacher of Hari's name; Gurudeva has realized the mantra;

Gurudeva is the embodiment of peace, truth and enlightenment; Gurudeva's touch is higher than that of the philosopher's stone.

Gurudevais the Tirtha [place of pilgrimage], the tank of nectar, immortality, there is nothing beyond immersion in Guru's knowledge.

Gurudeva the maker is the destroyer of all evil.

Gurudeva is the purifier of all fallen ones.

Gurudeva is primal, before ages, in every age; by repeating his Hari-Mantra we are saved, uplifted from the ocean of samsara

O Lord, favour us with Gurudeva's company, so that linked to him we deluded sinners may swim [across].

Gurudeva, the true Guru, is Parabrahman, Supreme Lord; bow to Gurudeva Hari.

—Guru V, Bavanakhhri

———

O mother! I rejoice, for I have found the true Guru.

—Guru III, Ramkali

———

Let him fix the Guru's word in his heart.

And cease to associate with the five persons [desire, wrath, etc.]

Keep the ten organs under control.

Then in his self the light shall shine forth.

—Guru V, Gauri

———

Finally, it is said:

> One has become a shriven Sannyasi, and another a Yogi, a Brahmachari, a Yati, is considered; a Hindu, a Muslim, a Rafazi, Imamshahi. But understand thou that **humanity is one. The Maker, the Compassionate, is the same**, the Nourisher, and the Kind One is the same; **fall not into the error and delusion of the difference of duality**. One is to be served; the Gurudeva of all is one; one is the Nature and know thou the Light to be one. **The temple and the mosque are the same, Puja and Namaz are one, all men are one, but many in manifestation**; so Gods and demons are one, Yakshas and Gandharvas. **Hindus and Turks are due to the different nature of the garbs of various lands**. The eyes, the ears, the body, the make is one, a combination of earth, air, fire, water; the signless Allah is the same; Puranas and Quran are the same; one is the nature and one is the make.
>
> As from one fire a crore of sparks arise, and becoming separate merge again into the same fire; as from one heap of dust many particles fill the sky and these particles again disappear in the same dust; as in one river many ripples are formed, but these ripples of water are called but water; so from the Universal Form conscious and unconscious beings have manifested, but they shall lose themselves into That from which they have come.
>
> —*Guru X, Kavitu*

Such is the teaching and such is the heart of Sikhism. Is there anything in it which can serve to bind men together in love? When you think of Guru Nanak, think of one of those great prophets of peace who, from their love of God draw the blessed fruit of love to men.

If our Sikh brothers are faithful to the teachings of their Guru, they should be friends and unifiers, builders-up and constructors of the national life.

❑ ❑ ❑

Editor's Postspeak

REMEDY FOR MODERN TERRORS: HINDU + BUDDHA + JAIN

Only eight religions—in an almost equal billions of people living on the earth—with one, the second major religion of the world, co-religion of the Aryan Vedism developing in Hinduism and Zoroastrianism, religion of the Parsis living in Iran (Aryaan), almost totally eliminated out of existence, alongwih its base community...

for which one of the last Parsi brilliant journalist, dear Bachi Karkaria, rightly laments in the *Times of India*, 15.11.2013: 'It is ironic that though the Parsis may have produced more than their share of crorepatis in their past, demographically, they have never approached even a 10% of that magic number, ...we are down to barely 10,000, our flame is dying...in all Gujarat settlements...even Udvada, the last "throne" of our sacred fire, the ancestral "wads" stand bereft, forlorn.'

And another, the equally famous Judaism, religion of God YHWH's self-selected 'chosen people', is making strenous efforts to reorganise itself in its tiny belt of land known as Israel.

The remaining religions—two of which are openly Godless (the prime condition for being denominated the high falutin title of 'religion')—as also non-violent—a relative rarity in this life-governing hoary area, playing their games as their teachers think fit.

A good news published just two days ago—on 16 Nov. 2013—is very heart-warming—that the Thais have sent about 300 kgs of gold to cover the Mahabodhi Temple at Bodh Gaya—the spot where lord Buddha attained enlightenment—to cover it with it. The work has already started and a former Deputy Prime Minister of Thailand, Gen. Pricha, is personally guiding it. Hurrah to the total-renunciation propounder of the great religion of Lord Buddha! Let the gold glitter in all its shine—along with the other kind of light spread by the venerable Dalai Lama! Let Buddhism be known worldwide once again and shape itself to subdue the horrors of terrorism, the gory son of a sister religion, totally against the values given by its revered founder.

Non-violence as the central point of a religion has been a major contribution of Indian thought and behavioural social culture to the world—but, unfortunately, its significance has not been suitably recognised till now. It may even be said that 'Non-violence itself is religion, the only religion.' Since the present day religions were born, more or less with the beginning of their particular communities, they were of need guided by the survival requirements, but now the change to humanity in its totality has come to be recognised, the concept of religion is also likely to be redone rather drastically. How it would happen, is not clear, but Hinduism does provide a system which can go a long way in doing it—and the West seems to be activating this idea. An amalgamation with Buddhism will provide an attractive life-program—Jainism, with its Syadvada, or Anekanta (several paths), has the potential of making a basic contribution; its 'No God' dispensation is another unique theory—totally ignored so far—which might help the very large non-believer segment in the world, to come along. India Ahoy! Bharat—'bha' means light—Ahoy!

Life—absurd, meaningless, with no purpose, and no exit even if one wants to—a compulsion—given with pretty little food (though the Bible says that God will take care of it)—does need to be intelligently tackled—Yes, there is no other way.

• • •

One genuienly interested in the study of human society—which everyone should be, because he himself is a human creature—can't escape the study of religions, which he will find not only enlightening, but unexpectedly interesting. Men like Zarathustra, Moses and Muhammad were chiefly social systemisers, who found it useful to develop it around some kind of religion centred around a God—whose dictates could not be discarded by the people; it didn't matter if these leaders did not really believe in the existence of their god—it was generally secondary for them. All of them had very difficult tasks to do, but they had to succeed—which they remarkably did, also perpetuating their propounded beliefs till long. Zarathustra's Avesta is strangely revealing because it starts by accounts of Ahura Mazda settling countries after countries to give people support and stability. The rules of social behaviour are also very detailed—which were followed with minor or very few changes by the Jewish Torah and Muslim Qur'an.

Indian religions were totally different—not only in basic concept but also their aims and objectives. They developed the idea of spirit—Atman, Soul, Brahman, etc.—in a variety of ways; spiritualism being not only power and recognising tool, but also an equaliser—in modern times, the intellectuals prefer to call them 'spiritualistic' but not religious. They were essentially thought and/or conscience religions, while others born elsewhere were power religions.

Then, though countries like China and Japan did not develop high profile religions of their own—they accepted the patently foreign Buddhist religion;—India's interest in religion, infested with a multiple variety of fancy ideas, seem to be rather unusually immense. King Harshvardhan is said to have found, while visiting Vindhya forests, seated on the rocks and reclining under the trees Arhata (Jain) begging monks, Svetapadas, Mahapasupadas, Pandara-bhikshus, Bhagvatas, Varnins, Kesalunchanas, Lokayatikas, Kapilas, Kanadas, Anupanishadas, Isvarakarins, Dharmasastrins, Pauranikas, Saptatanvas, Sabdas, Pancaratrikas, etc. all listening to their own accepted tenets and zealously defending them.' The famous work of Madhavacharya, 'Sarva-darshana Samgrah', discusses as many as 16 religious systems of India; and six systems of Indian philosophy are well known.

Was'nt this a little too much?—one would question. May be, may not be!—who would finally decide!

It would be interesting to learn that an equally large country, or even larger, than India, China, devoted, its intellect to an entirely different idea: to increase their living age. They thought that sex was basically life-giving, so it can, and should, be used to increasing one's life-span by sleeping with as many women as possible—a king is said to have done so with over 100 young girls—as by other means also. Their seers exercised in various curious ways and for unbearably long periods. Their literature is full of such materials.

Finally, in the zeal of religion, materialism, or our material needs, have been totally disregarded. I am surprised by narrations in the Bible, the basic need of food, and clothes etc. has been in a number of places been described rather strongly as unworthy of human beings and replaced by worship of God—underlining that He will look after their mundane matters—but, does He? Poverty and related matters remain our chief concern, and will remain so till a movement like Communism does not absolutely succeed. Whatever the new global religion, it must take note of the vast difference between the powers of creation and the availability of eating materials to sustain the easily—and much pleasingly—created life. It is strange, as well as unforgivable, that philosophy has not taken note of the iron-hard fact, and for no sufficient reason is involved in god-religion-spiritualism, etc. We should without delay straighten our lop-sided thoughts and practices governed by them.

In olden times life and people were limited but now they are increasing by leaps and bounds. Fortunately, science and technology is developing, and we must make use of these in sustaining our unasked for given-life. Amen!

❑ ❑ ❑

26. Learn Rajayoga From Vivekananda	250/-
27. Colossus Vivekananda Select	250/-
28. Intellect India	250/-
29. Culture India	250/-
30. My Experiments with Truth	250/-
31. Mahatma Gandhi The Bhagavadgita	125/-
32. Shirdi Sai Baba	80/-
33. The Ramayana For Every Home	125/-
34. The Mahabharata For Every Home	125/-
35. Sai - The Age of Cosmic Family	80/-
36. Sathya Sai and His Miraculous Powers	95/-
37. To Bloom Like a Lotus	225/-
38. The History of Sikh Gurus	225/-
39. Indian Mythology	195/-

Unit No. 220, Second Floor, 4735/22,
Prakash Deep Building, Ansari Road, Darya Ganj,
New Delhi - 110002, Ph.: 32903912, 23280047, 09811594448
E-mail: lotuspress1984@gmail.com, www.lotuspress.co.in